"With no holds barred, Omodt and Matter rip back the curtain of seedy reality and toss you headlong into the complex relationships of biker gangs and the cops whose job it is to pursue them. The writing is graphic, truthful, revealing and explores both sides of the law—the right side, and the wrong side—with equal detail. For lovers of true crime writing this is a must-read."

— **Mark Reps**, author, *Sheriff Zeb Hanks* crime series

"The story of an adversarial relationship that turned into one of the most unlikely, remarkable friendships I've ever been exposed to. And, as written by the two protagonists, *Breaking the Code* is told in the most authentic voice you'll ever read. Beyond the true crime audience, this is a story filled with so much humanity it must be experienced by all readers."

— **Ali Selim,** writer and director of the award-winning film, *Sweet Land*

"Up until *Breaking the Code* I knew Pat Matter to be a formidable but fair motorcycle drag racer and a competent professional as leader of Minneapolis Custom Cycle. This book fills in the blanks about the other 'dark' side of his life as a Hells Angel—a must-read to get the whole story."

— **George B. Smith**, Executive Chairman and CEO of S&S Motor Company, Viola, WI

"*Breaking the Code* takes you on a real-life crime adventure ... a fascinating behind-the-scenes look at Hells Angels, and what it took to take down one of their most prominent leaders."

— **Tom Chorske**, retired NHL player and commentator for FSN Sports

A TRUE STORY

*BY A HELLS ANGEL PRESIDENT AND
THE COP WHO PURSUED HIM*

PAT MATTER & CHRIS OMODT

THE REAL DEAL, LLC.

Dedication

Patrick: To Trish, my wife who never lost faith
and has always been there for me.

Chris: To my children, Rachel and Matthew,
I am so proud of both of you.

Breaking the Code

*A True Story by a Hells Angel President
and the Cop Who Pursued Him*

Pat Matter & Chris Omodt

FIRST EDITION

ISBN: 9781939288684

Library of Congress Control Number: 2014940507

eBook ISBN: 9781939288738

Published by The Real Deal, LLC.

THE REAL DEAL, LLC.

www.therealdealllc.com
facebook.com/RealDealLLC

Contents

Pat's booking photo from DEA the morning of February 15, 2002.

Prologue

"Pat Matter?" The short, but solid man walking into the sally port, the secured entryway of the Anoka County jail, turned towards me. "I'm Chris Omodt, detective with the Hennepin County Sheriff's Office."

"Yeah, I know who you are." The reply took me by surprise. In retrospect, knowing all that I now know about Patrick Joseph Matter, founder and twenty-year president of the Minneapolis chapter of the Hells Angels, it should not have. Pat knew his business. He ran it well and he ran it with a tight fist. And knowing his business meant knowing about guys like me—guys who had been investigating him for years.

Pat had just spent the night at the Anoka County jail—Valentine's Day, 2002. I had helped put him there. Five years before, just one day shy of five years, as a matter of fact, my special operations detail was able to tie two kilograms of cocaine to Pat. He'd had it hidden in a friend's garage. The garage had been broken into in the middle of the night. The thieves came to steal six Harley-Davidson motorcycles but they took the cocaine, too. That was a bonus for us. We'd been investigating the recent rash of motorcycle thefts in the Minneapolis-St. Paul metro area but the stolen coke was about to put us on to something bigger.

After the theft, all hell had broken loose. At Pat's direction, a private investigator was hired. Flyers were posted in the neighborhood bars offering a three-thousand-dollar reward for information on the stolen bikes (no mention of the cocaine, of course). Then Pat and his guys took to just beating people up for information. The thieves were in over their heads but you can't say they hadn't been warned. Each stolen bike had a Hells Angels support sticker on it: "This bike belongs to the Hells Angels—Fuck with it and find out."

Eventually, one of the thieves would come forward. We'd get other guys to talk, too. The scope of our investigation grew and we began looking closely at Pat Matter and his entire operation. I learned all I could about him. It's my way. When I'm investigating someone, I become intensely focused. Pat might have known who I was, but I could guarantee I knew more about him. I knew all about his youth in Fort Dodge, Iowa. I knew about his time with the Grim Reapers Motorcycle Club and his entry into the Hells Angels. I knew about the arrests and the jail time and the bar fights and the shootouts. I knew he'd lost a best friend in a hail of bullets in Fort Dodge and I knew he'd almost been killed himself when a rival gang blew up his truck in Minneapolis. Pat had quite a history.

He had quite a run of success, too. We'd come to learn that his drug distribution business ran into the multimillions of dollars. His Hells Angels chapter was the envy of other outlaw motorcycle gangs. And his custom motorcycle shop—his one business that had eventually become legitimate—had been featured nationally in countless cycle magazines. I couldn't help but admit to myself some respect for the man, even as I cuffed him and led him out of the county jail and into our waiting car.

U.S. Drug Enforcement Administration agent Jeff Harford drove, while Pat and I sat in the back. We were headed to the DEA where Pat would be processed. From there it would be to the U.S. Marshals' office downtown and then an appearance before a magistrate in federal court. It was strange to be sitting next to the man I'd been after for so long. I could have met him the day before, during the arrest at his cycle shop, but I had remained out of view, in a vehicle across the street, ready to assist if the arrest had gone badly. But Pat had been cooperative, even polite.

Nobody on the special operations detail had wanted to be the one to have to pick Pat up the next morning for processing; we'd all worked hard to remain unknown to him. Finally, as team leader, I figured what the hell, I'd take him. Turned out he knew me anyway.

In the backseat of the car I tried to break the awkward silence with some small talk. I don't much care for silence, and besides, I know that building a little trust and rapport never hurts. I knew Pat built his own V-Twin motorcycles at his shop and I'd been a motorcycle enthusiast since my teens. It seemed a good way to start a conversation.

"So who builds your frames?" I asked, even though I already knew.

"Oh, c'mon," he said, "you don't really want to know who builds my frames."

"No, I'm interested. I like bikes. Really."

"Daytec," he said after a long pause.

"Well your bikes are beautiful."

"Well thank you." The rest of the ride was quiet.

At the DEA office, I processed Pat, which included mug shot and fingerprints. Then, filling out the subject worksheet, I asked, "Do you still use the alias 'Silver Tooth'?" Now it was Pat's turn to be surprised.

"I haven't been called that for quite some time," he chuckled.

"How about 'Mad Hatter'?"

"Nope, haven't been called that for years," and he chuckled again. He knew I'd done my homework.

After the DEA booking, we went to the U.S. Marshals' office where Pat was processed again and then I escorted him to a temporary holding cell where he would await his appearance in front of the magistrate. He was all of five feet six inches, and for all he might have known at the time we had enough on him to put him away for life. But he carried himself with confidence and self-assurance and I remembered something my father always used to say. I imagined there was some truth to it: *little man, big balls.*

While Pat was in the holding cell, the other agents working on the case and I met with Jeff Paulsen, lead prosecutor. I liked Jeff. He was smart, effective in the courtroom, and he knew how to talk to cops. We discussed the case. The truth of the matter was that we *didn't* have enough to put Pat away for life. We were on shaky ground and we knew it. We'd had him indicted for conspiracy to distribute cocaine based on the promise of testimony from the people who knew about the cocaine theft five years prior—people who weren't exactly pillars of the community. It was all we really had and with the five-year statute of limitations set to expire, we'd had to move quickly, maybe too quickly.

On the other hand, we knew we could build a case. We knew that the people who were now talking could point to other people. We knew that in time, more and more evidence could be revealed. The case against Pat Matter was there, we just had to keep following it and hope Pat didn't invoke his right to a speedy trial. We were all hoping for a superseding indictment—something that could put Pat Matter, if convicted, away for a very long time.

Pat made his appearance in front of the magistrate and was released that day on an unsecured bond, pending a trial date. Later that night, I thought about Pat. He wasn't exactly what I'd expected. He wasn't the prototypical Hells Angel. There was something about his demeanor. In addition to his confidence, there was a certain gentleness that belied the stories of violence—the fights, the beatings he'd delivered to those who had crossed him. And he was obviously intelligent, despite the fact that his formal education ended somewhere in the eighth grade. After twenty-plus years of police work, I'd become a pretty good judge of character. He was quiet and we'd only spent a few hours together that day but Pat seemed ... well, there's no other way to put it. He seemed like a good guy. Was there another side to the man? Or was that all just a façade? Who was Patrick Joseph Matter, really?

I was about to find out.

CHAPTER 1
Grim Reaper

If Chris felt some grudging respect for me, I couldn't quite admit to the same for him. Not then anyway. He was a cop and my experience with cops was anything but good. But when he introduced himself to me, he at least shook my hand firmly and he looked me directly in the eye like a man. I told him I knew who he was, though in truth I had never seen him before. But I'd heard about him. I knew there were some cops investigating me and his name had kept coming up. I didn't know how deep they'd gone, though. When Chris brought up aliases from years ago, I knew I was in the presence of a guy who took his job seriously. And it made me wonder what else he had turned up.

If he'd gone back far enough, he'd have gone back to Redwood Falls, Minnesota where I was born in 1951 to a well-digger and his wife. They'd had four kids before me, two girls and two boys. I was the youngest by eight years. By the time I came along the marriage had just about played itself out. Dad was an alcoholic and Mom ultimately had enough, leaving Dad and taking us with her to Fort Dodge, Iowa in 1954 where she had a sister.

Dad eventually followed and he and Mom tried to repair the relationship, but it didn't work out. Mom went to work as a waitress at a restaurant at the Fort Dodge train station where she met Gene, my future stepfather. Shortly after, she went to work at a bar and grill called G.I. Bill's, working nights until midnight or later and then spending the rest of the night at Gene's place. Gene didn't especially care for kids. By the time I was a little older, my brothers and sisters were out of the house and most of the time I was left basically alone, getting myself up in the mornings and getting myself off to school. From time to time my father would stop by to check on me, but for the most part he kept himself busy drinking. My sister Lucille looked after me sometimes but, like the rest of my siblings, she was looking to get away and would eventually move to Minneapolis in 1966.

By then, I would sometimes spend time at Gene's. We might play cards, but I never considered him any kind of father figure. The truth is, I resented him for spending so much time with my mother and there wasn't a whole lot he could have told me that I would have listened to.

When I was fifteen, my friend Ron Linder and I broke into a bar in Clare, Iowa and stole a bunch of beer and cigarettes and got caught. It was my first arrest. I was sent to the Iowa Boys' Reformatory in Eldora where I stayed for three months. I went back to Fort Dodge Junior High, but I didn't make it through the eighth grade, dropping out in December of that year and going to work in a pool hall called Musty's where I cooked burgers and bussed tables and collected the money for the hourly pool games. Musty—Mustafa Habhab—paid me thirty-five bucks a week. Mom supplemented my income, maybe out of some sense of wanting to compensate for not spending any time with me.

With $250 from her, I bought my first real motorcycle, a 1955 Royal Enfield. I'd had smaller bikes before; I'd always been intrigued by them. My father had bought me an 80 Yamaha once and before that, a little Doodle Bug mini bike with a Briggs & Stratton that he found in a pawn shop. I rode that thing all over the place.

At Musty's I made friends with some older guys, Johnny Klinger and Mike Ulicki. Johnny had a Norton motorcycle and Mike had a 650 BSA and they'd let me ride them. I started hustling pool back then, too, getting pretty good at it and making myself some extra money. I was hanging out a lot with my brother Rusty about that time. He was sort of looking out for me and we became close. Rusty had a friend named Finnegan who was a member of a motorcycle club called the Banshees. It was the first time I'd really heard about bike clubs. I met other members: Denny "Hog" Swanson, Denny

Grunwald, Leonard Johns, Denny DeGroote, Rick Wingerson. Something about these guys resonated with me. I liked their attitudes, the way they never took shit from anybody. They led outlaw lives and they rode powerful bikes. I think I knew right away that one day I'd be riding with them.

I was back in reform school in '67 and again in '68. Little things. Driving without a license, breaking and entering. By then, Rusty had moved to Omaha, Nebraska. Our older brother Don had moved there earlier, taking work as a roofer, and together the two of them sometimes raced stock cars. I got in trouble again in '69 and it was decided that rather than stick me back in reform school, maybe it would be best to send me someplace else altogether. So they paroled me to the custody of Rusty and it was off to Omaha.

Rusty was twenty-seven and going through a divorce at the time. I was seventeen and I'd use his I.D. to get into bars. A lot of times we'd both go out and drink and hustle pool. We'd hit the road sometimes, too, traveling to Sioux City, Iowa to a pool hall there. One night in Sioux City we were doing especially well, to the aggravation of those we were playing. We were betting a hundred dollars a game and we weren't exactly making friends. Two of the guys were becoming more and more pissed off and I could sense we were getting close to having a fight on our hands. I was all of 120 pounds. Rusty might have been 160. But we'd earned the money fair and square and I was prepared to keep it by whatever means might have been necessary. I'd been in fights before. Scrapes in school and around the neighborhood. Hell, Rusty and I had even gone at it with each other once or twice. I was small, but I was never intimidated by anyone. I'd take my share of licks, but I'd always give as good as I got.

On this night it didn't come to that. Two other guys had been watching, —a couple of bikers, and they didn't particularly care for the guys threatening us. One of the bikers was six foot eight. I'd find out later they called him Tiny. The other was a guy named Tom Fugle. Both were founding members of a club called the El Forasteros. Tiny walked up and turned to me and said, "Don't worry, kid. We got your back." We didn't have any trouble after that.

I went out with my brother Don sometimes, too. Don sometimes had a tendency to get a little out of hand after drinking. One night at a place called the Stadium Bar, Don had become obnoxious to the point where the bartender cut him off. Don jumped on the bar in protest and began kicking beer bottles off the bar. That was met with a bunch of guys—maybe eight or nine particularly big guys—picking Don up and tossing him out the back door. I got thrown out with him. Out behind the bar Don turned to me and said, "If you don't go back in there with me, I'm going to kick *your* ass." Wasn't much I could do. We went around front and stormed in and I hit the first guy that came at me as hard as I could and broke his nose. Don hit a couple guys and then we got chased out the front door and down the street. Rusty happened to be a block away, working with some friends on a stock car. They all saw the commotion and came running towards us and the whole parade suddenly switched direction and now we were chasing the guys from the Stadium Bar. We chased them back inside and figured that was enough for one evening.

I stayed in Omaha for six months, then Rusty decided he wanted to move back to Fort Dodge so I tagged along. But Rusty couldn't find work in Fort Dodge, so he moved again. "You'll have to stay," he told me. "You can live with Mom and Gene." But Gene had just found a job with Chrysler in Belvidere, Illinois and exactly two days after Rusty left, Mom and Gene moved away, too. But they left Mom's Fort Dodge apartment to me. I was all on my own, but at least I had a place to live.

It wasn't long after that that I did my first stint in jail. I had a '59 Chevy at the time for which I'd bought a pair of Cragar mag wheels. The wheels were cheap. Too cheap, as it happens. Thirty bucks. I turned around and resold them and both the guy I sold them to and I got busted for receiving stolen property. I did sixty days in the county jail for grand larceny. I was eighteen.

Shortly after my release I got into a bike accident on my cousin's motorcycle that sent me to the hospital for a couple days. I guess that was enough for my sisters who had gotten wind of my troubles and that I was on my own and they came down and took me back to

Minneapolis with them. I lived with Lucille until December of that year but when Rusty decided, once again, to move back to Fort Dodge, I went to live with him.

In Fort Dodge in 1971, I met a girl. Jackie and I became serious pretty quickly. But I needed to find work. Don was still roofing in Omaha and I decided to join him there. Jackie came along but she was never really comfortable in Omaha. Her parents and friends were all still in Fort Dodge, and so we moved back. We broke up once, but got back together soon after. The only problem was that she'd become pregnant in the meantime. The baby wasn't mine. I didn't care, I told her, and we got married in October. Rusty tried to talk me out of it the night before the wedding. I was twenty by then, but Rusty figured I was too young for marriage and a family. The discussion escalated and we ended up throwing fists at each other. I said my vows the next day sporting two black eyes.

Nikki was born in 1972 and I accepted her as though she was my own. I found work in Eagle Grove, about twenty miles outside of Fort Dodge, and Jackie and I found a house. Things were good. But by that time I'd acquired a 1948 Harley-Davidson Panhead and I was hanging out with Denny Swanson and Rick Wingerson. By then, they'd met some of the guys from the Des Moines chapter of a motorcycle club called the Grim Reapers and they'd given up their Banshee membership and now wore the Grim Reapers patch. Denny had become president of the Fort Dodge chapter. And so I was out of the house a lot with the guys from the Grim Reapers, drinking and carousing, sometimes getting in fights. Jackie ended up leaving in July, moving to Oklahoma where she had family.

I found a little farmhouse that I moved into and Denny Swanson got me a job at Rosie's Tire Service in Fort Dodge. Denny wanted me to join the Grim Reapers. They liked me; thought I was a stand-up guy. They knew I was tough, knew I was a scrapper. I'd be the first one to jump into a fight to defend one of the guys and I'd stick around for as long as it took. I wasn't afraid to use any edge I could find to compensate for my size—a pool cue, a beer bottle. I used to wear a chain belt that I made from the primary drive of an old Harley and

Pats first Harley. 48 Panhead. At farmhouse outside Fort Dodge. 1972.

that came in handy more than once. I told Denny, sure, I'd love to be a Grim Reaper. It was what I'd bought the Panhead for, after all.

To join the club—to join any motorcycle club—you start as a hangaround. It's just what it implies. You hang around the guys, you get to know them, they get to know you. If it looks like you'd be a good fit, they'll make you a club prospect. As a prospect, you have to prove yourself. Basically, you run errands for the guys; you chase beers, you make yourself available whenever they need you for something (even just as company to go drinking with), and you do any number of things that allows the club to size you up and see if you're worthy of membership. When you're done prospecting, typically after ninety days, they vote on you. If the vote goes your way, you get your club patch.

I became patched, but right after, Jackie moved back to town. She said she wanted to try again. So did I. I told the guys I was going to stop hanging out and I traded the Panhead in for a minibus and some cash and eventually traded the bus in for a '64 Chevelle. Jackie and I moved to Minneapolis in October of 1972 for a fresh start, living for a time with my sister Lucille. The guys in the club understood and wished me luck.

Jackie and I soon found an apartment. I took a job at a manufacturing plant and Jackie went to work at a department store. We bought furniture and then a new car. In May of 1973 we had a baby boy, Joseph.

From time to time through '73 and '74, Rick Wingerson or Denny Swanson would come up and visit. They'd bring their wives and stay with Jackie and me. They'd visit the Minneapolis chapter of the Grim Reapers and take me along, introducing me to the Minneapolis guys: Tramp, Red, Corky, and a bunch of others. I started becoming interested in the Grim Reapers again. I bought a 1972 Harley-Davidson Super Glide and at a Minneapolis Grim Reaper party in '74, I let them know I wanted to join. Denny had told them I was a full patch member back in Fort Dodge, but the Minneapolis guys were insistent that if I wanted to join their chapter, I needed to prospect for them.

So I began prospecting. But the process became tiresome quickly. In Fort Dodge the club had maybe six guys you needed to do gofer work for. The Minneapolis club had fifteen. There wasn't a night that went by that at least one of them didn't want to go out. And there were the requisite fights and scuffles. Defending Tramp in a bar fight one night, I had to use my chain belt to knock a guy out. It was night after night. I'd get calls from members at all hours. Once they called at four in the morning about some bullshit party and it woke up Joseph and Nikki. Prospecting was interfering with my job, not to mention my marriage. Finally, I figured I'd had enough. They knew me well enough by then. If I was worthy of the club patch, then give me the club patch. If not, screw it. I was done prospecting.

By then my brothers Don and Rusty had been visiting me, trying to talk me into going back to Fort Dodge. Don had moved back there by then. Jackie's parents still lived in Fort Dodge so she was all for it and I figured what the hell? I quit my job, quit the club, and in August of 1974 we moved back to Fort Dodge. Denny and Rick and the rest of the guys in the Fort Dodge Grim Reapers welcomed me back in. Rusty joined, too.

I loved the Ft. Dodge Grim Reapers. Mostly, I loved hanging with the guys. I'd practically grown up with them and they were like family to me. They gave me a sense of place. We drank together, we chased women together, we rode motorcycles together. Denny would one day name his son after me. Rick Wingerson was like another big brother to me. During the times when Jackie and I would be apart, I'd often stay at Rick's for a week or so. He was married with a couple of cute kids. We became tight. Rick had been my best man at my wedding and I always knew I could count on him and that he'd do anything for me. I didn't know at the time just what that would one day mean.

But the club and the late nights and the womanizing didn't sit well with Jackie. Before long, she moved out of our place and into her folks' house.

I went out with the Grim Reapers and I went out with Rusty and Don a lot, too. At a bar one night, Don picked a fight with the bartender. He'd been hitting on the bartender's girlfriend. One thing led to another and the two ended up outside and I jumped in, smacking the bartender over the head with a beer bottle. The cops came and I was arrested for aggravated assault, though the charge was later reduced to assault and battery.

In November of 1974, Don got into a fight with two brothers. The fight turned into a feud of sorts. One night Rick and I were out and somewhere around midnight we walked into a bar we frequented called the Blue Bomber. The bartender told us that a couple guys had come in earlier looking for Don. It was the brothers. The Chadas. I knew them. And the Chada brothers knew me, knew I sometimes carried a gun, though I wasn't carrying one on that particular night. The bartender said the brothers had armed themselves. Rick thought it'd be a good idea if we did the same. "We'll go back to my place," he said, "then we'll find Don. Warn him."

Fifteen minutes later we were walking through the cool night air towards Crinnigan's, a bar where we figured Don might be having a

Rick in his Grim Reaper colors. My best friend at the time.

drink. We were across the street from it, cutting across a bank parking lot when we spotted the Chadas coming out of the Silver Spur, a bar next to Crinnigan's. And they saw us. Without saying a word, one of them pulled a .357 magnum and started shooting at us. Rick pulled his .22 and fired back, hitting one of them. The other started firing as Rick took a few steps towards him. Three times Rick was hit. I came up behind him as he fell backwards and as I put my hand on his back I could feel the warm blood soaking through his jacket. I heard a single gasp and then he was quiet. Rick Wingerson was dead in my arms.

The paper the next day called it an old west shootout. It even made national news on Paul Harvey's radio news segment. At least sixteen shots had been fired and bullet holes could be seen on several of the surrounding downtown buildings. One Chada went to the hospital to have a bullet removed from his spine; both brothers would eventually plead guilty to manslaughter and be sentenced to eight years in the state penitentiary.

Rick's death wasn't easy to take. It was all a part of it, of course, a part of the outlaw biker lifestyle. There was risk. There was danger. And yet that was also part of the allure. And there was the camaraderie—being around guys who would fight for you, even die for you. It was a special bond that I don't imagine very many people understand, let alone experience. It made me all the more determined to stick with it. Being a Grim Reaper was just the beginning.

At Stillwater Prison Run 1978.

Front Row L-R: Rusty, Stinger, Pat, Skezzicks.

Second Row L-R: Bernie (facing backwards), unknown, Geno, unknown, Robert "Red" Miner, Paul "Rooster" Seydel (standing).

Back Row: L-R: Unknown, John, Dave Benedict, Dave "Moose" Smith, Ed "Fast Ed" Dias, Jim "Mort" Morrow, Gunner, Shotgun and Robert "Maggot" McCollough.

CHAPTER 2
Gramps

In the summer of 1975, I decided to get out of Fort Dodge. I couldn't find work and it was too small a town for me. I preferred Minneapolis and moved back, signing up for unemployment and being sent to a welding school for three months. That enabled me to land a job back with the same manufacturing company I'd worked with before. By then, Jackie and I were back together and she came along. The four of us, Nikki, Joseph, Jackie, and me, moved into an apartment in Bloomington. Eventually I would become the manager of the apartment complex.

I began hanging with the Minneapolis Grim Reaper guys again, although I'd continue to wear the black and white Iowa patch until the following year. In December of '75 we were all at a bar called the Barbary Coast in Shakopee, about a half hour outside of Minneapolis. Drinks were two for one and we were all having a good time. Then Tramp got himself into a fight with a couple locals and a brawl quickly broke out. I jumped in and grabbed one of the locals and started punching and I didn't stop until he was down on the floor and then I kicked him in the head for good measure. By then someone had called the cops so we all ran out of the bar and jumped into our cars and started heading back to Minneapolis. Four miles away the cops pulled us over and I was identified and then arrested.

Joe Friedberg, an acquaintance of Tramp's, was more or less the club attorney, a young aggressive guy just starting his career. Today, he's one of the top lawyers in the state of Minnesota. He defended me on the charge of aggravated assault. I was facing five years. A request was made by the county attorney to prohibit the identification of witnesses to the fight; we might have made a threat or two before leaving the bar that night about what we might do to anyone who talked.

Joe's partners, Jack Wylde and William Mauzy, ultimately represented me and rather than risk a jury trial, we decided to plead guilty to a misdemeanor. In court, the judge asked me about the fight.

"What have you got," he said, "a short fuse?"

"No," I replied. "Not really."

"What caused the fight?"

"Well, I believe I was rather intoxicated and … I don't know, there were a few words between me and the man I assaulted. I'm sure he was very intoxicated, too." Then the judge asked me about my work, how I made a living, about Jackie and the kids. I had to support them. He sentenced me to eight days in the county jail and allowed me to serve them over four consecutive weekends. I thought it was pretty decent of him.

But there would be another fight a month later. A more serious one. Glen Breeden—"Gorilla"—was an officer in the Des Moines chapter of the Grim Reapers. I liked Gorilla. I didn't know him real well, but he was a good guy; he kept coming up to Minnesota after Jackie and I had moved back, trying to get me to move to Des Moines. Said the club could use me down there. And my Iowa patch from Fort Dodge meant that I was a member in Des Moines as well. I told him I'd think about it.

At the end of '75, Gorilla came up and told the Minneapolis chapter that he needed their help. There was another club out of Boone, Iowa called the Last Chapter. The Iowa Grim Reapers had been partying with them, courting them. The Last Chapter guys wanted to fold their club into a bigger one. Everything had been going well until a club called the Sons of Silence began courting the Last Chapter guys, too. They were even willing to waive the prospecting process and just give them all Sons of Silence patches. The Grim Reapers insisted on having the Last Chapter guys prospect; they wanted to do things right. When the Last Chapter guys spurned the Grim Reapers in favor of the Sons of Silence, needless to say it didn't sit well with the Iowa Grim

Reapers. Gorilla had come up to Minneapolis to ask for help in setting things right. The Last Chapter was going to be having a party on January 2nd, and he knew where. "We need to take care of business," he said.

I went down to Boone with some of the other guys about a week early to scout things out. We saw the bar where the Last Chapter would most likely be hanging out, a place called Wilson's Tavern. A week later, January 2, 1976, the Minneapolis guys hooked up with the Fort Dodge and Des Moines guys and we all headed for Boone. There were probably thirty of us. I was driving my '70 Barracuda and Red and Tramp rode with me. When we got to Wilson's we didn't see any of the Last Chapter members around. About half of us left the bar and started walking down the street to another bar where we figured they might be when all of the Last Chapter guys suddenly came up from the basement of the first bar. They had as many guys as we had, maybe more, and the fight spilled out onto the street. There were chains and clubs being swung around and I was cracking guys with a baseball bat.

After the melee, we all jumped into our cars and started heading back for Des Moines. Somewhere around Ames, maybe ten miles outside of Boone, Red and Tramp and I got pulled over by the cops. They'd surrounded us and had us at gunpoint. Then they loaded us up and took us to the Boone County Courthouse where they told us there'd been a killing. One of our guys had been stabbed to death. It was Gorilla.

The cops drove the three of us to the hospital where several members of the Last Chapter had ended up—I think I may have put a couple there myself—and asked if we could identify anybody who might have used a knife on Gorilla. I hadn't seen Gorilla go down and neither had Red or Tramp, but I don't think any of us would have said anything anyway. That's the biker code. We told the cops no one looked familiar and they took us back to the courthouse where a news van had pulled up and the news people began filming us as we were led inside. Then the cops told us we'd need to come back to appear before a grand jury to testify and we said sure, we'd come back. But we just wanted to get the hell out of there; for one thing, I had a trunk load of guns in the Barracuda. They let us go and we made for Des Moines to meet up with the rest of the guys. We never did go back to Boone to testify to any grand jury.

The next day I was given the Minneapolis Grim Reaper patch. To this day, Gorilla's death remains unsolved. A grand jury report stated that it was impossible, despite the testimonies of forty witnesses, to say with any certainty who had stabbed Gorilla to death in the chaos of the brawl.

Later that year, Jackie and I had another son, Chad. But things weren't getting any better between her and I. I wasn't paying much attention to the family. I was hanging out with the guys, partying and fighting and picking up women.

I had a few scrapes with the law over the course of the next couple years, too, including a conviction for what's known in Minnesota legalese as defeating security on personalty. It's a kind of fraud. A buddy of mine let me take his truck and then he reported it stolen for the insurance money. They caught him and he made a deal by turning me in. I admitted to changing the VIN numbers. But it wasn't like I'd stolen the truck. Joe Friedberg represented me once again and though I was facing potentially two years in prison, I ended up with two years' probation.

There was a disorderly conduct charge, too. "Dirty" Bill Daun, a club member, built custom bikes, including mine at the time. He came over one day and said let's go for a drive and we jumped on our bikes and headed downtown. Both our bikes had straight pipes, meaning no muffler or baffle, and they were loud as hell. We got pulled over and cited for disturbing the peace and we figured, well, so long as we got the ticket, we might as well get our money's worth. The cop was getting back in his car and we took off, making as much noise as we could and the cop pulled us over again. This time we were arrested, our bikes were impounded, and we spent the next seven hours in the county jail.

In September of 1977, I met a girl named Leslie. She was twenty and slender with long, dark hair and she was a lot fun. I was still living with Jackie but I started seeing Leslie and I found myself falling in love. On our second time out, we spent the night together and she offered me something I'd never tried before—crystal meth. I liked it. It kept you up, gave you energy. It acted as an alcohol repellent; you could drink as much as you wanted and not get drunk. I started thinking a guy could make some serious money selling the stuff.

It turned out that Red had a brother who was able to introduce me to a guy named Dallas Wildey. Dallas could get me meth—grams and quarter ounces. I was still working at the manufacturing plant, night shift, and I began selling dime bags of the stuff to the guys there. I was making three or four hundred dollars a week selling it at work and soon I started selling it to other Grim Reaper members, too. Then I started looking for bigger suppliers, expanding my business. By February of 1978, I quit my job and started dealing full time.

Jackie meanwhile had moved out a couple months after I'd started seeing Leslie and by March of '78, she'd taken the kids and moved back to Iowa. In July, she moved all the way back to Oklahoma.

Leslie and I kept seeing each other. She seemed to appreciate my lifestyle and even joined in. Together with an old Fort Dodge buddy of mine named Mark who came up to visit and another guy named Ron, we decided to rob a drug dealer I knew of. We burst into his house and held him at gunpoint and scored some meth, about five pounds of pot, and about a thousand bucks in cash. Later, back at my place, the four of us got into a card game for the cash. I won most of it.

In 1979, I moved to north Minneapolis. Jackie, still in Oklahoma, filed for divorce. By then, I'd been spending a significant amount of my free time with the Grim Reapers. I never missed a function and kept pushing us to do more. I'd more or less settled into a leadership position with the club and one day they made it official and voted me president. There were a few more scrapes with the law, including the suspension of my license for speeding and a ten-mile police chase through Minneapolis to a friend's house. They took me downtown for that one.

Around that time I began hearing about a guy named Roger "Gramps" Sheehan who had just gotten out of Leavenworth. Gramps, along with a group of other guys, had been busted for dealing drugs.

They were all members of the Minneapolis chapter of a little motorcycle club called the Hells Angels. Most were still in prison and consequently, the chapter was essentially defunct. I loved being a Grim Reaper and I even had a grudging respect for other outlaw motorcycle clubs, but there was nothing else like the Hells Angels and I knew it. Everyone did. The Hells Angels was *the* club and I had thought they were cool as far back as I could remember.

Gramps & Dago. Gramps inspired me to rebuild a Minnesota Hells Angels Chapter. Dago and I were always up to mischief.

Through an acquaintance of mine named Scratch I met Gramps. Gramps had been wearing a Nebraska bottom rocker that the Omaha chapter had given him but he was looking to start the Minneapolis chapter back up again. I liked Gramps right away. He always wore a cowboy hat with a big hat band and he was personable and funny. He'd tease me about my height. We started hanging out together. Gramps liked to party, always doing weed or coke, trying to make up for the lost years in Leavenworth. More than anything, Gramps loved the Hells Angels. The club had been his whole life. And he knew how active I was with the Grim Reapers and what I'd been up to. "You're a mover and a shaker," he would say. "A money maker. And you got style. You could be a Hells Angel."

Soon Gramps was introducing me to other Hells Angels that came into town. Lightning Les from Omaha, Thunder from Charlotte, Mitch from Rochester. They all liked me. At a bar one night I backed up Mitch in a fight with another club called the BPMs (Beer, Pussy, and Motorcycles) and that seemed to impress everybody. Thunder told me to move down to Charlotte. He was president of the chapter. "We'll sponsor you," he said. "We want you in the club." Lightning Les said I could join in Omaha if I wanted to.

I knew I was going to become a Hells Angel almost right away. There was just something about these guys—the way they carried themselves, the way they dressed, their gold rings. The iconic Hells Angels patch. They were sharp as hell and they knew how to take care of business. They were a huge step above the typical, grungy, old-

Lightning Les. Inspired me to be a Hells Angel. Wanted me to move to Omaha.

school biker dudes with the dirty jeans, my Grim Reapers included. You needed six members to make a chapter and I became determined to start one in Minneapolis. I'd take Lightning Les up on his offer and go to Omaha if I had to, because I was going to be a Hells Angel no matter what, but I was sure going to try like hell to put together a chapter right where I lived.

Then in July of 1980, Lightning Les was killed, shot at a party in north Omaha by a guy who was later found innocent by reason of self-defense. Apparently an argument had broken out in the wee hours of the morning between the killer's wife and a friend of Les's. Les stabbed the guy in the leg and the guy shot Les.

I went to Les's funeral where I met a lot more Hells Angels, all good guys. I wanted to be a part of their club more than ever. But I was keeping my thoughts pretty much to myself around most of the Grim Reapers. The guys knew I'd started spending a lot of time with Gramps and some of the other Hells Angels, but I didn't want any animosity between us. When the time was right, I figured I'd enlist several of them to make up the new Minnesota Hells Angels' chapter.

In September of 1980 about fifteen of us Grim Reapers went to the annual Defeat of Jesse James Days in Northfield, Minnesota, a big outdoor festival that commemorates the town's successful thwarting of a robbery attempt of the First National Bank of Northfield by the James-Younger Gang. In September of 1876, local citizens apparently armed themselves and killed a couple gang members on the main street and the rest of the gang was eventually cornered in the nearby town of Madelia; that is, all except for two of them. Frank and Jesse James managed to escape west into the Dakotas.

In any event, the town celebrated it annually with the festival and we all went down there and there was a big party one night at a nearby farmhouse hosted by the Timberwolves Motorcycle Club. There were maybe four or five hundred people there with a band playing in the barn. A lot of motorcycle clubs were in attendance—the BPMs, the El Forasteros, the Sons of Silence, the Choppers. We didn't really get along with any of them, which is one of the things the Hells Angels liked about us.

Gramps was there and he got into a heated argument with a guy named Corky from the BPMs. Turns out Gramps had belonged at one time and in fact the original Minneapolis Hells Angels' chapter had come out of the BPMs. I told Gramps I had his back, but the argument never got too serious. But a little later, out in the yard, we Grim Reapers found ourselves in a confrontation of our own with some members of the Choppers. They were wearing Sons of Silence patches. Like the last Chapter, the Choppers had at one time considered joining the Grim Reapers before spurning us for the Sons of Silence. There was bad blood between our clubs. I don't know how it started but a big melee broke out. The Timberwolves joined in, taking sides with the Sons of Silence and one Timberwolf rushed me, swinging a club. I pulled my 9mm Browning and shot him in the leg and he went down but other guys started coming. Along with fellow Grim Reaper Paul "Rooster" Seydel, I pistol whipped a couple of them. During the fight we managed to take some patches from some of the Sons of Silence. And then another one of our guys, Moose, sprayed his Mini-14 semi-automatic overtop of everybody, bullets flying through the roof of the barn. That kind of slowed everything down and we all went for our bikes, huddling up two by two and riding the fuck out of town. Later, we hung the Sons of Silence patches upside down on the wall of our clubhouse.

The papers the next day talked about the shooting but mentioned that no charges would be filed because nobody was talking. A member of the Dakota County sheriff's department acknowledged that lots of drinking and fighting had gone on. "A good time was had by all," he said. Then he added, "But I wouldn't know because I wasn't there. You'd have to be crazy to go in there with hundreds of members of motorcycle gangs."

The shooting helped my reputation; I wasn't afraid to stand up to anybody and use whatever force was necessary. Thunder came up to visit Gramps and Gramps told him about the incident. Thunder was impressed and invited me down to the Charlotte Hells Angels' first anniversary party. Thunder was six-two with thinning hair that he pulled back into a ponytail. He had a big gut that hung off a small chest and he had heavy thighs, too. Sort of a funny build, but there really wasn't anything funny about Thunder. He didn't smile very often and he had a full beard and intense, dark brown eyes that could pierce right through you. We flew down to Charlotte together. My first time on an airplane. Thunder's new red corvette was waiting for us when we landed and we drove directly to a motel room where we met another Charlotte member named Ronnie. Ronnie had four girls waiting for us there, all from a local strip club and all regulars at the Charlotte clubhouse. The dancers liked having the Hells Angels around. The guys acted as protectors and the dancers felt safe. Naturally, there were sexual favors.

At the anniversary party I was wearing the Minneapolis red and white Grim Reaper patch which happened to be the colors of the Hells Angels. A couple of the Angels said they didn't allow those colors to be worn around there by anybody besides their own club members. "We see red and white patches, we take 'em, you know?" These guys were real southern boys and I wasn't feeling exactly welcomed. But then I smiled and said, that's funny because where I come from we shoot people for trying to take our patches. "You know?" It was a really ballsy thing to say, but it was what I knew I needed to say. And I could tell they respected me for saying it. We got along from then on.

In Charlotte, I got my first taste of how serious the war was that had been going on seemingly forever between the Hells Angels and the Hells Angels' major rivals, the Outlaws. The hatred between the clubs had given rise to a catch-phrase often uttered by Outlaw members: ADIOS. It was more than just a way to say goodbye. It was an acronym that stood for Angels Die In Outlaw States. At the party, I noticed a Hells Angels prospect stationed on the roof of the bar we were in with an AR-15 semiautomatic. "Guard duty," someone explained to me. "He's watching for Outlaws. Lots of guys been killed on both sides." Thunder mentioned to me that the on the Fourth of July, 1979, five Outlaws had been shot to death in a house in Charlotte. Dubbed the July 4th Massacre by all the papers, it remained an unsolved crime. Thunder didn't say who did it. I didn't ask.

There was another club that had been invited to the party.

Thunder had invited six El Forasteros, guys he knew well. I knew a few of them: 8-Ball and Shifty from Kansas City and Websie from St. Louis. But they were kind of huddling with each other while I was mingling with everybody. Harry, a Hells Angel from Cleveland, turned to me at one point and laughed, "You know, all those El Forasteros could be wiped out with a single lightning bolt, seeing as how they all hang together so close." He liked that I was getting around, making friends. "What are your intentions?" he asked.

"I'm becoming a Hells Angel," I said.

"Well you know what? I think that's a good idea. I like you already."

All in all, it was a great time. Ronnie took me back to the airport the next day. If my mind hadn't been made up about becoming a Hells Angel before the trip, it certainly had been by the time I got back to Minneapolis. Strangely, though, I never saw Ronnie again.

Upon my return I told some of the Grim Reaper guys that I was going to be a Hells Angel.

"Oh c'mon, Pat," said Tank. "Fuck those guys." Tank was six feet four and 420 pounds. But he was a gentle giant. Polite. You'd have to push him to fight, but he was surprisingly athletic and you wouldn't want to have to face off against him.

"Well, Tank," I said, "I'd planned on having you come with me."

"Oh. Well, I didn't know that," Tank said. "That's different. Okay, then."

Tank came along and so did Rooster, whom I'd known from Iowa. We'd become close. Rooster wasn't much taller than I was and maybe a little stockier. He had a little goatee and wore glasses and sported a long ponytail. He'd moved to Minneapolis in 1978 and even though I'd had to wait for mine, I'd made sure Rooster got his Minneapolis Grim Reapers' patch right away.

Along with Tank and Rooster were Bear, Foot, and Finnegan. With me, that made six from the Grim Reapers. Ron Fischl, an original Minnesota Hells Angel, and Bill Ellis, both friends of Gramps, made eight. There was still a long ways to go to become chartered. But the Minnesota chapter of the Hells Angels was about to be reborn.

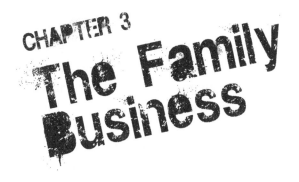

CHAPTER 3
The Family Business

Pat Matter's career as a Hells Angel started at exactly the same time as my career as a cop. While he was prospecting for a Minneapolis charter, I was doing some prospecting of my own, paying my dues in Edina, Minnesota as a CSO—community service officer—for the Edina police department. I was working less than a twenty-minute drive from where Pat lived, though it would be a few more years before I'd start hearing his name.

A city of less than fifty thousand, Edina is a wealthy, first tier sub-urb of Minneapolis. My work there started as an internship while attending community college, getting my associate's degree in law enforcement. I was nineteen. I took the job as CSO as a way to get my foot in the door. It wasn't easy to get police work back then. There would be dozens if not hundreds of applicants for every position that came open. I started part-time: dispatching, helping with inventory and evidence, picking up stray dogs, basically whatever grunt work the real, full-time police officers needed to have done. It wasn't exactly glamorous but I was determined. I was going to be a cop no matter what.

It's what I'd always wanted to be. Police work is what my father did. It's what my grandfather did. It's even what my great uncle did. Hans Martin Aamodt was a sergeant with the Oslo (then called Kristiana) Police Department. His brother, my great-grandfather Bernt Kristian Aamodt, came over from Norway in 1893. They called him Chris, just like me, and somewhere along the line the spelling of the last name changed to Omodt. Chris's son, Hugh Martin Omodt, my grandfather, was a St. Paul detective. Though he died when I was just seven, I grew up admiring him. My father would tell me stories. Grandpa was strong, with massive shoulders that he developed as a fishing guide on Big Stone Lake in western Minnesota. There were no outboard motors in his day and Hugh rowed his clients everywhere. For fifty cents a day. And he was apparently one hell of a cop. St. Paul was rough-and-tumble back then and Hugh was an experienced brawler and street fighter and preferred his fists to his gun or night-stick. But after being reprimanded for ruining no less than four uniforms, he reluctantly switched to his nightstick. As a detective he worked on some major cases and even had an encounter with John Dillinger. In the fall of 1933, Hugh and his fellow officers and some FBI agents combined in a raid on an apartment where Dillinger had been staying. Dillinger had apparently been tipped off. He fled the apartment just as the cops were getting ready to move in, but not before spraying machine gun fire everywhere. Dillinger got away, but at least nobody got hurt. And my grandfather had a good story to tell.

Hugh also spent a good deal of time as a top-notch auto theft investigator, something that would especially resonate with me during the course of my own career. Before detective, he was a patrolman and spent a few years patrolling on a Harley-Davidson, one complete with sidecar. And before patrolman, Hugh was a World War I hero, serving on a U.S. submarine that patrolled the waters off the Irish coast and single-handedly taking charge of a confrontation with two German U-boats, sinking them both and receiving a commendation for exhibiting "splendid discipline and coolness." The commendation now hangs on my wall.

But Grandpa experienced tragedy in his life. His daughter Marie, my father's sister, died in childhood after an illness. When she was near death, Grandpa took a night off from work and it so happened that on that night, his partner, and best friend, was killed in a shootout trying to thwart an attempted robbery. Grandpa's daughter died just a few days later and my father said my grandfather was never the same after that week.

Dad followed Grandpa into law enforcement, working with the

My grandpa, Hugh, and my dad, about 4 years old on grandpas Harley. About 1931.

FBI under none other than J. Edgar Hoover in Washington. He was also an attorney with a Ph.D. in law. He loved the Bureau and was proud of it. Eventually he was transferred from D.C. to Salt Lake City where a tragic incident with a gas leak in a hotel heater caused significant brain damage to my parents' firstborn child, my oldest sister. They stayed in Salt Lake for a time but then after a short stint in Chicago, Dad felt like he needed to be back home, back where he was from—St. Paul—to better care for my sister. He left the FBI.

Back home he got a job as criminal prosecutor for Hennepin County, in Minneapolis. In 1966, he ran for sheriff, won, and remained sheriff for twenty-eight years. I was born in '60 and Dad was still sheriff as I began my career nineteen years later. "I can make a place for you," he'd tell me. But I wanted to make it on my own. I needed to blaze my own trail and I never wanted anyone thinking I got a lucky break because my father happened to be sheriff. So I started in Edina as a lowly CSO. Dad understood.

In 1983, I became a full-time cop—a patrolman, humping a squad car as we called it, doing general police duties. What I really wanted to be was a detective. Deep down, it's all I'd ever really wanted to be. Dad had told me about a guy named Don Enger with the Edina P.D., one of the best detectives he'd ever known, and I kept my eye on Don and tried to learn as much as I could. The year I started fulltime, Don was digging up information on a motorcycle club—the Minneapolis chapter of the Hells Angels. An informant had told him who the president of the club was, a guy named Pat Matter. Matter was dealing a lot of dope, including meth. Don passed the information along to a task force that was doing some investigative work on the Hells Angels but I don't think too much came of it, and I didn't really give the matter much thought at the time.

The fact is I didn't know too much about motorcycle clubs at all. Of course I'd heard of the Hells Angels—who hadn't? But I just assumed they weren't a whole lot more than a gang of guys who rode Harleys and drank and got into occasional bar fights. I certainly wouldn't have thought of them as being any kind of sophisticated criminal enterprise.

My first direct experience with a motorcycle club was in 1984. Early on a Sunday August morning, I was running radar on a stretch of County Road 62 when a Harley came by doing 75—twenty miles an hour over the speed limit. I turned on my lights and pulled the Harley over and through my rearview mirror I suddenly saw about a dozen or so bikes following. I walked up to the guy I'd pulled over and glanced behind me to see all the other bikes pulling over behind my squad car. I had no idea what the hell I'd just gotten myself into but I knew I wasn't going to show any fear. I cited the first Harley driver and he pulled out and the rest of the bikes followed him, having waited patiently and respectfully for me to conclude my business with him, and I was finally able to exhale. The bikers all wore patches, I'm sure, but it didn't occur to me to see what they were, to see what club they all belonged to. Could have been the Hells Angels for all I know, although I suspect it was one of the smaller clubs, one of the clubs I didn't even know existed back then. Looking back, based on the time of year, I can guess they were probably all returning from the annual motorcycle rally in Sturgis, South Dakota. But that wouldn't have occurred to me at the time either. I knew damn little about biker clubs. What an education I was going to get in the years to come.

But if I didn't know about biker clubs, I at least knew about bikes. I loved them. I road mini bikes as a kid and got my first real motorcycle just after I'd turned sixteen and gotten my driver's license. It was a '73 Yamaha CT3 Enduro, and my acquisition of it was actually my father's idea. Not that he wanted me riding a motorcycle. What he wanted was to keep me off the back of my buddy's Yamaha 175. That was my ride to school every morning. "I'd rather have you at least driving your own," Dad said. Needless to say he didn't really need to twist my arm.

Later, I'd buy myself a Honda 450. After I got married, I'd ride my father-in-law's Harleys when we'd visit him at his place in Bismarck during the summers. I loved the Harleys, the weight of them, the way they looked, the way they felt. There's nothing like a Harley.

At any rate, I humped a squad car for most of the 1980s. Then I heard talk about Edina wanting to put a narcotics investigator on the force. We didn't have one. It would be a way to learn investigation, be a path to detective. I'd learn about illegal drug distribution, too, something I was pretty naive about back then. My first brush with the drug trade had actually happened a few years earlier, though I had no idea at the time. I was grouse hunting in the woods of Cloquet Valley State Forest when I encountered a rough-looking dude in denim overalls holding a shotgun. He wasn't a fellow hunter; that much I could tell.

"Get the fuck off my land," he said evenly.

I had a map with me and I knew where I was. "This is public land," I said and I started to unfold the map.

"I said get the fuck off my land." I put the map away and decided not to argue. Or tell him I was a cop. It was him and me, and we both had guns and I couldn't imagine a good ending to the encounter. I walked away. A week later, the guy was busted. He'd had a cabin back in the woods and he'd been operating a meth lab. They sent him to the federal pen in Rochester. You just never know where a meth lab is going to turn up.

Anyway, when the narcotics investigation position came up, I sent a memo to the chief telling him I wanted it and in 1990 they gave it to me. It was a six-month stint, kind of a trial thing to determine if having a narcotics investigator was worthwhile. They decided it was and I took the job full-time in '91.

By then I'd been working on various cases with other narcotics investigators in other agencies around the area, including a captain I really admired from the sheriff's office named Rocky Fontana. Rocky liked my work. I'd been involved in some big cases. One day Rocky pulled me aside and told me the sheriff's office was expanding their narcotics division from five to fifteen investigators. "You should apply, Chris," he said. "We want you there."

Don Enger, meanwhile, had kind of taken me under his wing and had been telling me to move on to something bigger than narc for

My ID card while working narcotics. 1993.

Edina, Minnesota. "Go somewhere where you can really put your talents to use," he'd said. I wasn't going to go to my father for a job in the sheriff's office, but in this case, his office had come looking for me. By then I figured I'd paid my dues. I applied and before long I was working for the Hennepin County Sheriff's Department.

For the next three years I did investigative work. It was great experience and a perfect road towards becoming detective. A lot of the action involved undercover work and in the course of one case I ended up buying pound quantities of weed from a biker dude in northeast Minneapolis, not far from the Hells Angels clubhouse. He was a Hells Angel, we were all sure of it. He rode a Harley, had tattoos, wore a leather jacket. What else could he be? Turned out he was just a guy who rode a Harley and smoked weed. I had a lot to learn about the Hells Angels, but so did the entire department.

The club was really kind of a mystery to law enforcement in general, at least in the Midwest. Around our part of the country, the

Pat's booking photo at the Hennepin County Jail, March 1981 – Friday the 13th!

Hells Angels flew pretty much under the radar through the 1980s as the crack epidemic exploded and narcotics departments were focused elsewhere. Nobody really bothered to monitor the activities of biker gangs. Nobody knew what a player the Hells Angels organization had become. But in the years to come, I'd make a study of them. I'd need to in order to bring down the local chapter's president, whose name started coming up regularly by then. It seemed Pat Matter was into a little bit of everything. That shooting at Jesse James Days helped build Pat's reputation amongst bikers, but it helped build it amongst law enforcement, too. In fact, there was a wanted poster floating around with Pat's mug shot on it and a note that said: *Known to have shot a Sons of Silence member at Jesse James Days.* The poster listed Pat's aliases, too. *Silver Tooth. The Mad Hatter.*

Pat was rubbing people the wrong way and not just us cops. He was making real enemies. The deadly kind. I remember hearing about an attempt on his life in 1993. Someone had blown up his truck. Other names kept popping up, too. Names like Rooster and Tank.

As for me, my daughter Rachel was born in 1991 and my son Matthew in '93. I worked for Narcotics until 1994 when I made detective. I earned a B.S. degree that year, too, from Cardinal Stritch College (now University) in Milwaukee. The next year my father retired. Minnesota Senator Paul Wellstone paid tribute to Dad with a short speech in the U. S. Senate, extolling Dad's years of exemplary service. It was quite an honor and I was proud to be an Omodt. Proud to be a cop.

CHAPTER 4
Thunder

So it seems as if Chris and I were starting our careers at the same time. But, man, were we going in different directions.

Over Thanksgiving of 1980, we Minnesota would-be prospects, just hangarounds at that point, went to Omaha. Since there were no other Hells Angels chapters in Minnesota, we had to go out of state to find a sponsor. The Omaha club was going to be our sponsors. I was voted on by our group to be president of our eventual chapter. In Omaha they told Rooster and Tank and me that if we wanted to prospect to be Hells Angels, we'd have to quit the Grim Reapers. Back in Minneapolis, we officially quit. There were still eleven or twelve Grim Reapers left and they weren't exactly happy with what we were doing. We had a few words about it, but that was it. I told them they could have the treasury, the clubhouse, everything. We'd go our way and they'd go theirs.

The Omaha chapter also insisted that we tell some friends of theirs in Minneapolis that we were planning on forming a Hells Angels chapter: the El Forasteros. "You gotta tell them," they said. "We gotta show 'em some respect." Ron Fischl and I met a couple El Forasteros at a place called the Chug-a-Lug and let them know our intentions. "We hope it won't be a problem," I told them, "because we aim to be Hells Angels up here and we'll do whatever we need to do. Fight, die, whatever." They respected that. They hated it, though. They thought of their club as the number one club around the area and they knew a Hells Angels' chapter would make them second fiddle. But they had to respect our intentions and they knew I was ready to back up what

I'd told them. I reported back to Gramps and the Omaha guys and let them know we'd talked it out with the El Forasteros and that there weren't going to be any problems. Not that they would have helped us if there had been. That's all part of wanting to be a Hells Angel. You need to show you can make it on your own. There's no asking for help. Not while you're a hangaround or prospect.

The Chug-a-Lug was a place we hung out in a lot, especially as Grim Reapers. I tended bar there at one time while Leslie waited tables. One night after we'd started prospecting, a couple of the Omaha guys were in town and hanging out in the Chug-a-Lug. I'd gone home earlier but got a phone call from one of them—Corky. Corky said, "Pat, you'd better get your ass back down here. We got a little problem with some Hells Outcasts guys." The Hells Outcasts, from St. Paul, were another motorcycle club, another Hells Angels wannabe club. I knew some of them. I grabbed my .380 and drove by Rooster's house and picked him up and we headed for the Chug-a-Lug.

When we got there, we stormed in and I fired a round into the ceiling and grabbed an Outcast named Smitty. "Do we have a problem, here, Smitty?"

"No, Pat!" yelled Corky across the bar, "It's okay. It's all over. We're cool with these guys!"

"Yeah, we're cool!" pleaded Smitty. "Everything's been worked out!" Sometime between Corky's phone call and our bursting into the bar, the bartender had apparently hit one of the Hells Outcasts in the head with his .38 and that slowed things down and reason had apparently prevailed. A disagreement over a game of 6-5-4 had started the scrap but everyone had talked it out and nobody wanted any more trouble. I put the gun away and let Smitty go.

It was another episode that helped build my reputation. I wasn't a guy to be fucked with. Thankfully, it never got to the point where I'd have to follow through, where I'd actually have to pull the trigger on someone. Unless it was self-defense, I knew I didn't really have it in me. But of course no one else knew that and that's the way I wanted to keep it.

Meanwhile, my drug business had been expanding. Since 1979,

I'd been buying meth and coke mainly from Dallas Wildey but once I met Gramps, I started buying a lot of meth from him. Wildey would eventually get himself shot and killed. Gramps introduced me to an ex-Hells Angels prospect named Romel Ferguson, a black guy, a real rarity for the Hells Angels. (In fact, in 1986, the club would put the unspoken rule in writing: "No niggers in the club.") Ferguson started supplying me with coke.

At the beginning of 1981, Gramps had a brain aneurysm that left him in pretty bad shape. He could barely walk let alone ride his bike. It was hard seeing him like that. Gramps had been instrumental in getting me involved in the Hells Angels as well as helping me to grow my business. Of course I'd always make sure he had a place with us.

By then, Gramps had introduced me to a guy named Billy West and I began getting supplied by him, as well as from Thunder who'd make trips up from Charlotte now and again. I was buying in large quantities, selling mostly to the guys in the club who were reselling it. We were all making good money. One time Billy and I made a trip to Charlotte to make a purchase from Thunder. Three pounds of meth. John, a friend of Thunder's and a fellow Hells Angel, drove us by way of back roads to the Greensboro airport, rather than the busier Charlotte airport. Billy was wearing a big vest with lots of pockets which he loaded with all three pounds of meth. We walked right through the airport and onto the plane. Billy was cool as ice. I was on edge until after we'd landed in Minneapolis and made it to the parking lot. But at the same time, I thought it was pretty damn cool to be a part of something so brazen.

In February of 1981, the Omaha chapter got raided by the cops. The charges were many and varied—mostly for using threats, torture, and even murder to corner the Omaha drug market. Collectively, it was called CCE: Continuing Criminal Enterprise, a federal law that targets large-scale drug traffickers. Our sponsoring chapter, for all intents and purposes, was now defunct. Stepping in was Thunder. He liked me. "Matter's a cocky little fucker," he'd say, "but he'll back it up." The Charlotte chapter would now be our sponsors.

Hells Angel Chapter Omaha, Nebraska.
Front Row: John Coffman
Back Row – L to R: Charles "Chaz" Miller, Calvin Davenport, Lamont Kress,
Bob LNU, Gary Apker. About 1985-86.

By then, Bear and Foot were out of the picture. Bear quit and we threw Foot out. Tank and Foot had gotten busted crossing the Minnesota-Iowa line with some stolen John Deere tractors. I signed Foot's bond for him and then he jumped bond and fled to Iowa. I sent Rooster and Tank down to get him. They found him and brought him back and I handcuffed him to a pole down in my basement. I asked Thunder what I should do. "Well, you can't turn him into the cops," he said. "You have to either turn him into the bail bondsman or kill him."

The way Thunder said it I could tell he didn't much care one way or the other what the choice would be. It was the first of many hints into Thunder's personality that I would start picking up on. Over time, I would learn that Thunder was a bona-fide psychopath. As for Foot, we took him to the bail bondsman.

By then, we'd also lost Finnegan. At least temporarily. Turns out Finnegan had caught his wife cheating on him. He chased the guy up a flight of stairs at his apartment building with a.45 Thompson submachine gun. The guy jumped off a second story balcony while Finnegan shot the gun into the air. So Finnegan was doing a little time in prison and that left us with five guys, not enough for a charter. Thunder suggested I move to North Carolina and join the Charlotte chapter. But Finnegan would be out of prison in a few months and we'd be six again. I was staying put in Minnesota.

Later that summer was the Hells Angels' USA Run, held at Kerr Lake along the border of North Carolina and Virginia. The USA Run is an annual event, kind of a Hells Angels' convention. Everyone comes and guys often bring their wives and sometimes even their kids. At that time, it was a two-week affair. Nowadays it's usually just five days. As still just hangarounds, we Minnesota guys couldn't attend, but we knew that one of the orders of business there would be a vote as to whether we'd be bumped up to prospect status.

We made our way down to Charlotte to spend some time with the North Carolina chapters before they headed for Kerr Lake. It's what we knew we had to do. We wanted everyone to know who we were. Once in North Carolina, we split up, with Tank and Ron going to Durham, Bill to Winston-Salem, and Rooster and I going to Charlotte. At the Charlotte clubhouse, we found that Thunder had already left for Kerr Lake. As chapter president, he had to be there at the start of the Run. But he knew we were coming and before he'd left for the Run, he made sure we were taken care of—several of the girls from the strip club were at the Charlotte clubhouse waiting for us.

Soon after we arrived, Thunder called from Kerr Lake and told me to go to the strip club to get Holly, his girl at the time. For a little support, I took Fred with me, a Charlotte hangaround. The Hells Angels weren't the only motorcycle club that frequented the strip club. The Outlaws came by from time to time, too. We got Holly and I brought her back to the clubhouse and talked to Thunder on the phone. "Okay, I got her," I said.

"Good. Now punch her in the mouth."

"Do what?"

"Punch her in the fucking mouth." I didn't know if Thunder was mad at Holly or just wanted to test my mettle, or maybe both, but I could tell he was serious. I held back a little, actually a lot, but I punched Holly in the mouth and got back on the phone.

"Okay, I punched Holly in the mouth."

"Good," Thunder said. "Now take her into the back and fuck her." He was serious about that, too. Thunder was insane, it was becoming obvious. Still, Holly was an attractive, sexy girl. I took her into the back.

I pulled guard duty at the clubhouse that night and I was more than a little wound-up. At 5:00 in the morning the newspaper delivery man came by and I pointed my AR-15 at him through the window. "Pat!" yelled Fred. "It's okay … it's just the newspaper guy." If Fred hadn't said something I might have opened fire.

L-R: David Benson, a Charlotte member who had been shot and paralyzed, Michael "Thunder" Finazzo. The AR-15 hanging on the wall is the one that I used for guard duty where I almost shot the newspaper delivery man.

We continued to hang around the Charlotte clubhouse as the Run got underway up at Kerr Lake. Mid-week, we got a call from Thunder. "Get your asses up here," he said. We'd been officially voted in as prospects.

At Kerr Lake, in an expansive campground, there were Hells Angels chapter tents everywhere, each with their respective chapter flag out front. As new prospects, it would become our job to do guard duty, make sure everyone had plenty of firewood, and more or less do gopher work whenever it was asked of us. But as excited as we were to be official prospects, I wasn't ready to take a bunch of shit from anyone. A big tough guy named Butch from the Cleveland chapter came by once and told Bill Ellis that there was going to be a "patch and boots race" for the prospects.

"What's that?" said Bill.

"It's when you guys strip down to nothing but your patches and boots and then climb a tree as fast as you can." Bill told Butch he'd talk to me about it and when I heard Butch's idea I went and had a word with him.

"Fuck that idea, Butch," I said. "We ain't doing that. Now I don't know what we have to do—fight with you and have it out or whatever—but we're not doing any boots and patch race."

"This guy's all right!" said Butch, pointing to me. "That's what we wanted to hear! You think we want a bunch of guys who're willing to climb a tree naked just 'cause we told 'em to?"

There were a few tests like that at Kerr Lake. Chip, a New York member, went up to Rooster while on guard duty and asked to see his gun. "Sure," Rooster said, and he handed it to him. Chip immediately started firing it off in every direction. "Never!" he said, after he'd emptied it, "Never give anyone your gun. Don't matter *who* asks for it!" Then he asked to see Rooster's chapter president—me, "Your man just handed me his gun," Chip said to me. I could see Rooster was getting pissed.

"Well, what do you want to do, Chip?" I asked "Do we need to fight about it, or what?"

"I'll take care of this," said Rooster. And so Rooster and Chip fought it out, neither one beating up the other too bad and that was that. Everything was okay with Chip from then on.

We needed to get firewood for everyone, so I made sure we got plenty of it. I noticed that on the outskirts of Kerr Lake someone was taking down trees and sawing them into firewood and he was working a pretty large area. I got us a truck and we drove to where he'd started. We could hear his chainsaw about a half mile away and so we loaded up the truck with wood and took it back to the campground. Then we made about nine more unseen trips. We drove around the campground dropping off wood by the cord to each Hells Angels site. Nobody in any of the chapters messed with us after that.

In early September of 1981, the court trials for the Omaha guys started getting underway. We rode down there often, wearing the colors and showing our support. Ultimately, five of the Omaha members would get convicted for drug and firearms possession with sentences that ran from one to three years.

Also in September, Thunder came up to see me with two pounds of meth. He stayed a couple days and we partied and he was as crazy as always. He went back to Charlotte and just a few days later, I got a telephone call from John. Thunder and another Charlotte Hells Angel named Yank were found stuffed into the trunk of a car. They'd been shot execution style.

There must have been a couple hundred Hells Angels at Thunder's funeral. Mostly it was to pay respects to a fellow club member, not necessarily to pay respects to Thunder. The truth of the matter was that Thunder didn't have a lot of friends. We were all a little crazy. To be a Hells Angel you needed to be a little out there. But Thunder had taken it to a new level. And it could have been any number of people who killed him. Maybe it was the Outlaws exacting revenge. Was it Thunder who was behind the July 4th Massacre that he had talked about back when I'd visited him for the first time? Turns out he was a suspect in another mass killing, too. Back in January, six bodies had been found in a house outside of Richmond, four men and two women, all members or associates of the Invader Motorcycle Club. All shot in the head.

Michael "Thunder" Finazzo, Artie Ray "John" Cherry & Tyler "Yank" Frndyk (lower right).

Or maybe Thunder's murder had something to do with a drug deal gone bad. But rumors began to circulate that Thunder may have been done in by another Hells Angels chapter. John, Thunder's friend who had driven Billy West and me to the airport that day with three pounds of meth in Billy's vest, told me he suspected guys from Durham and Winston-Salem. Why, I don't know. A disagreement over drug territory? Or maybe someone just felt as if Thunder had to be stopped before he brought the whole damn club crashing down around him.

Whatever the reason, the whole thing freaked me out a little. Especially so when John insisted that a couple guys had better escort us back to Minneapolis to keep us safe. Scotty from Cleveland and a guy nicknamed Oats from New York City came along with us.

Scotty turned out to be a good guy and he stuck around and partied with us for a few days and soon it was decided that with Thunder out of the picture, Cleveland would be our new sponsor chapter. John, meanwhile, became president of the Charlotte chapter. But in January of 1982, John was shot and killed in a shootout by the manager of a bar in South Carolina called Rock Hole in the town of Rock Hill. And it was only then that I learned John's real name—Artie Ray Cherry—and I also learned he'd been wanted for stabbing a guy to death.

There was an Outlaw who had been shot, too, in a phone booth, killed by a .45. Cherry had mentioned something about that to me once. He mentioned the shooting, but he never said who did it. But I learned that he was the prime suspect. Turns out Cherry was as psychopathic as Thunder. I'd be lying if I said that by then I wasn't having some second thoughts about becoming a member of the Hells Angels. Shootings, murders, stabbings—these guys played hardball. I didn't mind the occasional fights, but being a Hells Angel seemed to mean taking your life in your hands. And yet, there was really no turning back. Part of me was apprehensive. But part of me loved it. Looking back, this much I'm pretty sure of: had I taken Thunder up on his offer to move down to North Carolina and join his Charlotte chapter, I'd probably either be dead by now or I'd be doing life.

Artie Ray "John Delmonico" Cherry.

CHAPTER 5
Bona Fide

In April 1982 there was the Hells Angels South Run, kind of an officers meeting where representatives from all the chapters gather. That year it was right outside of Charleston, South Carolina, and as prospects, we needed to be there. We rode down and somewhere around Kansas City it started to pour rain and it didn't stop the whole way down to Charleston. It got so bad we rented a U-Haul to put the bikes in and drove the rest of the way. We caught a little flack for it when we got there. William from the Durham chapter said, "Hey, you guys didn't fucking ride your bikes the whole way!" A day or so later, we came up for a membership vote and William voted no. The results have to be unanimous. Every East Coast chapter has to say yes. We were disappointed but we weren't going to let it slow us down any.

In the summer of that year, some of the Omaha guys were released from prison. The chapter was soon back in business and they became our sponsors again. In August, the annual USA run was held in Frisco, Colorado. We Minneapolis prospects rode to Omaha and then we all rode to Frisco. Even though we were prospects, Omaha treated us with real respect. They treated us like men. While the rest of the chapters hung out in Officers Gulch—a huge campground—Omaha rented themselves a chalet. So did we. Of course we didn't tell anybody. We were just prospects, obligated to be on the campground premises making sure everyone was being taken care of. We put up a tent for appearances, but stayed most of the time at our chalet. To keep anyone from looking too hard for us, we made sure once again that everybody was well stocked with firewood. This time I happened upon a stack of telephone poles about five or six miles away and Tank and I got ourselves a U-Haul and swiped a bunch of them and took them back to Officers Gulch where we cut them all up with chainsaws.

At one point during the week I saw a guy I recognized. It was hard to miss him, actually. The last time I'd seen him—all six foot eight of him—he was an El Forastero in Sioux City and I was just a kid hustling pool. But I'd never forgotten Tiny. Now he was a Hells Angel. I asked him if he remembered backing me up that night. "Yeah," Tiny laughed, "I think I do. Good to see you again." Small world.

In Frisco we were brought up for patch again and, again, we got turned down. This time it was the Salem, Massachusetts chapter. Harvey from Salem said he didn't feel like he knew us at all. We hadn't been out enough, at least not to his chapter. Again we were disappointed. But partying with the guys from Omaha almost made up for it. We'd all had a great time.

A month later, we got word of a chapter anniversary party in Bridgeport, Connecticut. We figured it would be a good chance to go see the guys in Salem. Ron Fischl and I flew out and attended the party and then told Salem we'd be coming up there to spend a few days. Picking us up at the airport were John-John and Burt from the New York City chapter, a couple of New York's finest. Burt had lost an arm while trying to make an explosive. John-John was a heavy guy who had just had his stomach stapled and was in the process of losing a lot of weight. In the car, they went absolutely nuts, running toll booths, crossing lanes, driving thirty or forty miles per hour over the speed limit. I turned to Ron. "Fuck this," I said. "Hey, fellas, you keep this up and we're all going to end up in jail. I'm gonna ask you to knock it off. Now if you want to pull over and have it out with us, Ron and I are okay with that."

Turned out to be another test. "You guys stand up for yourselves," John-John said. "That's what we wanted to see." They drove normally from then on.

In Bridgeport, we had a chance to hang out with Harvey. Harvey was a tough guy, a boxer. He said that although he voted against us at

Frisco, he had nothing against us. "I just don't know you," he said. We spent a couple days with him and by the time we left, Harvey promised us his vote next time. Ron and I flew back to Minneapolis and celebrated with the rest of the guys.

At the East Coast officer's meeting in September of 1982 in Rochester, New York, we were officially voted in. There would be no more prospecting. On September 18, 1982, Minnesota became a bona fide Hells Angels chapter. We celebrated hard and I was proud of having originated the idea, but I also knew that the chapter would never have come together without guys like Rooster and Tank. And especially Gramps.

Original chapter of the Minnesota Hells Angels voted in, September 18, 1982
Front Row – L to R: Me, Michael "Finnegan" Carroll, Paul "Rooster"
Seydel & Dale Ray "Corky" Haley (Omaha member).
Back Row – L to R: Dennis "Tank" Fenstra, Ron Fischl & Bill "Sick Bill" Ellis.

Through it all, my drug business kept rolling along. Ron Fischl got busted selling meth and had to do some time in Leavenworth. But before he did, he hooked up Billy West and me with his brother in Vegas. His brother was a big-time supplier. Billy and I flew out there to pick up ten pounds of meth at a price of $10,000 per pound. My old friend Tramp was out there and he fixed me up with a gun. I didn't walk into meetings with $100,000 in cash and no protection. But it went smoothly. We met in a casino parking lot and then Billy and I swung by a drugstore and picked up some tin foil, envelopes, and talcum powder and we broke it all down ourselves and shipped everything UPS to Billy's house.

By then, Billy had introduced me to Curt Anderson who owned a place in Minneapolis called the Roaring Twenties, a lively strip club with private parties in the back complete with cocaine and sex. Curt was supplying cocaine to Billy. I met other suppliers, too. Steve Manson, an ex-Minneapolis cop of all things, was a coke supplier and he eventually introduced me to Brad Jacobsen from whom I would start buying coke by the kilo. Brad was a clean-cut, sharp-looking dude who always dressed well. He was a solid businessman, smart and savvy. Brad and I made a lot of money. Steve, meanwhile, would eventually join the Hells Angels.

I dealt in marijuana a little bit, too. A dude named Country came up one time from Charleston and I sold him 150 pounds of it. The next day I was driving with Finnegan in my 1978 Corvette and the cops pulled us over. By then, of course, I was a marked man. The cops knew I was dealing in large quantities. Naturally they could never get me on anything. I was careful. I never kept shipments at my house, for example. If I couldn't move the stuff through the club quickly, I'd store it someplace safe. One time I stored several pounds of meth at my mother's house, unbeknownst to her, of course.

The cops couldn't get me on anything that day with Finnegan, either. They pulled me over exactly one day too late. One of the cops spotted a bag on the floor in the back. "What's in the bag?" he asked.

"Oh, that. Those are the numbers we use to stamp hot Harleys." The cops grabbed the bag and poured out a collection of lug nuts.

Finnegan and I couldn't help but laugh. The cops didn't think it was all that funny. "Get the fuck out of here, Matter," one of them said. I didn't need to be asked twice.

With all my drug money, I bought a bar in Shakopee called Cactus Jack's. It had been kind of a dream of mine and I partnered with Jerry Smith, someone I knew through my brothers from the Iowa days and someone I'd been reintroduced to through Gramps. Jerry had been an El Forastero in Omaha and became the first Omaha Hells Angels president when the El Forasteros were patched over. We'd talked about someday running a bar and Cactus Jack's was our kind of joint—loud , rowdy, and just a fun place to hang out. The guys from the club came around, of course, although Jerry was a little apprehensive about having guys with Hells Angels patches sitting in the bar. "I can't very well tell 'em to leave their patches at home," I said.

Naturally the bar saw its share of fights and, truthfully, I probably wasn't mature enough to run it like a business. I was having too much fun. The cops would eventually shut us down and eventually Jerry and I would sell it.

In February of 1983, Rooster and I went down to Charleston, South Carolina for a Hells Angels officers meeting. Among other festivities, Johnny Rodriguez was scheduled to come by the clubhouse and we were fans of his. We took our girlfriends; I was still with Leslie at the time. We spent an evening in the Electric Keg bar with the club and then the four of us left to go back to the motel, but Rooster and I ended up doing some Quaaludes and decided to return to the bar where a couple of the Hells Angels were still hanging out. The Electric Keg was a casual, oyster bar kind of place, with peanut shells on the floor, and a couple of pool tables in the back. We were enjoying some beers when a group of sailors on leave from the port wandered in. A girl who was with one of them saw my Minnesota patch. "Hey, I'm from Minnesota!" she said. We started talking and I guess the sailor she was with didn't like it and he told me to stop talking to her. I told him it might be a good idea to just leave it alone.

"Fuck you," he said. That was all I needed to hear. I smashed him over the head with my beer mug and then all hell broke loose, with

Rooster and one of the Charlotte prospects jumping in against some of the other sailors who decided to join the melee. I grabbed the dude I'd hit with the beer mug and started punching him in the face. I wore gold rings on each finger and it was like hitting the guy with brass knuckles. I cut him up pretty bad and blood was flowing everywhere and then I just threw him into a wall. One of the sailors flung a pool ball at me, hitting me in the chest and bending my flat Death Head pin into a semicircle. Rooster, meanwhile, was busy cracking one of the sailors over the head with a pool stick. Soon the other sailors started coming toward us and there must have been a couple dozen of them. I pulled out my .380 and hit one guy over the head with it and the bottom of the clip broke off and all the bullets came cascading out of it, bouncing all over the floor. But the sight of the gun was sufficient to make everyone stop long enough for me to wave the gun and yell out, "There's still one in the chamber, fuckers!" And then we all got the hell out of there before the police came. A hangaround named Sam drove us back to the hotel where I noticed I was covered head to toe in blood. I stepped into the shower fully clothed and let the blood run down the drain. Then Rooster and I decided we'd better get out of town and we took the girls and left for home. I never did get to see Johnny Rodriguez.

Back in Minnesota a week later, the cops knocked down both my door and Rooster's. The South Carolina police had identified us through our Hells Angels patches and had the Minneapolis police bust us. Then they were going to extradite us. They found several pounds of pot in Rooster's house and some handguns in mine, along with some Valium and Diazepam. They arrested us and held us until we could make bail. My Cactus Jack's partner Jerry happened to know a judge. "Pat," he said, "give me ten thousand dollars in cash that I can pass along to this guy. He'll stop the extradition." Three weeks later Jerry came back and said no deal. "He says you're too hot," Jerry said. Otherwise he would have. I won't mention names. But there's at least one judge I know of out there who, given the right circumstances, can be bought. Who knows how many more there are?

In Minneapolis I pleaded guilty to misdemeanor possession of

Diazepam. But then it was on to South Carolina for the charge of assault and battery with intent to kill. My attorney, Larry Rapoport, flew down with me and we managed to work out a plea bargain for assault. I had to pay restitution of $5,700 (the sailor I punched out needed a bit of plastic surgery) and do two years of probation, but I managed to avoid prison time. Rooster had to pay a fine, too, but he didn't have the money so I paid it for him. After the hearing, Larry and I went to the Charleston Hells Angels clubhouse to celebrate. Turns out Johnny Paycheck was in town for a concert and the guys had invited him over. Johnny of course was something of a hell raiser. I missed Johnny Rodriguez but I didn't miss Johnny Paycheck. We all had a good time partying at the clubhouse that night.

That year the USA Run was sponsored by us. That meant we had to make all the arrangements and set the whole thing up. We held it in Custer, South Dakota. 1983's Run was also a World Run. Hells Angels from all over the world came in. We had three Germans who flew into Minneapolis and rode with us to Custer, two from the Hamburg chapter and one from the Stuttgart chapter. The Run went smoothly. We had a little trouble at first with cops issuing way too many tickets, all for petty stuff, but we talked to the city council about it. We were bringing in a lot of money to the area, after all, as well as publicity. The cops backed off. And the Sunday paper did a nice feature article on us.

When we came home the cops came by Bill's place where our German friends were staying and arrested them. Turns out they were wanted back in Hamburg for prostitution, gambling, narcotics, and a bunch of other shit. Germany was cracking down on motorcycle clubs at the time; it had become illegal to even wear a Hells Angels patch.

Meanwhile, while we'd been away, someone had stolen a bike from an El Forastero. That club had never gotten over the Hells Angels opening up a chapter in the area and replacing them as top dogs. I guess they thought we were behind the bike thefts because a couple of them had broken into Rooster's and Finnegan's houses. Both Rooster's and Finnegan's girlfriends were home at the time and the El Forasteros swore at them and insulted them and tore things off the walls. Mitch from Rochester had ridden back with us and so had Ron from Binghamton, Bear from Bridgeport (the second Bear I had known, the first being my old Grim Reaper club mate), and Bob, a prospect from Rochester. We decided we needed to pay the El Forasteros a visit. We knocked on their clubhouse door and when nobody answered, we decided to break in, to make sure none of the El Forasteros were hiding from us. Bear boosted me up to a side window which I broke and climbed through. I found some of the club's handguns and a shotgun and passed them back through the window to the other guys outside and they proceeded to toss them up onto the roof of the place. It was a flat roof and it had been raining for a couple days and there must have been a foot of standing water up there. Then we went looking for the El Forasteros.

At the Sun Saloon we came across Pat Smith, one of their guys, and we grabbed him and took him back to Tank's house and slapped him around a little and then handcuffed him to a toilet. Then we called some of their guys and let them know we had Pat. "We'd better meet and get this straightened out," we said and we took Pat and headed for our clubhouse.

As we turned down the access road that ran in front of the house, we noticed a van suspiciously parked down the street from the house, maybe a hundred yards from it. I guess the El Forasteros hadn't planned on knocking on the front door. We drove up from behind and parked around the back of an old gas station out of view from the van. Then we climbed out of the car and snuck around to the back of the van and I yanked the rear door open and leveled my .380 at the occupants—several armed El Forasteros. "Okay," I said, "I think we'd better get in the clubhouse and talk."

Once in the clubhouse there wasn't much talking. We just sort of split off one on one in the living room and had it out. We got the better of them and ended up loading some of their guys back into their van, along with Pat Smith, and off they drove, heading for the hospital.

A couple days later the Des Moines chapter of the El Forasteros got involved. They called our Oakland chapter and spoke to Irish, our

Oakland chapter president, explaining that they wanted someone to go to Minnesota to settle the situation down. Irish agreed. Neither side wanted things to get ugly all over the country between the clubs. Irish and some other Hells Angels from Oakland flew out and some of their guys flew out and everybody met and I had a lot of trouble keeping my cool. I was still thinking about that vanload of El Forasteros bent on ambushing us. Irish kind of got in my face about making things all right with their guys and I got in his while the other guys tried to settle me down.

Finally, Irish said, "Look, Pat, what do you want to do?"

"Well fuck, Irish, what would *you* do?"

"Yeah, Pat, I know how you feel. But we gotta settle this somehow." Finally I hit upon the idea of me fighting their president one on one. I was maybe 150 at the time; their president was 185, maybe more. We met at a body shop that night and fought it out. Neither one of us got banged up too badly and that more or less resolved it. From then on the El Forasteros and the Hells Angels were okay.

In 1984, Leslie and I moved into a house I bought in the Minneapolis suburb of Robbinsdale. By then I had built a couple custom bikes, something I'd become interested in doing. I started making them in the garage in Robbinsdale and thought it could become a profitable sideline, although the drug business was what was making me wealthy. But the drug business was risky. When there's so much money involved in an industry where people aren't concerned with the law and aren't afraid of the cops, you come up against some dangerous dudes.

That's what happened to Scratch, the guy who had introduced me to Gramps. Scratch called me in a panic at two o'clock in the morning one time, said I owed him money for drugs. I didn't. Scratch was, at best, an acquaintance of mine. We'd never had any dealings. "What the fuck are you talking about, Scratch?" I said. I told him he was nuts and hung up. I guess maybe Scratch was just desperate for money. He must have owed somebody somewhere, because that's the last I heard from him. Not long after, they found his body on an island in the Mississippi south of St. Paul.

Meanwhile, I was taking my presidency of the Hells Angels seriously. I never missed an event. That year my brother Rusty moved up to Minneapolis and began to prospect as a Hells Angel. He'd get patched in '85. We had another guy join in 1984: Steve Manson, my coke supplier and ex-cop. He'd been a cop for all of nine months and got kicked off for fighting. Being a cop wasn't anything he'd really wanted to do. He originally applied for civil service work as a fire fighter but for whatever reason they offered him a position as cop instead and he took it. He wasn't a very good one and figured he'd make a much better Hells Angel. We agreed. He prospected and everybody was fine with it and we patched him.

By 1985, Leslie was finally tiring of my lifestyle. It took her a little longer than it had with Jackie, but eventually she left and went down to Clearwater, Florida. I followed her down and talked her into coming back. Nine months later, our son Cole was born. We stuck it out some more, although things were getting rockier and rockier. Then right after Cole's birth, the cops kicked in my door again. It was part of their "Operation One-Percenter."

One-percenters were what we outlaw motorcycle clubs called ourselves. It comes from the claim often used by motorcycle enthusiasts to defend their interest in bikes: ninety-nine percent of motorcyclists are law-abiding citizens. I imagine that's true, but the Hells Angels and clubs like them, like to turn the claim on its head and take the one percent part as a kind of badge of honor.

At any rate, the cops were intent on breaking up the outlaw motorcycle clubs in the area and they managed to find a way to bust me, even though it meant having to go back a few years. They used my conviction for defeating security on personalty back in '77, which was a felony, and my possession of a firearm from when they busted down my door back in 1983, and arrested me for felon in possession of a firearm. It would take a year for the case to go to court.

That year, the USA Run was in Missouri. Sonny Barger was there, one of the founders of the Oakland chapter which went all the way back to 1957. Sonny had gotten a lot of press over the years. He still does. People often mistakenly think he's some high-ranking official of the Hells Angels, even the president or a past president. But that's not the way the club works. It's not a top-down organization. It's more democratic with each chapter more or less responsible for their own actions, although of course there are rules all the chapters abide by and votes need to be taken for issues such as membership. The chapters are divided into two main regions—East Coast and West Coast. Each region takes care of its own. When we came up for patches, for example, all we needed was the approval of the East Coast chapters.

Sonny got wind that we had an ex-cop in our chapter. Of course we'd had it okayed by everyone on the East Coast, once I'd explained Steve's history; how he'd only been a cop for nine months and been kicked out. But now Sonny started saying that the West Coast, too, needed to approve Steve. And they weren't likely to do so. "We can't have ex-cops in the club," Sonny insisted. Sonny pulled a lot of weight. Some of the East Coast guys even started rethinking the matter. We kept getting heat about it, even after the Run, and Steve began to feel more and more uncomfortable. Finally he came to me and said, "Pat, I probably ought to just quit. I'm becoming a real distraction and maybe my getting out of the club would be the best thing." And so Steve quit the club and shortly after that, another unwritten rule became a written one: "No cops or ex-cops in the club." In fact, that rule was officially adopted on the same date as the other one, along with another new rule about snitches. On August 3, 1986, the official Hells Angels Rules were amended to include these:

No cops or ex-cops in the club.
No niggers in the club.
No snitches in the club.

In 1987, my felon in possession case finally made it to trial and I ended up taking a plea: two years and a ten-thousand dollar fine. Someone must have caught the judge's ear beforehand because I found out right afterwards that Larry Rapoport had actually been offered a plea deal of eighteen months with no fine. Nobody had bothered to tell me. I was furious. We filed some paperwork and I was able to take the eighteen months, even though I still had to pay the ten grand. But on good behavior, I got out in thirteen months, five months of which was in a halfway house and the final month on house arrest.

By that time, Leslie's mother had moved into the house. Leslie and I had actually tied the knot back in May, before my sentencing. I couldn't live with my mother-in-law so during the final weekends of my time at the halfway house, I stayed with Rooster. When Leslie's mom finally moved out, I moved back in. But I hadn't changed much. I was still intent on partying hard and chasing women. In 1988, I went to a Hells Angels officers' meeting in Rochester. When I returned, the house was empty.

CHAPTER 6
A Way of Life

"Gramps" was Roger Sheehan, and in 1970, he and several other Hells Angels in the Minnesota chapter were arrested and convicted for selling narcotics, including heroin, to undercover agents in a sting. That essentially ended the Minnesota chapter until Pat Matter, encouraged by Sheehan and joined by Dennis "Tank" Fenstra, Paul Michael "Rooster" Seydel, Mike "Finnegan" Carroll, Ron Fischl, and Bill "Sick Bill" Ellis, started it up again, becoming an official chapter in September of 1982. Prior to the arrests in 1970, the chapter had been very active. The USA Run, in fact, had been held in Minnesota just a year prior.

Pat was introduced to Sheehan by "Scratch"—Thomas Carroll. Yes, Carroll's body was exhumed from a shallow grave on an island in the Mississippi near Cottage Grove, Minnesota. He'd been shot five times, four of the shots to the face. Convicted for the murder were Jim "Big John" Johnson and Johnson's wife Sondra. There were rumors that Jim Johnson was involved in the kidnapping of Virginia Piper in 1972, an unsolved case and one of the most famous in Minnesota history. Piper was the wife of a wealthy investment banker. The kidnappers demanded a million dollars. My father, as a matter of fact, as Hennepin County Sheriff, was involved in the investigation of the case. He also transported some of the ransom money. Piper was subsequently found chained to a tree in a wooded area but nobody was ever convicted of the kidnapping.

And then there was Curt Anderson, owner of the Roaring Twenties, a notorious place of illegal drug use and illicit sex. Anderson would get busted along with his friend Jimmy Box, a guy who Pat rented a clubhouse from. Box was big time. One of the largest drug dealers in the state, maybe the country. He sold to motorcycle gangs and was also believed to be connected to La Cosa Nostra—the Mafia. Pat's connections, and *their* connections, sure make for an interesting community of people.

Pat doesn't overstate the involvement of the Hells Angels in drugs. If you haven't picked up on it yet, these clubs are often sophisticated criminal enterprises populated by intelligent, often dangerous guys, who know their business. And their business is dealing drugs— cocaine, methamphetamine, heroin, you name it.

Jerry Smith, Pat's partner in Cactus Jack's was a drug dealer, too. Originally from Omaha, he was an El Forastero in the early 1960s and became the first president of the Omaha chapter of the Hells Angels when the El Forasteros got patched over. He'd eventually get busted and sent to Sandstone Federal Prison.

Some of the names Pat has mentioned are big-time players. They may not be members of the Hells Angels, but various Hells Angels chapters comprise a good piece of their clientele. The Hells Angels' own vetting process (prospecting), as well as their rules ("no cops, no snitches") provides a degree of safety for these suppliers. Obviously, there's still some risk. No drug deal is without it. But you don't get to be a big-time player without assuming some risk. Take William "Billy" West, for instance. Here's a guy who wasn't afraid to load his vest pockets with three pounds of meth and walk onto an airplane. Billy was successful. Brad Jacobsen was another high roller. I heard their names a lot back in my early days in narcotics. In fact, I'd heard West's name as far back as my early days in the Edina P.D. West owned property in the Brainerd Lakes area in northern Minnesota, an especially pricey locale. Jacobsen owned a limo company—a good cash-intensive business by which to launder money, incidentally. You can say you had thirty customers one night and who's to say you didn't? It gives you a legitimate excuse for where you get your money.

My interest in narcotics investigation quickly became a passion. It's discouraging to see how much crime is caused because of drugs.

And I don't mean the selling or buying of it. Since it's illegal to buy or sell, it's axiomatic that the buying and selling is a cause of crime. I'm talking about the guy who's trying to fuel a two hundred dollar-a-day drug habit. Someone like that will stop at nothing to feed his addiction. He'll rob, he'll hurt, he'll kill. Families get destroyed. People die.

But trying to stop the flow of drugs when you're up against smart guys like West or Jacobsen or Matter isn't easy. We used to say that you never catch the bright ones. If you do, a lot of times it's almost accidental—a routine traffic stop or something along those lines. But we put a lot of time and resources into going after these guys and if we never get them, we can at least make their lives difficult. Every day, for as long as they live, they're looking over their shoulders, wondering if they're being followed, wondering if the guy they're dealing with can be trusted, wondering if today's the day their door gets broken down by the cops. It becomes a way of life. It's not a way of life I would want, but I'll let Pat speak to that.

If they do get busted, however, they're certainly not without their resources. The Hells Angels are famous for taking care of their own. There's no shortage of attorneys who run successful practices just defending Hells Angels members. It's a constant stream of business. And there's the club support that Pat talked about when he and his guys rode down to Omaha during the trials of the Omaha members. It's a common practice. What it means, a lot of times, is you attend the trial in your Hells Angels colors and spend a good deal of time staring down the jury members or prosecution witnesses and generally just intimidating everybody in the courtroom, without even having to say a word. Frequently it works. In the case of the Omaha trial, security was exceptionally tight, often with ten deputy U.S. marshals stationed around the courtroom. And Pat's not exaggerating in his description of the judge that his buddy tried to buy. Like Pat, I won't mention names, either, but Pat's not alone in his opinion about that particular judge. Rumor has it he's tied in with the Hells Angels.

Of course, sometimes the biggest risk for a gang dealing drugs isn't law enforcement; it's the competition—other gangs dealing drugs. Or maybe just other gangs period. Forget the drugs; some of these guys just don't like each other. The July 4th Massacre that Pat referenced may be a perfect example of that. Four men and a girl were all found shot to death at their Outlaw clubhouse in Charlotte in 1979. One guy was found slumped outside on the front porch where he'd apparently been posted as a guard. Probably an Outlaws prospect. A gun was resting in his lap. There was no sign of struggle inside the house and each victim had been shot several times. The girl was just seventeen. Rumors fly around to this day. Some say it was the Hells Angels. But others say it was an inside job—a couple Outlaw prospects who were denied membership.

But the killings outside Richmond of Invader Motorcycle Club members were not an inside job. Police closed the books on those killings in 1986, coming to the conclusion, through cooperating witnesses, that the slayings were the result of a drug deal gone bad. The killers? Artie Ray Cherry, Tyler Duris "Yank" Frndyk, and Michael Franklin Finazzo, also known as "Thunder." There may have been a fourth as well.

Thunder. He made the Charlotte chapter of the Hells Angels into a force to be reckoned with. At one time, he was the president of the Omaha chapter. Leslie Fitzgerald—Lightning Les—was his vice president. Thunder and Lightning. Thunder had a lengthy criminal record and did some time in the Nebraska penitentiary. Somewhere around 1976, he was released and moved to North Carolina. He was with the Durham chapter of the Hells Angels for a little while and then he started the Charlotte chapter.

In Charlotte, Thunder and his cohorts were into drugs and theft and prostitution. And murder. Finazzo had been supplying the Invaders with drugs, but when the Invaders started getting their drugs from the Pagans motorcycle gang, Finazzo, according to an unnamed witness, "went nearly berserk with anger." He and his buddies went to the Invader house and were let in peacefully. They just wanted "to talk." Then the six Invaders were all quickly, coldly, executed. Each was shot between the eyes. The thermostat in the house was turned up in what was believed to be an attempt to confuse the issue of time of death. High heat causes bodies to decompose faster.

The case was closed because, by then, there was no way to try the Angels. They were all dead. Finazzo was killed as Pat described, executed in September of 1981 along with Frndyk and stuffed into the trunk of a car. There was evidence the two had been made to kneel before being shot. But Finazzo's leg was broken and it would be reasonable to conclude that maybe he wasn't too keen on the idea of kneeling. Probably someone chopped his leg out from under him.

And then there was Artie Ray Cherry, Finazzo's second-in-command. Cherry was a former Green Beret in Vietnam. On October 17, 1979, a man was stabbed to death outside a Charleston nightclub. Cherry was the prime suspect. Then there was the 1981 killing, outside Charlotte, of Samuel "Tommy" Stroud, an Outlaw member. A Hells Angels prospect at the time would later make a statement while in witness protection: Artie Ray Cherry came into the Marshville clubhouse one night and had the prospect gather up all the.45 ammunition he could find. Cherry left the next morning. At about midnight, he came back, carrying a.45 handgun and directing the prospect to melt it down. The gun was cut into slag and the grips were burned and Cherry wouldn't leave until the gun was destroyed. Tommy Stroud was found dead in a phone booth, killed by a.45. That's the phone booth killing Cherry mentioned to Pat. Cherry, meanwhile, kept himself out of sight. Called himself John, according to Pat. To authorities he was known as John Delmonico. Then in January of 1982, Cherry got into a barroom brawl at the Rock Hole. Evidently, members of several motorcycle gangs were on hand that night and the brawl turned into a real free-for-all. Cherry got shot in the head and died a few hours later.

The possible fourth shooter of the Invaders killings was rumored to have been the friend of Finazzo's who had taken Pat back to the airport after his first trip to Charlotte as a Grim Reaper: Ronnie. Authorities knew Ronnie to be Randall or Rondall "Ronnie" Branch. And so it may not be so surprising that Pat never saw Ronnie again.

One of the cooperating witnesses who had pointed to Finazzo as a killer in the Invaders murders was a Charlotte prospect named Percy Barfield. He'd heard Finazzo admit to it. In a statement to police in

1982, he also clued them in on the Finazzo murder, saying it had been carried out by the Durham chapter of the Hells Angels. Donald Edward Crowe, the president of Durham, was behind it. At least that's what Barfield reported that Artie Ray Cherry had told him. Apparently there had been a feud between the two chapters and between Crowe and Finazzo in particular. Barfield would later go on to prospect for the Minnesota chapter of the Hells Angels, as a matter of fact.

But the July 4th Massacre in Charlotte remains unsolved, as do the executions of Frndyk and Finazzo, notwithstanding Barfield's statement, which may or may not be accurate. The Finazzo murder case, as it happens, came with some clues. His body had been stripped of seven of eight rings he wore. Two Hells Angels were pulled over in South Carolina and the cops found a bunch of rings in their truck. But it wouldn't be until the following day that Finazzo's body would be identified. The cops didn't know what they had and the two Hells Angels in the truck were released. Funny thing: in Barfield's 1982 statement, he admitted to being pulled over by the police in South Carolina the day after Finazzo's murder (although he claimed it was before) and that the police had taken "a" ring. He was with Artie Ray Cherry at the time. Maybe it wasn't Crowe after all. At any rate, no one's ever been able to conclusively connect the dots.

Then there was the report from a cooperating defendant. A friend of Thunder's, he claimed Thunder once told him that if he was ever killed, it would be by Ralph "Squeaky" Logner from the Durham chapter. Strange that very soon after Thunder's murder, Logner left the Hells Angels and moved to Florida. Crowe, Cherry, Barfield, Logner … who knows who was behind the murder of Thunder? There were plenty of unsavory characters all around, that's for certain.

How come the cases aren't solved? It's tempting to think that there are just not enough people who care. These weren't pillars of the community being taken out, after all. But that's not an entirely fair portrayal of how the police do their job. Would more resources be spent on the investigations if the murders had been of high school honor students from wealthy, influential families? Maybe. But the fact is, no matter who these people are, they've most likely got loved ones somewhere. Mothers and fathers and brothers and sisters. Maybe spouses, maybe kids. They're missed by somebody. We're not insensitive to that.

And truthfully, there's always an investigator somewhere looking to make a name for himself. There's always motivation to solve a previously-unsolved case, no matter what it is. It's a real feather in an investigator's cap. And then, of course, there's the desire to simply get a killer off the streets. Nobody's comfortable with the idea that there's someone out there roaming around who's perfectly okay with the idea of walking into a house and pumping several bullets into the heads of other human beings (no matter who those human beings are or what motorcycle gang they belong to). When one gang member is killed by another gang member, we've got a justifiable reason to put someone away where he belongs. I heard guys on the force call it a twofer: one gang-banger dead, one in prison.

Pat was obviously right to have some second thoughts about immersing himself into the lifestyle. But immerse he did. And clearly he held his own. Pat could take care of himself. So could "Rooster" Seydel. The fight at the Electric Keg with the sailors was about as ugly as it gets. Pat tells it more or less accurately. The fact is, he beat the shit out of his guy and there's just no other way to put it. Seydel kept one of the guy's buddies from jumping in by beating the shit out of him. Then for good measure, Seydel kept kicking Pat's guy after he had fallen to the floor unconscious. Witness accounts differ as to who, exactly, started the fight. Nobody seems to disagree about who ended it.

When Pat was arrested for felon in possession of a firearm, it was, as he said, Operation One-Percenter, a federal operation run by the ATF. Over a hundred agents were involved as well as local police agencies in thirty states. One-Percenter specifically targeted outlaw motorcycle gangs—eighteen different ones, including the so-called big four: the Outlaws, the Pagans, the Bandidos, and, of course, the Hells Angels. Coming out of Washington, D.C., the operation focused on the real movers and shakers. You really had to be somebody to make the list. Pat qualified.

There were over fifty arrests, the majority of them for firearms violations and drug trafficking. Did it change anything? Well, maybe for a little while. There were a few less guns on the street and a few less drugs. And it's another one of those things that keeps guys looking over their shoulders, making life just a little more difficult for them. The threat is always out there.

As for me, my interest in outlaw motorcycle clubs started in earnest in the early '90s—October of 1992 to be exact. We raided a local drug dealer's home in northeast Minneapolis and seized some meth. He later told us the meth came from Pat Matter. On another case, my childhood friend and fellow narc, Brad Erickson, had been making cocaine buys from Pearson's bar in south Minneapolis. The ultimate source of the coke was thought to be the Hells Angels. "Tank" Fenstra in particular. Tank was supposedly supplying to a guy named Brad Armstrong and Armstrong was in turn supplying employees at

L - R: Me and Brad Erickson, childhood friends and fellow narcs.

the bar. Brad Erickson was buying from a bartender, but unfortunately couldn't climb any higher up the ladder. But in talking to Brad, it was clear to me how involved the Hells Angels were in the local drug trade.

My curiosity grew through '93 and in January of 1994, I was asked to come along on a search warrant at an engine-building shop in northeast Minneapolis. Turns out these guys were building engines and transmissions for Pat. By then, of course, I'd been hearing his name, as well as some of the other Hells Angels names. I went out and bought Yves Lavigne's 1987 book, *Hell's Angels—Three Can Keep a Secret if Two are Dead*. Before the age of the Internet, this book was something of the go-to source for information for anyone, including cops, who wanted to learn more about the Hells Angels. And so I started learning. I haven't stopped since.

CHAPTER 7
Outlaws

About the fight at the Electric Keg that night: the newspapers reported that Rooster kept kicking the guy I had knocked to the ground. But that's not how it happened. Rooster was busy hitting another guy over the head with a pool cue, trying to keep him from jumping in. He never touched my guy. I was there. That's how it went down. I can't prove it, but I can tell you that the guys we beat up were pretty quick to settle, rather than allow the case to go before a jury. The fact is, we had the girl I had talked to that night—the girl from Minnesota—ready to testify that they had started the fight, not us. That's just for the record.

In any event, Leslie leaving me in 1988 was a bit of a heartbreak. Our divorce would become official in '91. But if I thought I knew what love was, I'd soon learn that I didn't.

Not until Trish.

Trish was a waitress at a restaurant that I began to frequent after my workouts in a nearby gym. I met her about six months after Leslie moved out and I liked her right away. I started coming into the restaurant regularly and talking to her and flirting with her and asking her out. She was reluctant at first. I had my tattoos, I was a bit rough around the edges, and she knew I was a Hells Angel. Not exactly her type. And she was living with another guy at the time, which didn't make things any easier. But I slowly kept working on her, bringing her flowers (a huge bouquet on her birthday) and one time even sending my jeweler into the restaurant with a solid gold bracelet for her.

Little by little, I wore her down. We started going out. I took her to a Tom Petty concert one night. The Hells Angels knew Petty and the club had backstage passes. We kept seeing each other and I became certain that Trish was the love of my life. More certain than I'd been of anything else. I'd been with a lot of women, but none of them had made me feel like Trish did. I hoped she felt the same about me—that I was the love of her life. "I'll know it," I joked to her one time, "when you drop by my place unannounced some night in nothing but an overcoat." On a February night in 1990, there was a knock on the front door. It was Trish. In an overcoat. I invited her in and closed the door behind her and she smiled and dropped the coat to the floor.

Not long after, she moved in with me. And shortly after that, we took a trip to Hawaii. I'd surprised her with the tickets before she'd moved in and the trip turned out to be the perfect way to celebrate our new life together. We went to the beach every day and out to dinner every night. I liked just being with her. She was beautiful, the kind of girl who turned heads when she walked into a room.

Trish and Pat on vacation.

But in the middle of the trip, I got a call from Tank. "Pat," he said, "the warehouse got busted." It was a kind of code. I'd stored seven pounds of meth at the house of Kenneth Bousely, a close friend of mine, along with a briefcase full of guns. The feds searched the place and found both the meth and the guns in the garage. Bousely said he didn't know the stuff was there and initially said it must have been mine. The information enabled the feds to obtain a search warrant for my house, too, but they didn't find anything. I rarely kept anything in the house. Still, they seized bank records, income tax returns, an address book, and some cash. Later, I would realize that they missed something in the garage—a quarter pound of meth I had stashed away.

Trish and I cut short our vacation and flew back home. I didn't tell her exactly what was going on, but I could sense she was starting to have some second thoughts about having moved in with me. Fortunately, nothing came of the discovery of the meth. Bousely refused to follow through with his statement that the drugs were mine, and the feds didn't have a case. The stuff they took from my house added up to nothing but to get it back, I had to go downtown and give them my fingerprints and a handwriting sample. I thought it was bullshit and said so, but they had a subpoena for both. I could have been held in contempt. So after they took my fingerprints, they gave me a sheet of paper and made we write: *Mary had a little lamb, its fleece was white as snow. And everywhere the lamb went, he had a Harley to go.* Funny guys. I imagine they made me write it for no good reason other than they could.

By this time I was ramping up my custom bike building, though I was still putting the bikes together in my garage. I was being supplied regularly by a couple friends who were stealing bikes around the area. At that time, to legitimately sell a bike, you needed a manufacturer's statement of origin for the frame, the motor case, and the triple trees. That meant that every other piece of the bike could be hot. (That would change in time, and I'd have a lot to do with it.) Once you put the bike together, you'd get it inspected by the state and obtain a reconstructed title. Then you'd be in business, with a bike that was suddenly worth ten to twelve thousand dollars. I was buying the stolen bikes for about five hundred bucks and putting about two thousand into them. You don't need to be a math whizz to see how much money a guy could make selling custom bikes this way.

In one fell swoop I sold a bunch of them. Tommy Lewis, a friend of mine who was originally a member of the Charlotte Hells Angels but was now living in Minneapolis, introduced me to a friend of his named Sean Gallagher. Sean bought a dozen bikes from me for $130,000. With the money, I decided to launch a legitimate custom cycle business. I knew there was a market. There was a waiting list for new Harleys, and custom bikes were in demand. In April 1992, I found a vacant NAPA store in north Minneapolis, rented the front of it, hired a couple employees—Mike Eason and Jerry Schiro—and started Minneapolis Custom Cycle. Mike would become my service manager. An older guy, he wore glasses and had a beard and red hair that he kept short except for a long, tightly-wound ponytail. Mike knew a lot about bikes.

The business grew quickly and before long I expanded into the back of the building. I hired more employees and we kept building bikes and the money really started coming in. We sold custom bikes in the $10,000 to $12,000 range, but we also sold them for $30,000 and up to $50,000. The first year in business we did a quarter-million dollars' worth of business and we tripled that in the second year. By the third year we were well over a million dollars in sales and we just kept growing.

It was a legit business and I was proud of it. I never had any formal business training, or any schooling beyond eighth grade, for that matter; but I was good with numbers and I felt as if I had a Ph.D. in street smarts. The only problem with the business was that others started seeing my success and very soon a lot of illegitimate custom bikes were being sold and that meant a lot of people stealing bikes. Motorcycle thefts spiked around the whole state. Eventually, I'd have to discourage that.

Helping to publicize my business was the fact that I was racing bikes. Rooster had a small, fast bike that he let me use and I raced in the annual Humboldt, Iowa motorcycle rally. Then I built a Pro Stock bike at the shop and started entering all the American Motorcycle Racing Association events. I did well. Cycle magazines would do profiles on me. It helped that I'd advertise in their publications. Over time, I became good friends with the editors: Dave Nichols of *Easyriders* and Howard Kelly of *Hot Bike*, to name a couple. I'd go to the events with some of my employees: Mike Eason and Richard Rohda, and some others. Richard, a stocky guy with long hair and a mustache, made a good crew chief and later he'd become patched as a Hells Angel and be our sergeant at arms.

Some of the guys from the club, prospects mostly, would come along, too, including Percy Barfield on a couple occasions. The thing about Percy and Artie Ray Cherry being stopped by the cops and being found in possession of Hells Angels rings like what Thunder wore— well, that doesn't mean a whole lot, really. Clubs would give rings away to other club members as gifts all the time. We'd swap pins and rings and chapter t-shirts and everything. But I never knew that Percy had made a statement back in 1982 to the cops about Thunder's murder or I would have never let him prospect. You can't know everything. And there were things about Thunder's life that I didn't really want to know anyway.

At the tracks, we'd sell Minneapolis Custom Cycle t-shirts as well as club support stuff. Problem was, a lot of outlaw motorcycle clubs attended the AMRA events, especially the events that were in their own backyards. Often, I raced in enemy territory. And I'd never race without my patch.

In 1993, I raced in Macon, Georgia. It was Outlaws territory. We were left alone the day we arrived but the next day, before the race, Rich, a Hell's Henchman and the guy who ran the AMRA came up to me. "Pat," he said, "there're about a hundred Outlaws here. They're down around the pit area, on each side of the lane, right where you're pitted. I thought you ought to know." Rich wasn't kidding. The Outlaws were there, some armed with AR-15s. But I was intent on racing.

We went to the pit area, seven of us in total including a couple club members and a prospect who'd come along; Richard, Mike, and another friend of mine. I could see from where we parked the van in the pit that the Outlaws had formed a gauntlet, leaving no more than maybe a six- or eight-foot path up the return lane to the line. I noticed some of the other racers were in the pit area with their families and I told them it might be a good idea to get their kids out of there.

Soon, two Outlaws sauntered over, neither wearing shirts, which was their way of showing they were unarmed. I started walking toward them, telling the other guys to stay back. We had guns in the van which I didn't necessarily want the Outlaws to see. One of the two Outlaws, "Big R," began to talk. "So, what are you doing here, man? What are you planning on doing?"

"I'm racing, Big R. Simple as that. I'm on a race team. I own a fucking race bike. And anywhere there's an AMRA event, I'm going to be there racing. With my club patch. I won't be hard to find, Big R." In fact, my leather racing jacket had the Hells Angels Death Head logo on the back, along with my name in bold letters across the top. I was the only Hells Angels member ever allowed to do this. Club bylaws say you can't have anything on the back of your jacket except "Hells Angels," the logo, and the state you're from. But my jacket had MATTER running across the top.

I took a breath and said to Big R, "Fuck, man, I'm not trying to make trouble. I just want to race my motorcycle."

Big R thought about it for a moment. "Hells Angel or no Hells Angel, we respect you guys. As men."

"Thanks, Big R."

"It's okay with me. I'll take it back to my people." Turns out another racer had stood up to the Outlaws, too. Benny Brulloths, a Bandido, had talked to the Outlaws, saying, "Look, you guys stop me or a Hells Angels or some other club member, then what's to keep the Hells Angels from stopping one of your guys in Hells Angels territory? Racetracks should be neutral. Keeping guys from racing—man, that ain't right." The Outlaws agreed, at least in theory. But they didn't want any support stuff being sold.

After my talk with Big R, I raced and the Outlaws left us alone that day. And we sold our support stuff, too.

But the Outlaws would continue to be a thorn in my side. Fortunately, I ended up getting a lot of support from the other racers—one-percenters as well as guys who just loved to race. We respected each other and I made friends with a lot of them. Of course other guys from the Hells Angels came along with me, but so did members of other clubs. A couple times, even various chapters of the Sons of Silence accompanied us. They all knew how hard the Outlaws were making it for me.

In June of '93, I entered the Harley-Davidson 90th Anniversary race in Milwaukee. I had a couple of former Green Beret friends of mine go on ahead and they reported back that at least three hundred Outlaws were on the scene. I took seven club guys with me and we drove there in a motor home full of guns. Kevin Cleary, the president of the East Coast was there, too. We found a Super 8 Motel where I noticed a lot of Minnesota license plates—a good place to kind of get lost in. But an Outlaw rode through and happened to spot us and our motor home. Not long after, the police showed up.

"We have a report that there's a bunch of guys hanging around a motor home with guns," they said. Of course it was an Outlaw who had made the call to the cops. "Mind if we search your vehicle?" Fuck yeah, I minded. Of course the cops had no probable cause and no warrant, so there wasn't anything they could do but leave once we declined their request. But I knew we were going to have trouble with the Outlaws.

Soon afterwards, "Taco," the president of the Outlaws, called Kevin and said he wanted a meeting. The next day, a group of Outlaws pulled into the motel parking lot. The first vehicle in was a black Lincoln and two guys jumped out of it, one of them placing a Mac-10 machine pistol on the roof, making sure we could all see it. I had a couple guys with guns of their own, positioned in upstairs rooms, facing the parking lot, their guns pointed out the windows. No fewer than twenty-eight Harleys roared in after the Lincoln, all in dual file, snaking around the parking lot. All of this in broad daylight. I wondered if the cops were watching from somewhere, staying out of it, waiting for shots to be fired. Maybe get themselves a twofer, as Chris might put it.

Kevin and I started walking from the motor home towards the Lincoln, just the two of us. I told the other guys to stay put. Taco had ridden in on a bike right behind the Lincoln and he stepped off it and came towards us as Kevin and I approached. Taco had long, black hair and a dark headband and he wore round, wire-rimmed sunglasses. He had a sort of Fu Manchu mustache but it was shaved clean at the spot right under his nose. Their other guys were getting off their bikes and standing by, no more than maybe fifteen feet away. I noticed Big R was one of them. "What the fuck, Pat?" Taco said. "This is our backyard, man. Our living room. You come here with your patches and disrespect us? You ain't gonna wear your patch. Not here." Taco's nose was running and it was clear by his demeanor that he was wound up on crank or meth.

Kevin was looking around at all the Outlaws and I could tell he was a little nervous. He started to talk but I cut him off. I was the one racing, after all. I got in Taco's face. "I'm wearing my patch, Taco. Talk to Big R over there. I'll tell you what I told him: wherever there's an AMRA event, I'm going to be in it. I'm involved in the point standings. If I'm going to be number one at the end of the year, I need to be in every race. And I don't race without my patch. Big R didn't have a problem with it in Macon."

"Well, what Big R said doesn't hold," said Taco. "You can't race and wear your patch. Not here. Try it and see what happens. Fair warning."

With that, Taco turned and got on his bike and the rest of the Outlaws followed suit, two by two out of the parking lot, the Lincoln bringing up the rear. The guys came down from the rooms and out of the motor home and Kevin turned to me and said, "Pat, let's all get a bite to eat and talk about this." We all went next door to a Perkins and Kevin tried to talk me out of racing.

"Fuck that," I told him "I'm racing. With my patch. I'm an AMRA racer and I'm a Hells Angel. Fuck Taco." The other guys agreed. We all talked about it some more. We didn't want anybody dictating to us. Somewhere in the midst of the conversation, with everyone talking at once, Kevin slipped out of the restaurant and went out to use the payphone. In a few minutes, he returned.

"Pat," he said, "Sonny wants us to give him a call. Will you talk to him?" I walked back to the phone and I got on the line with maybe the only person in the world who could talk me out of racing. It was a good play by Kevin to get Sonny Barger involved.

"Pat," said Sonny, "I'm not telling you what to do, but why get yourself killed?" I respected Sonny immensely. And he respected me. We'd gotten to know each other well over the years at all the Hells Angels' events. I listened to Sonny and he talked sense. "It's not worth your life, Pat. I can't stop you, man, but I sure as hell wish you'd respect my wishes."

I skipped the race. Sonny probably saved my life that day. Back in the parking lot, while I was loading up the bike, the desk clerk at the Super 8 came out. "One of you guys named Pat? There's a phone call for you." It was Taco.

"What are you gonna do, Pat?" Taco said. "I'll tell you once more. You can race, but not with your patch."

"I already told you, Taco. I ain't racing without my fucking patch." I hung up on him. Getting nose to nose with Taco in the parking lot of the Super 8 and hanging up the phone on him—I wasn't exactly becoming the man's best friend. From that point on, Taco had it in for me.

That wasn't the first time I'd crossed paths with Taco. Back in 1991 the Hells Angels and the Outlaws were all at the annual Sturgis Motorcycle Rally in South Dakota. Started in 1938, Sturgis draws about half a million people each year during the first full week of August, most of those people on bikes. In '91, Taco met with us at Sturgis at a big motel called Molly B's. Said he didn't want any trouble. And for the most part, there wasn't any, though I got a call one night; there were about eighteen Hells Angels in the front part of Gunner's Lounge in downtown Sturgis, with about a hundred Outlaws in the back. About forty of us made for Gunner's, just to make sure nothing got started, or, if it did, the Hells Angels would be well represented. We were still outnumbered but our show of force kept the Outlaws from trying anything, although some words were said back and forth. Eventually the Outlaws all left the bar. Big Wayne from our 'Frisco chapter went over to the jukebox and played Petty's "Won't Back Down."

Throughout the early '90s, lots of shit began happening between the Outlaws and the Hells Angels. A couple Hells Angels got beaten up and their patches taken by a gang of Outlaws in Wisconsin. Then an Outlaw got beaten up in New York City by a Hells Angel. Various incidents happened, some caused by us, some caused by them.

Meanwhile, I was making certain that no Outlaws were going to invade our turf in Minnesota. I didn't allow any new motorcycle clubs to organize within a fifty mile radius of our clubhouse in Minneapolis. People knew me. They knew if you even wanted to think about starting a club, you'd better run the idea past us first. The police were quoted in the paper as referring to me as the Godfather of Minnesota bike gangs. I'd tell anyone who came along that there were plenty of clubs already in existence. "There's no need to start a new club," I'd say. What I didn't want was a club to form that could ultimately become an Outlaws sympathizer club.

I made sure to convey the club's toughness. Perception was important. Rooster and I put in for our "Filthy Few" patches. The Hells Angels awards a Filthy Few patch to those who have taken care of the club's business. There are no written rules about what "taking care of business" means, but those on the outside have come to believe that if you're wearing a Filthy Few patch, you've killed for the club. There was a lot of shit people on the outside didn't understand about the Hells Angels, and don't understand to this day. I found it amusing that the cops would rely on books like Lavigne's to get their information. But I certainly wasn't going to do anything to counter the perception people had about the Filthy Few patch. Rooster and I wore our patches proudly.

I ran our chapter with a tight fist. I didn't want any problems to develop and I did my best to stop them before they even got started. Everyone in the club had to have a legitimate job. I wanted us to at least look like we were law-abiding. Rooster was the only one who really didn't have one. He had a couple belly dump trucks that he'd rent out from time to time, but Rooster made his money in other ways and used the truck business as a means of money laundering. Still, everyone looked more or less legitimate. I hired a professional polygrapher, too—Darrell Shaw, a private investigator. (A few years later, I would hire him to investigate the theft of some bikes and cocaine.) Anybody who wanted to become a hangaround had to pass a lie detector test.

Are you now or have you ever been associated in any way
with any law enforcement agency?
Have you ever cooperated in any way with any state
or federal prosecution?
Do you have any intention or desire to see any harm come to the
Hells Angels organization or any of its members?

Mostly, I wanted to keep the violence from the club. I was still making a lot of money selling drugs and I remembered something that Gramps had told me years before. "If you're going to go to jail," he'd said, "make sure it's only for making money." But it wasn't always easy to stay away from the violence. Club business often meant making enemies. Like expanding the Hells Angels into Outlaw territory. As early as 1985, I'd been approached by some Hell's Henchmen from South Bend. I got to know some of the guys from racing. They had three Henchmen chapters: South Bend; Rockford, Illinois; and Chicago, with about a hundred guys total. They wanted to become Hells Angels. The idea moved to the backburner after the guy pushing the most for it committed suicide in 1986. But the group approached me again in 1992. They began to prospect in '93. The Outlaws got wind of it and didn't much care for the idea. The region was Outlaws turf. It was just one more thing that helped fuel the fire between the two clubs.

Besides the Outlaws, we had the usual hassles with the police to contend with. One night in November of 1993, we had all come back to the clubhouse after the bars had closed. One of our guys, Scotty, was walking up when a couple of cops appeared and asked him to stop and show some identification.

"Fuck you, Barney Fife," Scotty shot back. The cops tried to grab him but he ducked into the clubhouse and we slammed the door shut behind him. Soon a bunch of squad cars showed up and the cops started pounding on the door. Richard Rohda and Willie Dougherty came by about then and we opened the door to let them in and the cops tried to enter. We started mixing things up and I threw a few fists while the cops tried to grab us and pull us outside. They had a hold of me at one point and I remember a couple Angels grabbing my pants and yanking me back inside. We slammed the door shut again. It was a standoff for a while with the cops outside yelling all kinds of shit at us. Willie decided to go out and talk to them and when he did, one of the cops grabbed him and in the process, he pulled Willie down on top of him and the two went tumbling down a hill. The cop ended up getting hurt and Willie would get charged with assaulting a police officer. It was bullshit.

Meanwhile the cops had the clubhouse surrounded and we grabbed pool balls and cue sticks and whatever else we could use as weapons and got ready for them to come storming in. But I decided to place a call to Bruce Hanley first, the club attorney, who drove right over and eventually the cops figured they didn't really have any legal cause to be camped out on private property and they started making their way off. But Bruce would tell me that he didn't want to represent us anymore. And he told me why: "I'll be here for you if you're in a bind, Pat," he said, "but these Minneapolis cops don't play by the rules and, frankly, they scare the hell out of me."

That night earned me my Dequiallo patch, the Hells Angels patch you get for fighting law enforcement.

If it wasn't the cops or the Outlaws, it seemed there was always somebody else to worry about. A DUI attorney by the name of Sam McCloud bought some custom bikes from me and we got to know each other. He'd come around, trying to get the club's business after Bruce left us. I got to know his wife, too, who also came around, flirting with me. I guess Sam must have had his suspicions about his wife and me because one day he decided to set me up. He came into the shop telling me he needed a gun. "Can you help me out?" he said. "Can you send me one? In the mail?" I don't know how stupid Sam thought I was but I said I'd get back to him and then I called Barry Voss, my attorney at the time. He came out a few days later and I sat him in Mike Eason's office close to the counter where he could hear everything and I called Sam back into the shop. When he got there, I made him repeat his request.

"Well, Sam," I said, "I think you just might be trying to set me up. That's why I called my attorney in here. He's sitting behind that door, listening to every word."

Pat's new 1993 Chevy Half Ton.

Sam stared at me for a minute, not sure what to say. Finally he said, "You made a good call." Then he turned and walked out of the shop.

But cops or lawyers, it was the Outlaws we had to worry about the most. How far would they go to stop us? I was about to find out.

On December 15, 1993, just about six months after the incident with Taco and the Outlaws in Milwaukee, I had a customer come into the shop and we went off to the DMV to transfer a title. I offered to drive in my new Chevy pickup but the customer insisted we go in his car. When we returned a half hour later, cops were all over the place.

The windows of the shop had all been blown out, along with the windows of all the buildings for a block around.

My pickup truck was sitting in the parking lot, blasted apart. A bomb had been placed under the driver's side. Somebody sure wanted me dead, and they weren't messing around.

Pat's truck and customers Bronco.

Back side of Pat's truck.

Front of Pat's truck. Thanks Taco!

Bomb was placed here
Pat's truck at forensic garage.

CHAPTER 8
War

The attempt on Pat's life was part of a war between the Hells Angels and the Outlaws that goes back decades. It continues still. I don't imagine anything's ever really going to stop it. The two sides have had some uneasy truces from time to time, but those were mostly public relations stunts, serving mainly to keep law enforcement out of the picture. The truces don't last very long.

Rumor has it that the bad blood started back in the early '70s when two of the Hells Angels Lowell, Massachusetts members were killed in Florida by some Outlaws, but tensions were probably running high even before then. The fact is, there are a lot of one-percenter clubs out there and each club takes its turf seriously. It's like a playground game; my club's better than your club. And you can't come into my territory wearing your club's colors. Maybe it's understandable if, say, one club is horning in on the other's drug business. But guys are getting killed just for wearing their club patch somewhere where they shouldn't. The mentality is mind-boggling.

A little-known fact is that the Outlaws once had a chapter in Minnesota. Bloomington, to be exact. They got busted in July of 1970 for stripping down stolen Harleys and sending the parts to Florida. Butch LaBerge, a family friend and old associate of my father's was the investigator on the case. The Outlaws haven't had a presence in the state since.

At any rate, one side of the war attacks and the other side retaliates. In the least violent cases, you might have members of one club beating up members of the other club and taking their patches. Pat mentioned the two Hells Angels who got assaulted in Wisconsin. It happened in a bar in Janesville called Slick's Tavern, and it came at the hands of several Outlaws, maybe six or eight of them. One of the Hells Angels, Joey "Bad" Badaracco, was knocked senseless, his nose and jaw both broken, but he remembered having his patch actually cut off his denim vest. It's reminiscent of the way Indians used to take the scalp. And in the biker world, it's considered a huge insult. A total humiliation. Sometimes you'll hear about the Outlaws having their girlfriends wear the stolen patches. They'll make sure the Hells Angels see the girlfriends wearing them. Naturally those antics are always going to be met with retribution somewhere down the line.

In the most violent cases, you have killings and even bombings. The clubs seem to like the shock and awe of explosives. Clubhouses get bombed, businesses get bombed, and, as in Pat's case, vehicles get bombed. Plans for bombings, as well as other forms of ambushing, can be pretty elaborate. For the most part, club members—notwith-standing Pat's requirement that his guys be legitimately employed—typically don't have real day-to-day jobs. They have a lot of time on their hands to scheme and figure out ways to get back at the other guys. For a lot of them, it's all they do.

The guy pulling the strings for the Outlaws back in the '90s was Harry Joseph Bowman. Nickname: Taco. He was the international president of the gang. The Outlaws work a little differently than the Hells Angels. It's more of a top-down organizational structure. You have five regions in the U.S., and, internationally, each country is con-sidered a region. Chapter presidents report to regional presidents, and regional presidents report to the international president. Bowman be-came the international president in 1984. Working out of the club's Detroit clubhouse, he lived in a wealthy section of the city and drove around in an armor-plated Cadillac.

On New Year's Eve 1993, Bowman called a meeting of all the Outlaws at a party in Fort Lauderdale. There, he announced that the Outlaws would escalate their war with the Hells Angels. From then on, things became even more serious. And more deadly.

There were skirmishes here and there throughout 1994, then in

September of that year things really came to a head at the Lancaster National Speedway in New York. A small contingent of Hells Angels members squared off against the Outlaws who were there in force. The melee came complete with knives, guns, clubs, ax handles, and fists. Bullets flew. An Outlaw by the name of Walter "Buffalo Wally" Posjnak was shot in the chest and killed. He'd escaped a threat to his life back in October of 1993 when his home had been firebombed, presumably by the Hells Angels, but he didn't escape Lancaster. Meanwhile, Michael Quale, a Hells Angel, was stabbed in the neck and bled to death. Fourteen people were injured at Lancaster. Harry Bowman's war was heating up.

One of the Outlaws at Lancaster was a guy named Donald "Big Don" Fogg. Fogg became a suspect in Quale's death after being pulled over an hour after the melee and found in possession of Quale's Hells Angels vest. Apparently, Fogg then began secretly cooperating with the police. Bowman got wind of it and ordered his killing. A few weeks later, Fogg was found dead, lying face down in the snow outside of his truck. He'd been shot three times in the head and the Outlaws who killed him made it a point of making it appear as though the Hells Angels were behind the shooting.

Fogg's murder was just one of a number of murders and kidnappings and beatings and bombings that Bowman was behind. Taco was one bad man. When he would eventually go to prison, it would be for a laundry list of convictions that included multiple racketeering charges as well as murder charges (including Fogg's) and conspiracy to commit murder charges. At one point he was on the FBI's Ten Most Wanted list. Today, he's in prison with enough sentencing time that he's never going to see the light of day.

But in his prime, Bowman was a dangerous mastermind and he didn't exactly care for one Patrick Matter. He was particularly incensed at the Hell's Henchmen clubs around Chicago transitioning, with Pat's encouragement, to Hells Angels clubs. Illinois was Outlaws territory. Two months after Lancaster, Bowman approved a plan to set off a car bomb outside the Hell's Henchmen clubhouse in Chicago. A couple of the Outlaws constructed the bomb, built a metal box for it, took out the front seat of a Ford Taurus to accommodate the bomb's considerable size, drove the Taurus to the clubhouse, and set the bomb off, damaging half a dozen buildings around the immediate vicinity. It ended up being one of the largest bombs to ever go off on U.S. soil. It was 5:00 p.m. on a busy street. Amazingly, no one got hurt. I remember seeing a teletype come across not long after from the Ramsey County Sheriff: "Please be aware that this technique is being used by the Outlaw Motorcycle gang and use extreme caution around any suspicious vehicles or objects located at or near identified Hells Angels locations."

This is when law enforcement really gets involved. It's one thing when clubs keep their violence between themselves. It's a whole different matter when it seeps out into the public and innocent lives are put at risk.

The Hell's Henchmen is a club that's a good example of what's known as a support club. Some clubs keep to themselves but a lot of clubs often ally with other clubs, with the smaller clubs—the Henchmen, the El Forasteros—supporting the bigger clubs. It gives the smaller clubs a level of protection; it gives the bigger clubs a level of insulation, especially from law enforcement. For each Hells Angel dealing drugs or engaging in some illicit activity, there are probably several guys working for him, often members of a support club. He doesn't have to be as visible. His business can be conducted through the gang members he's surrounded by. That makes it more difficult to get to him.

Support clubs are a good source of recruits, too. It's a vetting process of sorts. A guy might prove himself worthy as a Hell's Henchman, for instance (or in Pat's case a Grim Reaper) and be invited to join the Hells Angels. It's a rare Hells Angel who got into the club without starting somewhere else in a smaller club.

For the rival gangs, intimidation is the name of the game. The "Filthy Few" patch is a good example. It's widely believed that it means the guy wearing it has killed for the club, or at least beaten somebody up pretty severely. If you're wearing a Filthy Few patch, you're the baddest of the bad. This intimidates other club members, but it also intimidates police officers. We're human. Your heart beats a little faster if you've pulled a biker over and you notice he's wearing a Filthy Few patch. Has he killed someone? You have the same kind of reaction if you see him with a Dequiallo patch. Has he assaulted a cop somewhere?

I imagine every club has equivalent patches. The Outlaws wear their "lightning bolts," kind of a Nazi-style "SS" emblem that supposedly means the Outlaw in question has committed murder, attempted murder, or exploded a bomb on behalf of the club. In time, however, as I would become more involved in the investigation of the Hells Angels, I started doing the math. I saw a ton of Filthy Few patches. It seemed as if everybody was wearing one. Same with the Outlaws and their lightning bolts. And I would wonder where all the bodies were. It just didn't add up. It turns out the patches are mostly flash. A lot of the guys get theirs just by asking for them. But as far as instilling a little fear, the patches work.

At any rate, the war between the Outlaws and Hells Angels continued and Pat almost became a statistic of it in December of 1993. The bomb idea was hatched after three Outlaws, two from the Milwaukee chapter and one from the Janesville chapter, came into town and followed Pat around for a few days intent on shooting him. They could never seem to find the right moment to get a shot off, so they went back and built a bomb instead. It was a C-4 plastic explosive, placed into a six-inch by nine-inch metal box with an aluminum top. It was attached to the underside of the driver's side of the truck and it had a mercury-activated switch that would cause it to go off with movement, such as if Pat would have sat down in the driver's seat or even stepped onto the running board. But apparently the switch was a bit too sensitive. One of the Outlaws accidentally set it off prematurely, destroying the truck and injuring himself in the process.

I remember hearing about the bomb. I was working in Narcotics at the time. Of course, by then we all knew who Pat was. "Camden Area Businessman's Truck Blown Up," the headlines said. That brought a chuckle from some of the guys. "*Businessman*, my ass," I remember one of them saying.

We had intel at the time about the war between the Hells Angels and the Outlaws and about Pat's intention to have the Hells Angels absorb the Hell's Henchmen chapters. Everybody pretty much assumed the war was behind the bombing. Pat had to know it, too. But he wasn't saying. "Who might have done this to you?" he was asked by one of the cops on the scene that day. "I don't know," he replied, in standard Pat Matter cocky wise-ass fashion. "That's your job. You figure it out." But from a law enforcement perspective, Pat wasn't exactly an innocent victim. He was a target and you don't generally get to be a target in the middle of a gang war for no reason.

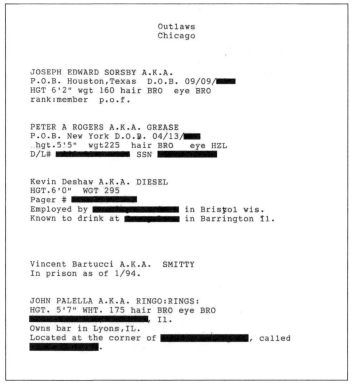

Chicago Clubhouse Members

Chicago Clubhouse

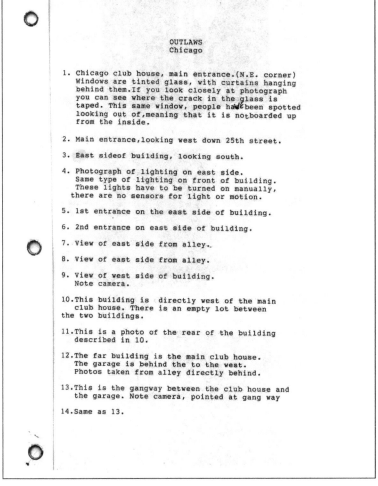

```
                        OUTLAWS
                        Chicago

1. Chicago club house, main entrance.(N.E. corner)
   Windows are tinted glass, with curtains hanging
   behind them.If you look closely at photograph
   you can see where the crack in the glass is
   taped. This same window, people have been spotted
   looking out of,meaning that it is notboarded up
   from the inside.

2. Main entrance,looking west down 25th street.

3. East sideof building, looking south.

4. Photograph of lighting on east side.
   Same type of lighting on front of building.
   These lights have to be turned on manually,
   there are no sensors for light or motion.

5. 1st entrance on the east side of building.

6. 2nd entrance on east side of building.

7. View of east side from alley.

8. View of east side from alley.

9. View of west side of building.
   Note camera.

10.This building is  directly west of the main
   club house. There is an empty lot between
the two buildings.

11.This is a photo of the rear of the building
   described in 10.

12.The far building is the main club house.
   The garage is behind the to the west.
   Photos taken from alley directly behind.

13.This is the gangway between the club house and
   the garage. Note camera, pointed at gang way

14.Same as 13.
```

Chicago Clubhouse Layout

An Outlaws Security File was recovered from the Minneapolis Hells Angels clubhouse in 2001. Every Outlaws chapter in Illinois, Indiana and Wisconsin had a file. The files included photos of each clubhouse, a description of each clubhouse and a list of each member along with their address and physical description.

As for me, I continued working Narcotics and in 1994, I was promoted from deputy to detective. I was thrilled. I got the shit cases at first—general investigative cases—minor thefts and forgeries and the like. But I was *Detective*, which was all I'd ever really wanted to be. And I did well.

In '95, I was assigned to a double homicide case. Two men had been shot execution style in Spring Park, a well-to-do area near Lake Minnetonka. A dope deal gone bad. Several of us were working on the case, under our captain, Rocky Fontana, the guy who had encouraged me to join the sheriff's office in the first place. Rocky liked me, liked the work I was doing. In roundtable meetings about the double-homicide case, I wasn't shy about speaking up and Rocky seemed to appreciate that. We developed suspects for the case and when one of them fled to Oregon and was subsequently arrested, Rocky sent me out there to interview him. I was the new guy and sending me sort of rubbed the others the wrong way. But I did a good job with it and the case against our suspects was ultimately successful.

Because of my work on the Spring Park case, I was sent on a temporary basis from the sheriff's office to Minneapolis P.D. Homicide. The homicide department needed all the help it could get. Gang bangers were causing murder rates to go through the roof and Minneapolis was being called Murderapolis. In seven months' time I worked on some thirty cases. I enjoyed it. I liked the challenge. It could be difficult, of course, and sometimes depressing. The urban gang members were mostly kids with no clue as to what life or death really meant. Most of them didn't have family. Sometimes there'd be a trial and there wouldn't even be anyone in the gallery for the victim. Seeing younger kids get killed for no reason was the worst. In the course of my duties I was once required to attend the autopsy of a ten-year-old. I didn't go. The final report was sufficient for me. There was nothing at the autopsy itself that I figured I needed to see.

For one case, I was awarded the Minneapolis Chief's Award of Merit. It was a case everyone was calling unsolvable. A local musician had been shot to death. He was a marijuana dealer and we all knew it had to be a drug robbery gone bad. But there were zero suspects.

I didn't start getting any solid information until a month or so after the fact when I had a couple informants independently approach me. The morning after the homicide I had executed a second search warrant on the scene of the shooting and found a bunch of evidence that was missed by the guys who did the first search. With that, and what I'd learned from my informants, there was enough to find the killers— a couple gang-bangers. The case went to trial and I had to testify and the gang-bangers got put away.

Success like that can be gratifying and working homicide can be addicting. At the same time, it's likely to burn you out. You take the cases home with you in your head. It's long days and often long nights. The experience was worthwhile for me, but I wouldn't want to do it forever.

After my stint in homicide, I went back to my investigative work at the sheriff's office. There was no shortage of it. Forgery cases had piled up on my desk. I recognized the perpetrators in a lot of them: a well-known, female-led crime family. The Loyds were notorious in Minnesota. Josephine Foreman was the matriarch and everybody called her Grandma. Her daughter was Betty Loyd and Betty ran everything. Check forgery, money laundering, bank fraud—they did it all. The people they had working for them were motivated by the crack cocaine that the Loyds would get them hooked on. I decided to go after the whole organization. I put together a task force and we got the IRS involved along with the U.S. Postal Inspection Service and the Minnesota Bureau of Criminal Apprehension. We spent a year and a half investigating the Loyds. In the end, we were able to indict them on federal charges. Betty went to federal prison and the whole experience taught me a lot about investigating criminal organizations. The knowledge would soon come in handy for another criminal enterprise.

Rocky took note of my work on the Loyd case, and in August of 1997, put me in charge of our Special Operations Division, the SOD unit. The unit was a proactive police team that concentrated on criminal organizations. I was young and I felt a little resentment from some of the others at being given the responsibility of leading the group.

But I was determined not to let Rocky down and in time I'd earn the respect of the other members.

Shortly after my assignment to the SOD unit, Mike Tamte, a detective friend who was big into Harleys, turned to me one day and said, "If you're looking for something for the SOD unit to investigate, how about all these bike thefts?" Rocky happened to walk past and he overheard Mike. There'd been a lot of motorcycles, mostly Harley-Davidsons, recently reported stolen all around the Twin Cities. "I'll back that one," Rocky said. And so we began to investigate the group that seemed most likely to be behind the thefts. The only group, to our minds, that it could have been was the Minnesota chapter of the Hells Angels.

CHAPTER 9
Enough's Enough

Not surprisingly, Trish got a little freaked out by the bomb that destroyed my truck. When the cops came to the house to do a search to see if anything else was amiss, I uncharacteristically let them. I had nothing incriminating on hand and the cops looking around made Trish feel better. She didn't really know a whole lot about the war between the Outlaws and the Hells Angels, or about Taco, or the Hell's Henchmen. She thought maybe the bomb had to do with my racing. Maybe I'd pissed someone off somewhere. I didn't tell her anything different.

My employees were a little freaked out, too. They all started to check the underside of their cars with sticks and mirrors. I joked that I was going to get us all red and white Plymouth Champs so that our vehicles would all look alike and the Outlaws wouldn't know which one to plant their next bomb under. And then I initiated a watch at the clubhouse. Each member would take a turn spending the night at the clubhouse.

The way I heard it, the war started in 1969 when Pete Rogers, who would go on to become the Outlaws' regional president, raped Sandy Alexander's girlfriend. Sandy was president at the time of another club but would eventually become president of the New York chapter of the Hells Angels. Sandy beat the shit out of Rogers and, shortly after that, two Hells Angels showed up dead in Florida. From then on, it's been one retaliatory act after another. I think Chris is right. I don't ever see it ending.

For my part, I couldn't allow the bombing of my truck to stand. For me to be who I was, the well-respected, well-known president of a Hells Angels chapter, I could not let the bombing go by unanswered. I just couldn't. And in addition to the truck bombing, there was Ed Murphy's kidnapping. Ed was one of the Hell's Henchmen and one night a couple Outlaws grabbed him near his home in Fox Lake, Illinois and threw him into their van. He saw body bags in the van and that meant only one thing: they were driving him somewhere to execute him. Ed managed to get out, rolling out of the van right into the middle of the street. The Outlaws kept going. When the cops came, Ed did what you're not supposed to do. He told the cops it was the Outlaws, breaking the biker code.

That year, 1994, it so happened that the Easyriders Rodeo was being held in New Ulm, Minnesota, not too far away. All the Hell's Henchmen prospects came up for it, at least fifty of them, including Ed, and I mentioned that something had to be done. "You need to take care of one of their guys," I said. "Somebody big."

But I also heard the story of Ed's kidnapping and his talking to the cops. I liked Ed and I hated like hell to do it, but I turned to him and said, "Man, I gotta let you go, Ed. You can't be a Hells Angel." I didn't even want him being a Hell's Henchmen at that point and although we let him ride with us to the Rodeo, he was ousted from the Henchmen, too.

The rest of the Henchmen got my message about taking care of somebody and a few weeks later, in late June, none other than Pete Rogers, regional Outlaws president, was shot as he rode his bike on the Dan Ryan Expressway in Chicago. A van pulled up beside him and the occupants opened fire. Rogers took a bullet in the leg and one in the gut. But he managed to escape up an exit ramp and eventually he pulled over in front of a deli where the owner called for an ambulance. Rogers survived. Later, after the Henchmen got patched as Hells Angels, I presented the two shooters, Mel Chancey and David "Pulley" Ohlendorf, with their Filthy Few patches.

I gave Filthy Few patches to Mel "Road" Chancey and David "Pulley" Ohlendorf for shooting Outlaw Peter "Grease" Lightning" Rogers.

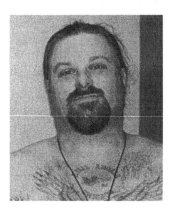

A couple days after the Rogers shooting, it was the Outlaws' turn. One of their prospects showed up at a Henchmen's motorcycle shop in Rockford. It was the shop of Monte Mathias, president of the chapter. Monte was a good guy, a friend and a business associate; he rebuilt motors for me. In fact, he had several of my motors in his shop that day. He'd finished the work and I was planning on driving to Rockford to pick the motors up within the next day or so. I wish I had gone the day the Outlaw prospect showed up. Maybe I could have stopped what happened.

David Wolf was the Outlaw prospect. Apparently he walked into Monte's shop on the pretense of buying spark plugs. He left, and then, confident that he had the right guy, he returned. Monte must have sensed trouble because he tried to leave through the back door of the shop. Wolf pulled out a.45 and shot Monte three times in the back. Then Wolf hit him with the gun so hard that he broke off part of the butt. Finally he picked up a screwdriver and stabbed Monte in the neck over and over. A newspaper reported later that the coroner used the phrase "frenzy wounds" to describe the nature of the stabbing.

I got a call that night at the clubhouse. I didn't recognize the voice. "Pat Matter? Tell me—how many members do you need for a Hells Angels charter? Isn't it six? Well I think you're going to find that you're one short in Rockford." Then he hung up. It was a hell of a way to get the news about Monte. Though he had yet to be patched over, I made sure Monte was buried in full Hells Angels' colors.

In July, the Outlaws firebombed Ed Murphy's house, thinking he was still a Henchmen. In August they bombed a tattoo shop in Chicago. But of course they hadn't forgotten about us in Minnesota. Taco still had it in for me. Ever since our meeting in the parking lot of the Super 8, he'd had me in his sights. And my bringing the Hell's Henchmen into the fold only infuriated him further. The fact is, I was supposed to be at Lancaster National Speedway in New York that September day in '94 when the big fight broke out and Michael Quale got killed. And the Outlaws knew it. That's why they were there. I was the target. I had just finished racing at Woodburn in Oregon and my next stop in the points standings would have been Lancaster. The guys from Rochester called wanting to know if I'd be there. Lancaster was only an hour away from Rochester and they wanted to come and give me some back-up. I said sure, but first I needed to stop in Minnesota with my racing bike. At Woodburn, I'd blown my motor. Once back home I quickly realized the motor couldn't be rebuilt in time. I called Rochester to let them know I wouldn't be able to race in Lancaster. A blown motor may have saved my life.

The Rochester guys went anyway. There were only seven of them. The news accounts said there were dozens on both sides, but I'm sure that's because it probably looked that way to the witnesses. Lots of guys in leather vests and club colors going at each other—from an outsider's perspective, it was probably hard to tell who was who. But I ran into Rich Mroch, an Outlaw, years later. He was there and he knew how badly we were outnumbered. "Pat," he told me, "when the Hells Angels pulled their guns and started firing, man, we all just scattered. Your guys were fucking serious." A few months after Lancaster, the cops charged Rochester Hells Angel Bob Herald with the murder of Walter Posjnak, the Outlaw who was killed at Lancaster. Bob was one of the guys who helped me break into the El Forasteros' clubhouse that night when we'd taken their guns and tossed them up on the roof. Ultimately, Bob would be acquitted of the murder charge.

In October, we fired back. Club member John Derks wanted to plant a bomb outside the tattoo parlor of an Outlaw in Milwaukee. I went along with the idea. Derks picked "Pee Wee" to go with him. Pee Wee was six-foot-eight-inches and four hundred pounds. He was an ex-Sinners Motorcycle Club member now prospecting for us and he knew Milwaukee well. Derks wanted to see if Pee Wee had what it took to be a Hells Angel.

But in Milwaukee, as Pee Wee would tell me, Derks went a bit over the top. He and Pee Wee drove past the Outlaws' clubhouse and Derks made Pee Wee drop him off. His idea was to hide in the bushes and just start shooting anyone who came in or out. The idea made Pee Wee nervous. Derks ended up not shooting anyone and the two planted the bomb behind the gas meter of the tattoo shop where it went off; then Derks told me afterward that he didn't feel like Pee Wee had enough mud to be a Hells Angel. We never did bring Pee Wee up for patch, but eventually he ended up in the San Francisco Hells Angels chapter.

Then in November came the monster bomb that went off outside the Henchmen's clubhouse in Chicago, the one Taco ordered. Soon afterwards I received an eight by ten photograph in the mail. It was a picture of Rich Mroch standing in front of the bombed clubhouse. On the back of the photograph, somebody had written, *Pat, come out and play. Charlie.* Charlie was the name given to the Outlaws' emblem—a skull with two pistons placed like crossbones underneath.

In between all these events there were numerous other incidents—bombings, beatings, shootings, stabbings; the war wasn't cooling off. Even some Hells Angels were second-guessing our expansion into Outlaws territory. A couple guys from the southern chapters told me, "Man, Pat, we sure didn't need this." But in December of '94, the Henchmen came up for patch and got voted in. The Hells Angels increased their membership by three chapters, all of them in Outlaws territory. Taco must have been livid.

Not only was I dealing with Taco and the Outlaws; I was also one of four Hells Angels who traveled to Bellingham, Washington to meet with George Wegers, national president of the Bandidos, over a territory dispute. I was there along with Greg Domey from the East Coast Hells Angels and Mark Perry and Cisco from the West Coast. The Bandidos made it clear they didn't want us expanding any further into their territory. "How would you like it if we put a Bandidos chapter in Oakland?" they said. "That's not fucking happening," we told them. The meeting was civil but we made it clear that if we wanted to expand anywhere we would.

In the meantime, the cops weren't letting up in their harassment of us. And I was amazed at how far they'd go. Some St. Paul cop named Andy Shoemaker got it in his head that some of our guys had threatened his wife. At least that's what I would later come to understand. There was some bullshit allegation he made about a bunch of Hells Angels driving on his lawn. All I know is that one night I was sitting in a bar called Waldo's when I got a call from someone identifying himself as a St. Paul policeman and he wanted to see me. He was furious. Said there was going to be a problem. I hung up on him.

Less than a week later, two cops came knocking on the clubhouse door. I wasn't there. Back in '93 when the cops had tried to grab Scotty outside the clubhouse that night, Bruce Hanley, our attorney at the time, advised us to videotape them if they ever tried anything like that again. So this time, when they knocked, one of our guys taped them.

The cops told him that I needed to call the St. Paul Police Department where there was a message waiting for me. I don't know. Maybe it was Shoemaker again. But I never called.

Three days later, the cops busted the clubhouse with a search warrant. There was apparently a rape allegation. They had a girl who alleged she'd been raped repeatedly in the clubhouse by several Hells Angels. She'd been taken upstairs and she gave the cops details about a yellow beanbag chair and wall paintings of dragons. She remembered nicknames being used. "Blue" and "Animal" were two of the rapists, she said.

There were just a couple problems with her story. We didn't have a yellow beanbag chair in the clubhouse. Or paintings of dragons. We didn't have any members named Blue or Animal, either. Fuck, we didn't even have a second floor. There was a girl and she'd been raped and apparently confused. That was enough for the cops. I don't know how much information they put into her head but somehow they got her to say Hells Angels and that was enough to bust the place. They took a shitload of personal stuff out as "evidence" including the videotapes we'd made of them. Eventually the cops couldn't get the girl to cooperate and that was the end of the case. We got some of our stuff back. But they held onto the videotapes. It got to the point where I was no longer surprised at just how far the cops would go to harass us. There was no line it seemed they were unwilling to cross.

For me, my involvement with the club wasn't slowing down even though my cycle business was taking off and my time was being spread thinner and thinner. Earlier that year, during the World Run in San Francisco, I was brought up in a vote for president of the east coast. I said I didn't want it; I was too busy. They had the election anyway and I lost by a couple votes. Had I campaigned for it, I imagine I'd have won, but not having to take on the extra responsibilities was fine by me.

Getting to San Francisco that year for the Run was an experience. We Minnesota guys went to Omaha first. The Hell's Henchmen, still prospecting at the time, met us there. So did North Carolina and South Carolina and a few other miscellaneous chapters. And then I led the pack—more than a hundred bikes heading west. We left on a

Monday and made it to Cheyenne, Wyoming where we spent the night. From Cheyenne it was on to Wendover, right on the Utah-Nevada state line. We stayed in Wendover Tuesday night and then Wednesday morning we made for San Francisco, getting in at around 9:00 that night. It was three days of sunup to sundown riding, mostly at around eighty to ninety miles per hour, and two nights of partying, which of course we carried on with once we got to 'Frisco. It was a lot of bikes to move at once and it was a hell of a thrill leading them.

We got pulled over once, though we didn't make it very easy for the cops. I wouldn't pull over and about half the pack stayed with me while the cops managed to pull over the back half of us. They checked everyone's I.D. and ran warrants and let everyone go, then circled around in front and ultimately pulled over the front of our pack, but not before having to shut down the freeway. Then they checked our I.D.s, too. They let us go eventually, but I've never seen cops so pissed off. A convoy of a hundred Harley-Davidsons doesn't exactly make for a routine traffic stop.

Trish and I at Sturgis Raceway along with Percy "Scotty" Barfield.

But even with everything that was going on with the club, my time was going more and more to the cycle business and my racing. Racing was an addicting rush. I loved the speed. And I loved the fans, too, and I was popular with the other racers and the events were just a hell of a lot of fun. And I was good. With my custom drag bike, I won about seventy-five percent of the races I entered, winning the Sturgis Nationals in both 1994 and 1995. I was beating guys who had more money and better technology. The racing helped the shop. Cycle magazines kept doing articles on me. We'd sell five to six thousand dollars' worth of Minneapolis Custom Cycle t-shirts at the events.

Pat's Pro-Stock Race Bike at Sturgis Raceway

And the business was becoming more and more legitimate. I was selling drugs, of course, netting probably between half a million and a million dollars a year, but the cycle shop was making it on its own. I was buying fewer stolen parts all the time, but it was hard to stop completely. Pee Wee was providing me stolen transmission gear sets for about two hundred bucks each that would have otherwise cost me about fifteen hundred. He was getting them from a Sinners Motorcycle Club guy named Patrick Fengier, a Harley-Davidson employee in Milwaukee. Fengier was selling parts all over. Rooster was buying from him, too, and reselling the parts.

In 1996, the cops got wind of it and two of them showed up at my shop wanting to talk. I let them in and said we could talk in my office and we walked in and I suddenly remembered I had a water gun sitting on my desk that looked just like a Mac-10. I figured it was a good opportunity to fuck with the cops a little. I made sure they both spotted the water gun, then I jumped up and said, "Nope, this is no good. You know what? Let's talk outside my office. Yeah, outside my office is much better." Then I led them outside and shut the door quickly behind me. For good measure, I went back inside and closed the blinds on the window that faced the shop and came back outside and had to keep from laughing at the looks on the cops' faces.

The cops asked if I had gotten any shipments recently from Milwaukee. I told them I get shipments all the time from a lot of different places. They asked some more questions and I told them to contact my attorney. On the way out, the cops ran into Rooster who had just pulled into the shop. They tried talking to him but he didn't tell them anything either.

The business continued to grow. I stayed committed to the Hells Angels, too, but in 1996, Tank quit the club. It was a real blow to me. Tank was as close as a brother to me. We'd gone back a lot of years and we'd been through a lot together. You get close to the guys in your club when you lead the kind of lifestyles we led. You come to depend on them for your very life, and they depend on you. Tank and I had been in fights together. We'd seen friends killed. We'd cried together. But Tank was getting out. He didn't care for some of the new guys who had recently joined the chapter and he'd also had enough of the drug business. I tried to talk him into staying but he ended up giving me food for thought about leaving. "Pat," he said, "when is enough, enough?"

L-R: Dennis "Tank" Fenstra and me at the Humboldt,
Iowa Racetrack about 1984.

For months after he quit, I kept thinking about what Tank had said. I'd made millions from the drugs. How much more did I need? The club was taking so much of my time. And the war with the Outlaws wasn't going away anytime soon. I found myself constantly looking over my shoulder and even wearing a bulletproof vest to the races. I wasn't afraid, exactly. Somewhere along the line I came to understand that I don't seem to feel fear the way most people do. But I was definitely aware. Plus, I wasn't getting any younger. And then of course there was Trish; I had to think about her. Trish was sticking with me, even through shit like the truck bombing. Meanwhile, Minneapolis Custom Cycle had turned into a well-respected, mostly-legal, highly-profitable business. Did I really need to be involved with the Hells Angels anymore?

I met with Rooster one day in 1997 and told him I was getting out. I told him enough's enough.

CHAPTER 10
Getting Close

I didn't hear about the clubhouse rape allegation in 1994. Years later, I would run into Andy Shoemaker and he'd tell me that the Hells Angels threatened his wife. That sounded odd to me. The Hells Angels, and Pat Matter in particular from what I would come to learn of the man, weren't stupid enough to call attention to themselves. It just didn't make sense. Neither did the idea of them driving all over some cop's lawn. These guys aren't idiots. Then I learned of the allegation, and upon close inspection, the only conclusion you can come to is that it was false. It seems clear from the report that the girl was, in fact, raped. Somewhere. But it wasn't at the clubhouse and it wasn't by the Hells Angels. The details don't add up. It's disappointing when you see something like that. It was pure harassment by some misguided cops and there's just no other way to put it.

Meanwhile, in my department, we were zeroing in on the Hells Angels lawfully and with good old-fashioned police work. I'd gained an understanding of the motorcycle theft problem even before I was assigned to the Special Operations Division. In March of 1997, I attended a meeting of the Minnesota Outlaw Motorcycle Gang Investigators Association. MOMGIA was a loose confederation of statewide investigators from law enforcement agencies as well as the insurance industry. Bob Henderson of the National Insurance Crime Bureau was at the meeting. The NICB interest was obvious; from 1993 to 1997, over 500 Harleys had been stolen in the state of Minnesota alone—virtually none of them recovered—adding up to more than ten million dollars in insurance losses. At the meeting, Bob Feinen, an investigator with Sentry-Dairyland Insurance out of Stevens Point stood up and put his hands together as if in prayer and pleaded with those of us representing law enforcement. "*Please* help us solve these cases," he said. "These thefts are *killing* us."

It wouldn't take long before we'd start getting some breaks. Shortly after I'd been put in charge of the SOD unit in August of 1997, we learned of three Harleys being stolen from a garage in south Minneapolis. One of the bikes had been crashed by one of the thieves on a highway on-ramp. The thief somehow fled the scene, even though we'd learn later he'd broken his leg in the crash. The bike was impounded and a report written up, but that was about the extent of it until I mentioned to the guys of my Special Operations Division that we should check the scene ourselves, see if we could find anything. John VanSlyke—Slick we called him—and detective Jim Skaja ran out to the sight of the crash and snooped around and found a pager. It belonged to a gal named Kami Gorham, girlfriend of one Tony Morales, a known thief. Morales was also an addict, but we'd quickly learn that the thing he was most addicted to was stealing Harley-Davidson motorcycles.

One of the phone numbers on the pager belonged to a Patrick Stevens in Brooklyn Center, north of Minneapolis. We didn't recognize the name but Jim Skaja had a good friend on the Brooklyn Center P.D., and he placed a call to him. Investigator Fred Moen confirmed that the name Patrick Stevens was probably an alias for Patrick Smith, an El Forasteros club member. It was the first we'd heard of the El Forasteros motorcycle club. The pager was a nice piece of luck.

A month later, we got another break. Morales was arrested in Burnsville, south of Bloomington. A homeowner heard noises from his garage in the middle of the night and called the cops. Morales was discovered a block away pushing the Harley he'd stolen out of the garage. He was wearing a cast on his broken leg that ran all the way up to his groin. Turns out that when he'd dumped the stolen motorcycle a month prior, he'd gone to the emergency room telling them he'd wrecked his bicycle.

Morales was charged and we got busy trying to collect all the information we could about Pat Smith and the El Forasteros. Morales was obviously stealing for them, although we'd learn later that he'd steal for anybody. And *from* anybody—even the Hells Angels. In turn, the El Forasteros—in particular Pat Smith and Jay Puig, who we would come to learn was Smith's right-hand-man—were most likely chopping the bikes up and making custom bikes to resell.

We began investigating Smith. We got mail covers from the U.S. Postal Service which allowed us to see where his mail was going to and where it was coming from. We got pen registers, too, which allowed us to see whom he called and who called him. Quickly we discovered a lot of calls going to and coming from one Paul Seydel: Rooster—vice president of the Minneapolis Hells Angels.

I got in touch with Joe Cludy from the local Bureau of Alcohol, Tobacco, and Firearms to see what he knew about the El Forasteros. Cludy suggested we talk to the ATF in Kansas City. The El Forasteros were more prevalent in Missouri and the ATF had a man in Kansas City who was supposedly an expert. Slick and Skaja and I took a road trip with Cludy and met with ATF agents at their office in the Kansas City federal building, only to be disappointed to learn that the supposed expert didn't seem to know a great deal more than what we already knew. But on our way out, we were stopped by another ATF agent who said that if we really wanted to know about the El Forasteros, we needed to talk to a man by the name of Steve Cook, a detective who was serving on the Jackson County drug task force. "He knows everything about 'em."

We called Cook and he met us at Kelly's Westport Inn, an Irish pub where a lot of the Kansas City cops hung out. Cook asked when we were going back to Minneapolis. "Tomorrow morning," I said.

"Can you delay it a bit? I think you're going to want to see what I've got." We said sure and spent the next morning at Steve's office where he had files and files on the El Forasteros. He'd been investigating them for years. Now we had the names of all the players.

Back in Minneapolis we really started our surveillance. Rocky added another detective to the unit: Tom Rainville, a tall guy nicknamed Rattler, with a deep voice and a short fuse. We followed Pat

Smith. We learned where the El Forasteros clubhouse was and we watched guys come and go from Smith's house, including Seydel and a former Hells Angels prospect named Charles Goldsmith, who was also known as "Pee Wee." There were more guys, too, that we'd start learning about, like Paul Shimek, an ex-El Forastero who had his own motorcycle repair shop in the rear of his residence in Brooklyn Park.

Then in December of 1997, an informant of Jim Skaja's, a guy named Ronnie Rowles, came into our office. Ronnie was a tweaker, a meth addict. Ronnie was one of those guys just destined to be one of life's losers. Always out of work, always out of money, always getting into trouble. But he seemingly knew everything that was going on in the north side of town. Rowles came in looking for a few bucks, probably to help support his meth habit. But mostly, he wanted his Plymouth Roadrunner back which he claimed had been taken while he was doing a stint in a workhouse. Said he had information. "Sure, we'll help you out, Ronnie," I said, "but we're going to need it on paper. We're going to record it."

Ronnie said okay and began to tell Jim Skaja and me a story about a certain bike theft on the south side. He'd been approached by Tony Morales and a guy named Burronnie Brosh to help pilfer a Harley out of a residential garage. On or about the night of February 18 of 1997 (Morales hadn't yet stolen the bike that he'd subsequently crash to suffer his broken leg), the three showed up at the garage to find not one, but four bikes and enough parts to make two more. They also found a lift and a bunch of tools. And they found something else: in a Nike shoebox they discovered two kilos of cocaine. It took about five hours, but they took it all, emptying out the garage and making several trips between it and Morales's house, stuffing everything into Brosh's van which had been custom-equipped for the job, complete with tie-downs and everything a thief would need to transport motorcycles.

But soon word got out that the wrong motorcycles had been taken. The garage they were taken from was owned by Mark Armstrong. Mark was a friend of Pat Matter's. The bikes had Hells Angels support stickers on them: "Fuck with it and find out." And Pat Matter and the Hells Angels didn't have much of a sense of humor about having the bikes stolen. At Pat's direction, Mark put up reward signs offering $3,000 for information. Pat was interested in more than just the bikes. It turns out the cocaine was his. When he eventually learned who the three thieves were, he imposed a $10,000 "tax" on each of them to help recover the costs. Ronnie had to sell his own motorcycle and snowmobile to pay his share. Morales waited for Ronnie to get sent to the workhouse, then took Ronnie's Roadrunner to help pay his own ten grand.

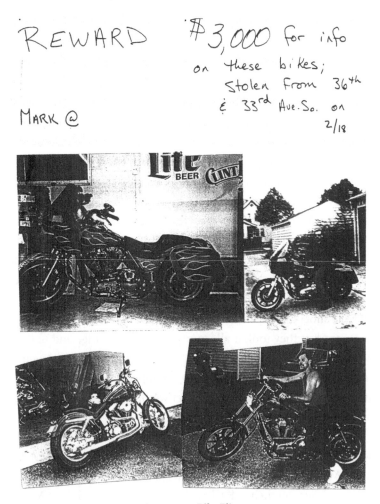

Armstrong Bike Flier

I imagine it was understood what the consequences would be if one's tax went unpaid. But just in case it wasn't, Pat Matter, according to a later interview by Ronnie, showed him and Brosh three body bags. I wasn't present at that particular interview and in retrospect, I imagine Ronnie was embellishing. I don't believe Pat carried body bags around. But there was no doubt that Ronnie was scared as shit by Pat. Ronnie would meet with Pat one more time, after he'd paid his tax, just to make certain he was all square. They met at a diner and after Ronnie was patted down to make sure he wasn't wearing a wire, Pat told him, "You're a ghost, Ronnie. I never want to hear from you again."

Three weeks after we talked with Ronnie Rowles, Officer Kerry Mraz, a beat cop on the north side, was patrolling early one morning and responded to a report of suspicious activity behind a detached garage. Mraz knew the garage. It belonged to Tony Morales. What Mraz found when got there was a stolen van parked behind the garage and one Shawn Anderson. Anderson was a friend of Morales's. Upon being questioned, he told Mraz his name was Eric Lambert and, when asked about the van Mraz had seen him exiting just moments before, replied with, "What van?"

Mraz arrested Anderson and then called us and suggested we execute a search warrant on the garage. The next day, December 23, we spent hours going through Morales's house and garage. There were countless bike parts, two fresh stolen bikes, and a parts catalog with the name Brad Armstrong on it. Brad was Mark Armstrong's brother. Ronnie's story was gaining validity, at least about the stolen bikes. Then I called the Armstrong residence and left a voice message that we'd found some of their stuff. Nobody ever called back. That seemed suspicious to me and helped substantiate in my mind Ronnie's tale about the coke.

Morales was arrested again and now we had bikes and drugs and even more names. I began building spreadsheets to keep track of everything. Meanwhile, we found out that the Bureau of Criminal Apprehension had been investigating a guy named Ralph Schluter for drug dealing. Schluter was a well-known former Hells Angel. And the

Hennepin/Anoka Drug Task Force was looking into a guy named Mike Eason for the same reason. Eason had been spotted coming in and out of Pat Matter's Minneapolis Custom Cycle. We knew about them both. Mike Eason, we'd learn, was M.C.C.'s service manager.

By then, our SOD team was aiming at a date of February 11, 1998, to execute search warrants on Pat Smith's house as well as other places. We encouraged the BCA and the Drug Task Force to search the homes of Schluter and Eason on the same day. I sensed that what they were investigating was connected to what we were investigating and I knew we needed to work together.

They agreed. The idea was to daze and confuse, keep everyone from knowing where in the hell we were coming from. We'd learned Pat Smith had multiple storage lockers, which we had placed cameras around and from where we had seen him and Jay Puig coming and going with bike parts. We had enough probable cause to search the lockers along with his house. As well, we planned to search Seydel's house and garage and the El Forasteros' clubhouse. Other houses and garages and storage lockers, too. We didn't have sufficient probable cause at the time to search Pat Matter's house and Minneapolis Custom Cycle, though we knew there had to be a connection. Seydel was a Hells Angels VP, after all. I imagine we could have probably manufactured some cheesy reason to search Pat's places but it was important to me that we do things right.

February 11 came and we swooped down everywhere. We utilized a SWAT team to make entry into Pat Smith's house and the team had to shoot a couple Rottweilers as the dogs began to attack. By the end of the day, we recovered a shitload of stuff, enough stolen bike parts to half-fill the Brooklyn Park patrol station. Tools, too, and several finished bikes. All told, at least three quarters of a million dollars' worth. One of the local papers ran a story about the search and confiscation, referring to Smith and the Forasteros as the "Forest Arrows." Slick kept saying, "Forest Arrows—men in tights!"

SMITH, PATRICK STEVEN

DOB 09/22/████   Age 38   Ht 5'11"   Wt 205   Hair color **BROWN**   Eye color **HAZEL**
Booking No   HCSO199805784   Person No   HCSO197713419
Booking Date 02/11/1998   Arresting Agency HC SHERIFF

02/17/1998 16:09 © hcso 04

Pat Smith's booking photo.

Jay Puig. Puig showed up at the Hennepin County Sheriff's Patrol office to pick up some property. In a bag was an filthy old pacifier which Jay promptly placed in his mouth.

Overwhelmed with the sheer amount of parts, unable to identify them, let alone inventory them, I called Harley-Davidson corporate in Milwaukee half in desperation. "Can you send someone to help us?" I asked. Pete Schemberger from Harley-Davidson agreed to fly out and bring with him Pete Simet from the Milwaukee Police Department. We'd end up referring to them as Pete and Pete. Simet was the resident expert in Milwaukee on Harley thefts and had been working closely with the corporate office.

When Pete and Pete flew out, I picked them up at the airport. They were older guys, older than I was. Simet was big—tall and stout; your prototypical beat cop. You looked at him and you knew right away he'd been around the block a time or two. I could tell by the look on his face that he was expecting someone older, more experienced. I knew he had to be skeptical of me for my relative youth and consequently skeptical of the work our SOD unit had done. What could we possibly know about motorcycle thefts? But when we pulled up to the patrol station and walked into where we were storing the parts, his jaw dropped. "Wow," he said. "When you said you guys were warehousing some stolen parts, I imagined a small garage. I've never seen so many parts in one place."

An overview of the parts and completed bikes seized from the
El Forasteross in February 1998.

We began to talk some more about what our respective agencies
had been doing. He told me about Pat Fengier. Fengier was a Harley-
Davidson employee at the facility where they made transmissions. He
was also a former member of the Sinners motorcycle club. Every day
he'd bring his lunch bucket to work and every day he'd take it home—
loaded with parts. Fengier was sending them everywhere: to Rooster,
to Pee Wee (whom he knew from when Pee Wee was a Sinner), and to
Hells Angels shops all over the country, including Minneapolis Custom Cycle. In fact, Simet had contacted Denny Roske, an auto theft
investigator for the Minnesota state patrol, and had recommended
that Denny investigate M.C.C. Denny had gone out there with another
detective back in 1996. These were the two cops that Pat stonewalled
when they asked about his receiving of shipments from Milwaukee.
"I get shipments from a lot of different places," Pat had told them.

Of course we hadn't forgotten about those kilos of Pat's cocaine.
But at the time, it still occurred to us that the best way to get to Pat
was through the stolen bikes. Besides, by then, I was thinking in terms
of a federal case. What we were seeing in Minneapolis was playing out
all over the country. We learned that Pat, for instance, was buying bike
frames from Tripoli bike frames in Red Deer, Alberta, and transmission cases from Delkron Manufacturing in Sacramento. The information we had at the time was that they were both known Hells
Angels-associated companies. Delkron, in fact, was operated by the
president of the Sacramento chapter. In my mind this was classic

money laundering at the national—international, in fact—level. We figured that all these businesses, manufacturing companies as well as retail cycle shops, had probably been set up for the purpose of providing legitimacy, to cover whatever illegal activities the Hells Angels organization was in to, mostly the stolen motorcycle business. Rocky and I thought we could eventually put a big enough case together to take down the entire organization, to shut down the Hells Angels Motorcycle Club.

We learned about Pat's suppliers after we'd gone to the state to request every title pack for every reconstructed bike in Minnesota for the previous five- year period. The state employees who had to dig out the information weren't exactly thrilled with the request; everything was on microfiche and it took them weeks to compile what ended up being hundreds and hundreds of pages. But we could see from where Pat was getting his frames and transmissions. And we also discovered that nobody was selling more reconstructed motorcycles than Minneapolis Custom Cycle. Pat Matter was a huge player.

We could also tell that some of the source receipts the cycle shops were producing for the other parts, receipts necessary to secure a title from the state, were often bogus. Some shops, like M.C.C., were listing a lot of the parts, particularly the internal engine and internal transmission parts, on their own receipts—not from the source. The shops were saying that the parts came from their own inventory. Well, of course that was true; but where did the inventory come from?

Small-time, "backyard" resellers like Pat Smith had a hard time finding legitimate parts dealers who would work with them. We'd eventually learn that Smith conned a few parts dealers into supplying him by sending them photos of his "shop"—North Country Custom. In reality, North Country Custom was a tattoo parlor set up for the photo shots to look like a cycle shop.

The bottom line is that the parts on many of the reconstructed bikes weren't coming from legitimate manufacturers and suppliers. They were coming from the likes of Tony Morales and Pat Smith and the El Forasteros, from chopped up bikes these guys were taking out of garages all over the state. And meanwhile, the state inspectors issuing titles weren't doing an adequate job. As long as they could see the manufacturer's statement of origin for the frame, engine case, and transmission case, they were satisfied. They didn't know to ask for the source receipts for the rest.

I talked to Rocky about it and we decided to meet with the agency in charge, the State Department of Public Safety. We told them our concerns and agreed to attend the inspections. About once a week we'd send someone. The very first day we seized a stolen bike. Word got out: it was going to be harder to get titles now. The program was a huge success. One hundred Harley motorcycles a year were being stolen around the state, mostly around the metro area, until we became involved. One year after we started helping with inspections, the number of bike thefts in Minneapolis fell to eleven.

About that time, Pat Matter decided to start taking his business legit. Was that coincidence, or did Pat see the writing on the wall?

In the spring of '98, we were still looking to put all the pieces together to go after the Hells Angels on a national level. The U.S. attorney on the Pat Smith case requested we do a complete inventory of the parts we had confiscated during the February searches, something I'd begun when Pete and Pete had flown in from Milwaukee. It was a massive undertaking and I had my suspicions that the attorney asked for it in the hopes we'd just drop the case. The fact was the case was a circumstantial one. A paper case, with motor vehicle titles and manufacturer's receipts and lots of little unexciting details. It was going to be a challenge. Most prosecutors prefer easy cases. Slam-dunk cases. And more glamorous ones. It's human nature. It didn't seem to matter that the Pat Smith thefts were part of something big and that we eventually may have been able to link everything together into a national case against the Hells Angels which would have included money laundering and who knows what else—probably drug distribution, for starters.

The same prosecutor expressed skepticism about the money laundering aspect to the case. "Where's the SUA?" he asked. To prove money laundering, you have to show a Specified Unlawful Activity for the money being laundered.

"Well, we've got interstate transportation of stolen parts," I said, "along with mail fraud."

"Hmm. What else you got?"

I said I'd get back to him. That weekend I took the federal statute book home with me and I painstakingly went through every page. I wasn't going to be deterred. I found our SUA: Title 18, section 513 of the U.S. Code. Motor vehicle titles are considered to be securities of the state. And doctored ones are therefore considered forged securities. I went into the prosecutor's office first thing Monday morning and pointed to what I'd found. He had to admit we had something we could move forward with.

I found the same foot-dragging attitude on the part of cops, too. At one point, I learned of a bike shop in Missouri, owned by an ex-El Forastero, that was receiving reconstructed bikes from Pat Smith and Jay Puig. The owner went by the name of Websie. It would turn out that Pat Matter knew him; Websie was at that Charlotte anniversary party, years before, when Pat, still a Grim Reaper, declared that his intention was to become a Hells Angel. Small world. In any event, I pulled every motor vehicle record from the shop that was filed with the state of Missouri and put together an impressive case. A circumstantial case. A paper case. To get a search warrant, I had to pull teeth. I went to every law enforcement agency I could find in Missouri. Nobody wanted to touch it. Finally I went to the FBI. "What have you got?" they asked. I detailed everything I'd found. Not strong enough, they told me. Finally I found a bike for sale on the shop's website that was identical in every way to a bike we knew that Pat Smith had built out of stolen parts, all the way down to the unique paint job. I wrote the search warrant affidavit myself and the FBI relented. I was there when they raided Websie's and then watched as they did a half-assed search. And then they never followed up. I'd literally opened the door for them, but they never took it any further.

It's a common mindset in law enforcement and a disappointing one. Everybody wants to be a part of the multimillion-dollar drug bust where big-time players are caught red-handed with thousands of kilos of cocaine and pictures get splashed on the front page of the newspaper and they interview you for the six o'clock news. But arrests are more often made on more mundane matters, matters that might involve a lot of background effort and chasing of obscure leads and the following of money trails—good old-fashioned detective work, in other words. But here's the thing: those are the types of efforts that, nine times out of ten, are what end up making the big bust. They got Al Capone on tax evasion, you know.

Anyway, when the prosecutor requested the detailed inventory, I said fine. I was bound and determined. I called Bob Feinen from Sentry-Dairyland Insurance—the guy who'd pleaded for us to help at the MOMGIA meeting—and I asked for some assistance. He sent some people to help with the inventorying. The NICB came in, too. Insurance adjusters were on hand to provide values for each stolen part. The prosecutor recommended we fly out Bob Kenney from the Connecticut State Police. Bob was a leading expert on Harley-Davidsons, and, more important to us, an expert on how to identify a stolen one. And then a guy by the name of John Rickerts from Harley-Davidson flew in to help us identify the parts. John was like a Harley-Davidson archaeologist. He knew every single part of any Harley ever built. It took us five weeks but we photographed and cataloged every piece.

If Harley-Davidson was helpful, I also managed to get a lot of cooperation from some of the aftermarket manufacturers, notably S&S Cycle, the leader in the aftermarket industry. During the time I was investigating bike thefts, I'd often call their 800-line with a number from a carburetor or engine case. I'd identify myself and they'd drop everything to track it for me, tell me what dealer it had been sold to, and when. They had a reputation for being a stand-up company and I could see why.

In June of 1998, Tony Morales was stopped for a traffic violation. He'd been out on bail while we were putting his case together. Truthfully, he was more valuable to us on the outside, where we could track his activities, see who he was dealing with. Morales was a small fish. We wanted the big fish. We wanted the Hells Angels. But in Morales's car was a Harley-Davidson transmission with altered numbers. It was the final straw for him. There was too much to ignore. He ended up pleading guilty to the theft in Burnsville, the one where he'd been caught in a full leg cast pushing the bike down the street. And then he was shipped off to state prison.

Meanwhile, we were surveilling and raiding certain cycle shops around the area that we could tie to Pat Smith and other El Forasteros. At one point, we raided Fast Lane Cycle, a shop owned by a former El Forasteros club member. Enough stolen parts were found, along with some guns and meth, that the business was shut down. We raided some other places, too.

In May of 1999, we got the opportunity to search the business of a Hells Angels member. John Quigley, nickname "Qwik," was riding a Buell sports bike one day with his girlfriend. A car cut him off—or more likely Qwik cut the car off—and the other driver honked. Qwik apparently pointed a gun at him. The other driver filed a complaint. With his description of the bike and the motorcyclist (Qwik was wearing his Hells Angels' colors at the time) we were able to have the driver pick out Qwik in a photo spread. Then we searched Qwik's excavation business in south Minneapolis.

When we got there we handcuffed Qwik and began our search. We came across some stolen parts but never did find the alleged gun. My theory is that Qwik probably pointed a ball peen hammer at the other motorist, making it look like a gun. At any rate, in his office, we came across an old cast iron safe. "What's in here?" we asked.

"Oh, nothing," said Qwik. "It's decorative. I don't even know the combination." We led Qwik into a garage area in the back of the business and sat him down while we kept searching. Back in his office some of the guys had begun to hammer on the safe. "What … what's that noise?" asked Qwik.

"Just trying to get into that safe, I guess," I said. Qwik started fidgeting. We brought the safe back to where Qwik was sitting and started really whacking at it. One guy used a pry bar to no avail. Another guy tried a sledgehammer. When we decided to use a cutting torch, Qwik started turning pale. But the torch didn't work, either. Finally, someone was able to use a pick ax to tear a small hole in the side of the safe. VanSlyke reached his hand in and felt something round which he pulled out. When he got it clear of the safe, we could see that the black, round ball Slick held—maybe a little bigger than a softball—had a wick attached to it. It was a bomb and it looked like it was straight out of a Wile E. Coyote cartoon. All it needed was white lettering on the side that said "Acme." The next few seconds resembled a Chinese fire drill. I don't think I've ever seen a room full of cops move so fast. We were all out the door in seconds.

When we caught our breaths, we called the bomb squad, which came and picked up the bomb and later detonated it. Probably meant for the Outlaws, the bomb had enough power that it would have leveled the whole building had it gone off in Qwik's office.

We learned a lot more about the stolen bike market in October of '99 when we took a proffer from Shawn Anderson, the guy Officer Mraz arrested that night at Morales's place. Anderson was about to go down on a huge meth bust. I wasn't involved with his drug case but asked to be present when he proffered. Before his arrest, we'd done a search of his house and had found a stolen bike. Anderson told me all about stealing bikes with Morales, stealing them for Pat Matter and Pat's employee Richard Rohda and delivering them to Dennis (Tank) Fenstra and Fast Lane Cycle. He'd get anywhere between two thousand and five thousand bucks a piece for them. Later, we'd learn that Anderson was mostly full of shit. He was facing over twenty years and ready to tell us anything.

Still, some of what Anderson said rang true. We learned, for instance, that one time Morales asked him to help strip a stolen bike. The bike had been taken from a guy named Mark Haymaker, a friend of Pat Matter's. Anderson saw a Hells Angels support sticker on the bike and refused to touch it. Not only that, Anderson actually went to Pat and told him he knew where the stolen bike was. Such was the fear that Pat apparently instilled in the bike thieves of the greater Minneapolis-St. Paul metropolitan area. Pat and Richard Rohda took Anderson and the three went to a garage rented by Morales where Haymaker's bike was. But we ultimately got to the bike before Pat did. He and Rohda tried to break in but the property manager spotted them and called the cops. The call enabled us to get a search warrant for the garage and discover Haymaker's stolen bike. We knew the garage was rented to Morales.

We also took a proffer about that time from Ronnie Rowles, where he essentially told us the information he'd told us previously about the Armstrong bike thefts. But now it was an official statement. We offered him immunity for the proffer. We weren't after Ronnie, after all. In fact, Ronnie would become a valuable informant for me over time. I grew to like Ronnie. Sure, he might have been something of a loser, but he always shot me straight and I treated him with respect. I think most of the time, Ronnie tried to do the right thing.

In January of 2000, we took a statement from Burronnie Brosh, too—the third player in the Armstrong theft. Like Ronnie, he also implicated Tony Morales. Brosh's street name was Bug. When he got nervous, his eyes would bug out of his head. And Brosh was nervous a lot. I'm not sure I've ever known anyone so ill-suited to be mixed

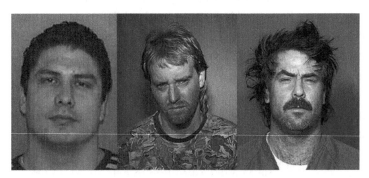

The Thieves
L - R: Antonio Morales, Burronnie Brosh, Ronnie Rowles

up in crime. The man was scared of his own shadow, yet there he was stealing bikes in the middle of the night and getting himself sideways with the Hells Angels. After the Armstrong theft, Pat Matter showed up on his doorstep. Brosh wasn't home at the time but his girlfriend was. Pat told her that Brosh needed to get a hold of him before Pat got a hold of Brosh. When the girlfriend asked who Pat was, he said, "I'm Pat with the Hells Fucking Angels. That's who I am." I can only assume Brosh's eyes bugged out even more than usual that night when his girlfriend told him who'd come calling. At any rate, in April of 2000, Jim Skaja and I picked Brosh up after he agreed to show us all the spots he could remember where he'd stolen bikes with Morales. We drove around half a day, past thirteen different places.

In the spring of 2000 we decided to begin surveilling the motor-cycle shop of a guy named Duane "Dewey" Selin, who was a member of the Los Valientes motorcycle club. Like the El Forasteros, the Los Valientes was another Hells Angels support club. We had information that Selin, too, was building bikes out of stolen parts. Selin's shop was in Brooklyn Center across from the municipal airport and we had planned to place a camera out there to catch the comings and goings. By pure coincidence one day, a buddy of mine in narcotics, Tom Sonenstahl, strolled by my desk and just happened to ask, "Hey, Chris, ever hear of a guy named Dewey?"

"Dewey? In Brooklyn Center? We're in the process of putting a camera on his shop. Why?"

"Because we're buying dope from him."

I knew we needed to pool our resources. To me, it seemed like another possible route to Pat Matter. We had come to suspect over time that the drug trade in town, especially that which was carried out by the motorcycle clubs, was dictated by the Hells Angels, specifically by Pat. I didn't know exactly what Dewey's connection was, but I knew there had to be one. And I knew our SOD unit had to team up with narcotics. Tom's task force was working with the DEA and the IRS. Before it was over, we'd bring them all together.

Things started really heating up. And Pat Matter was soon directly in our sights.

CHAPTER 11
Fuck with it and Find Out

Reinforcing my thoughts about getting out of the Hells Angels and the drug business was the fact that people around me kept getting arrested. In February of 1997, Billy West was busted during a traffic stop in Utah. The cops found what they thought was twenty pounds of meth. It would turn out to be amphetamine, not methamphetamine—a significant legal difference, but Billy was in trouble nonetheless. The thing is he was driving the twenty pounds back from California partly for me. He had gone out there with me for a race and we bought twenty pounds from a friend of mine while we were there, got it back home, tested it, and discovered it was weak. So I sent Billy back out to California to get another load for us.

Billy called me from jail. "Pat," he said, "you've got to clean out my houses." I knew what he meant. He had a lakefront home in Brainerd Lakes, probably worth upwards of a million bucks, and in the garage was a classic 1967 Corvette big block as well as a '67 Ford Bronco. Both looked like they'd just rolled off the showroom floor. The Corvette alone was worth over a hundred grand. Billy knew the feds could seize them both under the legal right of asset forfeiture.

A friend of mine lent me his flatbed tow truck and I figured I could load one of the vehicles onto the bed and tow the other behind. But the feds had already arrived at Billy's place and there was police tape everywhere. The way I saw it, there was only one thing I could do. I grabbed my employee Richard Rohda and the two of us put on official-looking tow truck jackets, showed up at Billy's house, removed the police tape from the driveway, backed the truck up, and right in

Billy West 1983 in Brainerd, Minnesota.

front of the cops proceeded to haul away the 'Vet and Bronco as
though we'd been ordered to. It was almost too easy. Then I rented a
storage barn to hide the vehicles away in.

Billy had a second house in town and I went there, too. I showed
up with Al Brown, a friend of mine, and apparently we beat the feds
to the house. But not by much, as it turned out. Al and I went in and
took out $10,000 in cash, two .45s, a shotgun, and three pounds of
meth, carrying everything out of the house in broad daylight. And just
as we pulled away, we spotted the feds driving up. One minute before
and they'd have seen Al carrying a shotgun and me carrying a paper
bag full of meth down the front walk of Billy's place.

Meanwhile, I sent my attorney Barry Voss out to Utah and we
got Billy bonded out of jail. He came back and the feds asked him
about the Corvette and Bronco. They knew I took them, but there
wasn't a thing they could do about it. I knew it had to piss them off.
Somebody said to Billy, "I'm sure you can thank Matter for getting

your vehicles for you. But, you know, we'll get him some day." Looking back, it surprises me that the cops around Billy's place didn't know the feds had an interest in the vehicles, or hadn't at least bothered to take the time to find out exactly who Richard and I were. But maybe it shouldn't. Over time, I've discovered that when it comes to law enforcement, the right hand doesn't always know what the left is doing.

Then, in addition to Billy's arrest, there was the arrest of my ex-wife. In August of that year, Leslie was busted in a Las Vegas bus depot with a pound of meth in her luggage. I bailed her out of jail and hired an attorney for her. She'd end up sentenced to seventy-two months in a federal prison, a sentence shortened eventually by good behavior and her enrollment in a drug program. Soon after her arrest, our son Cole, eleven years old, came to live with Trish and me. Just one more reason to say goodbye to my lifestyle.

Meanwhile, it wasn't hard to tell that the cops were closing in. I kept getting harassed by a big, oafy-looking guy named Roy Green who was with the gang strike force out of St. Paul. He'd sit outside the clubhouse doing surveillance. He'd come down my driveway. He'd follow me. He'd pull me over for the most asinine reasons. One time he pulled me over to ask if I had obtained a permit to start a fire that I had going in my yard a few days earlier. "You pulled me over for that?" I said. And then I took off and left him standing by the side of the road.

Another time he pulled me over and cited me for not using a turning signal. That one I took to court. It was a turn-only lane and you didn't technically have to signal. We drew Judge Jack Nordby. Years before when Nordby was a practicing attorney, I'd made use of his services. He knew me and he liked me. After informing the prosecuting attorney of our previous legal relationship, he said, "Do you still want me to hear this case?" The prosecutor said sure and had no one to blame but himself when Nordby ruled in my favor. Nordby didn't say so, but I knew he could tell Green's behavior bordered on stalking. And maybe Green got the idea because his harassment seemed to slow down after that.

But I knew Roy Green was just one of the cops out there. I sensed

Chris's guys were circling and I knew it was time to get out. But when I talked to Rooster about it, he ended up convincing me otherwise. "We need you, Pat," he said. "Look, I know the club takes a lot of your time, but the rest of us will start picking up some slack. We'll go to the officers' meetings on your behalf. We'll back you up, take care of the little details, free up more of your time. We'll make it work for you. We need you." I knew that the club did. When it came to the drug business, I was the one with all the connections. I knew there were a lot of people counting on me and I suddenly didn't feel right about leaving them high and dry. I loved the club. And I loved Rooster, a best friend from way back. In the end, I decided to stay, a decision made admittedly with no small amount of awareness that I was making more than a half-million dollars a year dealing in drugs, income I was understandably reluctant to give up. But the decision was also made out of the responsibility that I felt toward a lot of other people.

But Minneapolis Custom Cycle was becoming a legitimate business. And it had little to do with the involvement of Chris's unit with the Department of Public Safety overseeing the inspections. Yes, I was still receiving some parts here and there from Patrick Fengier in Milwaukee, who'd been smuggling them out of the factory in his lunchbox. But by and large, I hadn't used stolen parts in my custom bikes since the early 1990s. I didn't need them. I was doing enough volume that I was able to buy parts at wholesale pricing, often just ten percent over cost. By 1998, I was just as interested in stopping bike thefts as Chris was. I didn't need competitors out there putting bikes together with stolen parts. I had an inkling of what Pat Smith of the El Forasteros was up to. I knew him from way back, from even before we'd kidnapped him from the Sun Saloon back in 1983 after a couple of the El Forasteros had broken into Rooster and Finnegan's houses thinking they'd stolen an El Forasteros bike. Since that time, Rooster had become friends with Smith. Their girlfriends turned out to be sisters.

But as far as we Hells Angels went, we were never indicted on motorcycle theft. And companies like Delkron were legitimate, too. There was no money laundering going on. I knew Alan Mahon, who owned Delkron and who was also the Sacramento Hells Angels president, and I knew he ran an honest business.

If the number of motorcycle thefts decreased to eleven that next year, I'd argue it was more a factor of getting guys like Morales off the street, and not because the inspections were tougher. Morales and his guys were probably responsible for ninety-five percent of the state's motorcycle thefts. The inspections, from my standpoint, were just a pain in the ass and were unnecessary. Nobody ever found anything on me and, believe me, they were looking. Minneapolis Custom Cycle was a definite target. But I always had the appropriate receipts. That still didn't stop them from withholding titles for two of my bikes one time. Essentially, they withheld them because they could; the inspection process was without any kind of oversight. There was nobody inspecting the inspectors. I had to hire a lawyer to force them to send me the titles for those bikes.

At first, I decided to use the inspections to my advantage. I ran full-page ads in the Sunday paper: "Buy your custom bike from Minneapolis Custom Cycle—our bikes are inspected by the state of Minnesota and approved by the gang task force!" For that I received a cease-and-desist letter from the Hennepin County Attorney, Amy Klobuchar. Specifically, she didn't like the word "approve." But at the bike shows I'd post signs that bragged that our prices were so low, "It's almost like racketeering!" I knew that had to piss off Chris and his guys. But they could never get me on stolen bikes.

Eventually, I knew I had to do something about the oppressive inspection process. About that time, I helped put together a coalition of local motorcycle clubs. The coalition included the Hells Angels, El Forasteros, Los Valientes, the Fossils, and all the other clubs around. It was a good way for me to keep my finger on the pulse of the club activity in the area. We'd have meetings at the Hells Angels clubhouse and all over the state as well. It was an effective way to find prospective members, too. And all the non-one-percenter coalition clubs started sporting red and white support patches. At the big events, like the annual Sturgis rally, other Hells Angels chapters would see the coalition members and know they were H.A. friendly. The Outlaws saw them,

(612) 348-5550

CE OF THE HENNEPIN COUNTY ATTORNEY
C-2000 GOVERNMENT CENTER
MINNEAPOLIS, MINNESOTA 55487

January 6, 1999

Minneapolis, MN 55412

     Re: Star Tribune Classified Advertisement
            December 20, 1998 and January 3, 1999

Dear Mr. Matter:

Please be advised that I am legal counsel to the Hennepin County Sheriff. On December 20, 1998 and January 3, 1999 your business ran a classified advertisement in the Minneapolis Star Tribune Newspaper, a copy of which is enclosed. The ad claims that the Hennepin County Sheriff "inspected" and "approved" motorcycles built by your shop. As you must be aware, this advertising is false and misleading. I am therefore requesting that you immediately refrain from any such advertising or representations. If you do not so refrain, the Hennepin County Sheriff will take legal action.

While the Sheriff's Office, as part of an ongoing investigation, may have seen and/or inspected some motorcycles built by your shop, it is false to state or even imply that they have uniformly inspected bikes built by your company. Moreover, the mere fact that some Hennepin County bikes were inspected by the Sheriff's Office and subsequently licensed by the State of Minnesota does not establish that the Hennepin County Sheriff has in any way "approved" the bikes built by your shop. The State of Minnesota operates under its own guidelines in licensing.

I will seek a clarification and/or retraction of this ad directly with the newspaper. I am certain you desire to avoid litigation if possible, therefore it would seem prudent to cease any such advertising and avoid involvement of the court.

               Sincerely,

               AMY KLOBUCHAR
               Hennepin County Attorney

               KARLA F. HANCOCK
               Sr. Assistant County Attorney

The ad I placed in the Minneapolis StarTribune and the letter I received in
response from Hennepin County Attorney Amy Klobuchar.

too, and it made us look just that much bigger.

One of the coalition clubs, a non-one-percenter club called the Sovran Sons, refused to wear the support patches. We suspected that some of their members had friends in the Outlaws. I knew the Sovran Sons because they'd asked my permission to form way back when I was still a Grim Reaper. Even then, I'd held influence over the area. When I heard they wouldn't wear our red and white, I called them up and had them come over to the clubhouse. "Leave your club patches here," I said. "The Sovran Sons is, as of this moment, defunct. We know each of you. We know where you all live. If you try to organize a club again, we'll do what we need to do." That was the end of the Sovran Sons.

The Sons of Silence started coming to the coalition meetings, too. They were trying to put a chapter in Minneapolis. Of course we had a history with those guys and we weren't about to let them. At one meeting I cornered one of their members, a guy named Jazz, and I said, "Jazz, there ain't gonna be a Sons of Silence chapter in Minneapolis. If you have a problem with that, bring your club president next time."

Next meeting, Jim Jahnke, the regional president of the Sons of Silence, came to the meeting. So did about fifty Sons of Silence members. We had about seven Hells Angels there. Earlier I'd been on the phone with Sonny Barger. "I'm gonna have to knock their president out," I'd mentioned to him. "Do what you have to do," Sonny had said.

When the meeting wound down, Jahnke approached me and said he'd like to talk to me in private outside. Jahnke went probably two hundred pounds. I said sure. We walked out with Scott, one of his guys, and Richie, one of my guys. We got square to each other and I threw a fist and did what I'd told Sonny I was going to do. Jahnke went down in a heap. Then Richie and Scott started going at each other and Scott was getting the upper hand. Just then Rooster came around the corner. To help, I guess. He had his hand in his vest and he pulled it out and pointed his finger at Scott. Like it was a gun. A fucking gun. I said, "Rooster, what the fuck are you doing?"

To this day, I don't what Rooster was thinking. At any rate, Jahnke by then was trying to get up and I put a foot on his chest and said, "If I help you up, are we going to be all right here?"

Jahnke, who was bleeding from a pretty bad gash the rings on my fist had given him said, "Yeah, man, I just want to get the fuck out of here." I let him up and a group of Sons of Silence came around and saw Jahnke bleeding and they all just sort of took off, Scott included. That was the end of the Sons of Silence in Minneapolis, but it wouldn't surprise me if somewhere Scott's still laughing at the sight of Rooster pointing a finger at him.

As far as the coalition went, one of its main purposes was to press our rights as motorcyclists. The idea was power in numbers. For one thing, we were being collectively discriminated against in several of the bars and restaurants around town. It was perfectly legal for a bar owner to refuse to serve someone with a Hells Angels patch, for instance. We changed that. We got legislation passed that prevented that kind of discrimination—the Equal Access for Motorcyclists Statute: *A place of public accommodation may not restrict access, admission, or usage to a person solely because the person operates a motorcycle or is wearing clothing that displays the name of an organization or association.*

Working with us to get the legislation passed was a lobbyist named Bob Ellingsworth. Bob served on the board of the Minnesota Motorcycle Riders Association and was also on the governor's safety advisory committee. He got me appointed to the committee, too, but man, did he take some heat for that from law enforcement. A Hells Angels president on the safety committee? The idea was to have someone on the committee representing the coalition, but I guess nobody was ready for that someone to be Pat Matter, president of the Hells Angels. I stepped aside and recommended Bill Marvin for the job. He was a Fossil club member and clean. Bill was smart, too—a twenty-year executive for 3M Company in St. Paul. He worked on the committee under my direction, and although a lot of people didn't like it, there wasn't anything anybody could do about the fact that Bill soon decided to prospect for the Hells Angels. But Bill was driving a van one night in 1999 at a national coalition of motorcyclists meeting in Phoenix when a car ran a red light, broadsiding the van and killing Bill. I really liked Bill. It was a tragic, senseless loss and, as with Monte Mathias who also hadn't been patched when he'd been killed, Bill too was buried in full Hells Angels colors.

The national coalition had a meeting one time in Minnesota and they were impressed with the way we were organized and with my leadership, the way I was able to get all the different clubs to sit down together. Our coalition began to be used as a model. Meanwhile, the equal access legislation spread to other states. But while working with Bob Ellingsworth, the most important piece of legislation for me had to do with cleaning up the reconstructed title inspection process. With Bob's help, we were able to change the process into something uniform and specific. No longer were inspections up to the vagaries of inspectors run amuck. And the gang task force hasn't been involved since.

Meanwhile, if I was interested in discouraging motorcycle thefts for business reasons, I was just as interested in discouraging the thefts of Hells Angels bikes for club reasons. The Armstrong theft in February of 1997 was infuriating to me. Mark Armstrong was a friend of mine, and for that reason alone I would have been pissed. But the bikes had support stickers on them and my anger was multiplied. Who the fuck steals bikes with Hells Angels' support stickers on them?

I had Mark post the reward flyers and I had him hire Darrell Shaw, the private investigator that I had used for polygraph tests on prospective club members. I didn't want to hire Darrel directly because of the cocaine. Better to work behind Mark, I figured. Shaw came back with the name of Tony Morales and word got out quickly that I was looking for him. I asked around everywhere about Morales, but about anyone else, too. I talked to—or threatened—anyone I knew who might be even remotely knowledgeable about motorcycle thefts in the area. I made a lot of noise. Too much. It's easy to look back now and think that I should have just let it go. But it wasn't just the loss of the cocaine. It was my reputation at stake.

I learned of Burronnie Brosh and Ronnie Rowles through a

friend of mine by the name of Brian Weaver. Brian was a master car thief and he also dealt in marijuana. He knew Brosh and Rowles and when he found out they were behind the Armstrong thefts, he came and told me. Then he took me to Brosh's house. That's where I told Brosh's girlfriend I was looking for him and that I was the president of the Hells Fucking Angels. Brosh called and asked me to meet him at a strip club called the 22nd Avenue Station. When I got there I took him into the men's room and told him to take his clothes off so I could see that he wasn't wired. After he put his clothes back on, we went back outside. "I want all the shit returned," I told him. "All the motorcycle stuff and all the coke. And what's gone from the coke, you'll have to pay for." Brosh nodded. He was scared shitless and Chris wasn't kidding about the bug eyes. But I can guarantee that Bug was twice as scared of me as he was of the cops. For the amount of lost cocaine, I charged the three of them a total of $30,000.

As for Ronnie Rowles, I talked to him but I never showed him any body bags like he told the cops. Chris was right; Ronnie embellished. I didn't have any body bags. Ronnie got the message just from me talking to him. He was a real stooge and it's not surprising to me that the cops took advantage of him. When he eventually paid his share for the lost coke and met me at the diner to ask if he was square with me, I did tell him he was a ghost and that I never wanted to see him again, adding, "You're dead to me, Ronnie."

Morales ultimately came to me with his ten grand, knowing things would be much worse for him if I got to him first. I did pay a visit to a garage of his with Richard Rohda when I found out Mark Haymaker's bike had been stolen. Yes, Shawn Anderson came to me to tell me about that particular theft. I had known Anderson before. One time he stole a bike from an employee of mine. I paid a visit to his house and told him I'd break his fucking neck. It scared the shit out of Anderson and I got the bike back and Anderson knew not to fuck with me again. So when Morales enlisted his help with Haymaker's bike, Anderson came right to me, showing up at my shop.

I threw Anderson in my truck and he sat between Richard and me and we drove to an apartment complex in Brooklyn Center where

Morales had rented a garage. Anderson pointed out the garage and Richard and I tried to pry the door open. The property manager saw us and called the cops. Then he came over to us and asked what we were doing and I told him why we were there. "Wish you would have spoken to me first," he said. "I'd have let you in. Now the cops are on their way." We left and I called Mark Haymaker and told him where his bike was. He drove over to the complex and when the cops got their search warrant, he was able to identify his bike.

By then, Richard Rohda and I had been getting pretty close. He'd been working for me since I opened the shop and I knew him going back to 1985. In fact, he'd bought a couple custom bikes from me. He'd travel with me as part of my race team and would eventually join the Hells Angels, getting patched in 1993. In time, Richard would get involved in both my cycle business and my drug business. I trusted him. And he was always ready to help me out with a problem, like a stolen bike.

The fact is if a bike with a Hells Angels support sticker was stolen, we got it back. I made sure of that. Club member Willie Dougherty had his bike stolen once and the thief was ballsy—or stupid—enough to drive it right past me as I sat at a Dairy Queen just a few blocks from my shop. I was there with Trish and I recognized the bike immediately as it went past. "Sit tight," I told Trish, "I'll be right back." Then I jumped in my truck and gave chase, swerving in front of the thief right before he could make it onto the highway.

The bike went down and the thief took off on foot. Two guys in a car were following behind, friends of the thief, I guessed. They pulled over behind my stopped truck and I jumped out and the look on my face made them both turn pale. And I'm sure they must have known who I was. "You guys stay right here!" I yelled and then I started running after the thief, but he'd had too much of a head start by then. I went back to the truck. "Okay," I said to the two guys in the car, "one of you is going to drive my truck back to my shop while I ride the bike back." They both nodded. I never did find out who they were or who the thief was. But I had Dougherty's bike back and I'm certain those guys never messed with a Hells Angels bike ever again.

In the meantime, I kept racing. And still in enemy territory. In 1993, it was Taco and the Outlaws in Milwaukee. In 1997, it was Mongoose and the Pagans in Richmond, Virginia. Mongoose was from the Mother Chapter of the Pagans, thirteen guys who collectively ran the organization. I'd met him years earlier when Tommy Lewis wanted to start a Hells Angels chapter in the Richmond area, which was Pagan territory. I flew down there at the time with Kevin Cleary and we actually had a fairly civil meeting with Mongoose and the Pagans. The Hells Angels never approved a charter for the area, so it became a non-issue, but I did mention to Mongoose back then that I'd be racing from time to time at the Richmond Speedway. With my colors.

In 1997 I was there with Richard. Mark Armstrong came along, too. I was set to race. We were situated at the end of the racetrack with our trailer and there must have been about a hundred Pagans around. I was working on the bike when a big group of them walked over to us and started to surround the trailer. One of them moved towards it and I jumped over the bike and gave him a shove away from the door. We had a couple 9mm Glocks in there. Just about then, Mongoose came walking up. He remembered me from when I'd met him years before and he remembered that I told him I'd be racing in Richmond. But he said he didn't want us selling our support stuff.

"We're just selling our race team t-shirts, Mongoose, and we're gonna keep selling them."

By then, racetrack security had seen what was going down and they had put a call into the State Patrol. About a dozen State Patrol cops suddenly came onto the scene asking if there was a problem.

"No problem," I said. "No problem at all. Just having a couple cold ones with my friends." With that I reached into the cooler and grabbed four or five beers and handed them out to a few of the Pagans. The cops hung around for a little and then, apparently satisfied that a fight wasn't about to break out, they wandered off. I snatched the beers back out of the Pagans' hands. "Fuck, you guys aren't any friends of mine."

While this was happening, the other racers were having a meeting with the promoters of the race. They were nervous. Most of them had been at Lancaster in '94 when the fight broke out between the Hells Angels and the Outlaws and they didn't want to be in the middle of another fight in Richmond. But these guys had become friends of mine and they were concerned about my safety, too—about me being so outnumbered by the Pagans. I went and talked with them. "You can't concentrate with all these Pagans around, Pat," they said. "We'll cancel this one. We'll do a double points race at the next one in Georgia."

"I appreciate that," I said. "But I think Mongoose and I have an understanding. The racetrack is neutral. I'll be fine."

I raced that day while the Pagans lined up alongside the track and watched. George Smith, second generation leader of S&S Cycle was there, the leading manufacturer of aftermarket motors. S&S had sponsored one of the pro stock race bikes and George was there videotaping the races. It was a hell of a day for George to be taping and a hell of a day for the Pagans to be watching. I set a world record for speed and E.T. for the quarter mile in the pro stock class. The track announcer declared it the fastest pro stock pass ever.

We sold our t-shirts, too.

CHAPTER 12
Indictment

I won't argue with Pat that at some point Minneapolis Custom Cycle became a legitimate enterprise. Hell, I admired him for the bikes he built. They were beautiful. But the fact is that over a long period of time, Pat helped build his business by dealing in stolen motorcycle parts. Our case was circumstantial, but I truly believed that through detailed financial analysis, I could prove it. And as far as none of the Hells Angels being indicted on motorcycle thefts, we had the paper trail on that, too. Patrick Fengier was stealing parts from Harley Davidson and sending them to, in no particular order: Trust Me Racing, a shop in El Sobrante, California owned by a Hells Angel; a Hells Angels member in Salinas, California; a Hells Angels member in Rochester, New York; the Carolina Hells Angels vice president in Charleston, South Carolina; a Hells Angels member in Cleveland; a Hells Angels member in Phoenix; Minnesota Hells Angels vice president Paul "Rooster" Seydel in Brooklyn Park, Minnesota; and, let's not forget, Pat Matter himself at Minneapolis Custom Cycle. We even had a record of Fengier sending to Sacramento Hells Angels president, Allen Mahon, owner of Delkron Manufacturing.

Fengier, as it turned out, was a Hells Angels wannabe. The problem is he lived in the wrong state. Wisconsin was an Outlaws state. But that didn't stop him from helping out Charles "Pee Wee" Goldsmith and John Derks that time they made the trip to Milwaukee to blow up the tattoo shop. It was Fengier, we would later learn, who showed them where to plant the bomb.

The Hells Angels dealt in stolen motorcycle parts, pure and

simple. In time, we would have proven it. But as it would happen, we found a slightly different route to follow. In June of 2000, my task force joined forces with Tom Sonenstahl's narcotics unit which had already been investigating Duane "Dewey" Selin, the Los Valiente who owned a motorcycle shop in Brooklyn Center and whom we were investigating as well. Along with Tom's unit, we now had the IRS and the DEA, too, as well as a drug task force out of St. Cloud that had been working with Tom. The DEA Task Force included Detective Tom Billings and Special Agent Bob Bushman, both having been assigned to the Task Force from the Minnesota Bureau of Criminal Apprehension. I'd known Bob for years. In fact, his wife was working as a detective in our office at the time. Bob was a big guy with a mustache and a dimpled chin. Tom Billings was an old-school cop, a Columbo type, kind of rumpled, always with a cigarette dangling from his mouth. Analyst Tori Reisdorf of the BCA came in on the investigation, too. Later on in the investigation, Tom and Tori would actually get married.

On a tree across the road from Selin's shop, we placed a pole camera. The tree sat on the property of a municipal airport and from a little booth we set up, we could make note of the comings and goings of the shop. Eventually, we'd haul an old FEMA trailer over to the airport and work out of there. It became a little headquarters. We positioned chase cars nearby and anytime we saw somebody on camera driving up to the shop, we had the car swing by and get the plate number. We learned quickly who kept frequenting the shop and before long we could recognize the players by sight.

A guy by the name of Bob Fettig regularly came by. Sonenstahl's guys knew Fettig; they'd been buying meth from him undercover. Fettig was also supplying Billy "the Kid" Romig, a Los Valientes member and an employee of Selin's. Hells Angels member Jay Rankin was a frequent visitor to the shop. So was Pat Matter's service manager Mike Eason. And so it wasn't long before I began thinking in terms of drugs instead of bike parts.

Selin's shop was a beehive of activity and most of the visitors were motorcycle-club related. In August of 2000, two bikers pulled into the shop with Arizona Hells Angels rockers. One had a duffel bag we could only assume was full of dope. I hopped in a car and drove past the shop to get a better look, turning around in the parking lot like I was lost. One of the bikers took off his helmet. It was none other than Sonny Barger. We couldn't believe Barger would be that reckless, or that anyone in the Hells Angels would even allow him to be put into that situation. Making a drug deal himself? In broad daylight, with another member following him into a drug dealer's place of business with a duffel full of dope?

What we learned the next day was that the biker with Sonny was an Arizona prospect. And the duffel he was carrying wasn't full of dope. It was full of books. Barger was in town for a book signing that was to be held at Minneapolis Custom Cycle. Barger's memoir, *The Life and Times of Sonny Barger*, had just been released. There was a big article in the next day's paper with pictures of Sonny and Pat. I imagine Sonny had no idea that drugs were being dealt out of Selin's place, or, for that matter, any cause to know. Still, we'd come to find out later through Selin that two pounds of meth had been on the premises. Had we raided the place that day, it might have been a pretty sticky situation for Barger.

Pat Matter showed up at Selin's that day, too. We'd learn later that besides meeting Sonny there, Pat came to Selin's from time to time to use his dyno tuner since his own shop's dyno hadn't been working. But of course at the time, we had to figure Pat was there on drug business. That same day, while Barger was at the shop, Mike Eason showed up. So did Bob Fettig, Billy the Kid Romig, and others, including some Los Valientes members and a former Hells Angels prospect we knew to be a meth dealer. We'd learn that later that evening, at a Hells Angels meeting, Selin and Romig would become patched as prospects for the Hells Angels. It was the weekly club meeting—the church meeting, as they called it. Most of the outlaw motorcycle clubs refer to their regular meetings that way. Church night. Barger was in attendance on that particular church night and it made us think, with what we knew at the time, that maybe it was no coincidence; maybe he was so impressed with Selin and Romig's drug business that he gave them the patches himself.

Ralph "Sonny" Barger at Dewey's Motorcycle Shop.

L-R: Arizona Hells Angel prospect Dean Hiney, Ralph "Sonny" Barger
and Pat at Dewey's Motorcycle Shop.

The other agencies we were working with took a sudden interest in the information we had on the one-percenters and on the Hells Angels in particular. By then, I'd become the resident expert and they were all amazed at the information we'd collected. It was becoming clear to everyone that the Hells Angels were our targets. And that would mean Pat Matter, local president, in particular. But Pat was known to the IRS and I remember one of their guys saying, "No way you can take Matter down. We've tried."

"Bullshit," I said. "Anybody can be taken down." The IRS agent just shook his head and the conversation made me just that much more determined. I knew if we could get to the guys connected with Pat, we could get to Pat. Eventually someone would talk. That's the way these things work.

And I knew that the guys we had in place to continue the investigation were the right guys. Over time, the competent ones revealed their effectiveness. Others, not so much. Like Roy Green, the detective who'd harassed Pat. Green supposedly knew a lot about bikers but he was full of misinformation. He'd attend our meetings and chime in with, "Well, supposedly the Hells Angels do this," or "supposedly the Hells Angels do that." We started calling him Deputy Supposedly. In reality, he couldn't put a case together to save his life. Back in May of 1998, we'd raided Hells Angels member James Brady's house in northeast Minneapolis. We recovered two freshly stolen Harley bikes in his garage, along with some guns and meth. We found a trigger assembly for an MP-5 submachine gun. Green came along on the search. Back then, I assumed he knew what he was doing so I tossed the case to him. Brady was a convicted felon who was surely facing prison time. It was a felony just for him to have been in possession of the trigger assembly. But Green sat on the case, never following up on the work needed to prosecute it. The only thing that seemed to happen on the Brady case was that his Hells Angels colors, seized during the raid as evidence, later turned up missing. Looking back, I can guess who took them. Something similar happened that February when we'd raided Paul "Rooster" Seydel's house. A gold timing cover for Seydel's Harley was seized. Seydel would eventually sue to get it back, but it was gone.

Somehow it had mysteriously been removed from the motorcycle and had walked away from the patrol station.

Brady losing his patch, by the way, was grounds for dismissal from the Hells Angels. And from what we'd heard, Pat fined Brady fifteen hundred bucks on top of that. Apparently he'd gone into Brady's place of employment, a car lot called Malone's, asking where Brady was. When he didn't get the right answers he started breaking the place up with a baseball bat. I assume that eventually Pat collected the fine.

Anyway, besides Green, by the time we'd started to surveil Selin's shop in 2000, we had a nice little team put together. And we continued to watch as various interesting and unsavory characters came and went. One day in October a guy in a long leather European-style coat pulled up in a red Corvette. We had been informed that a member of the Forbidden Few Motorcycle Club out of Norway—a hit man by the name of Jan Hexeberg—was in town to commit a murder on behalf of the Hells Angels. The intel we had turned out to be inaccurate, but we got a photo of the presumed hit man in the 'Vette and I emailed it to a cop friend of mine in Norway. Our guy wasn't Hexeberg. But we knew he was somebody. We ended up following him to his house in Corcoran, a huge home on a big parcel of land that abutted the residence of Pat Matter. Turned out the guy was a car thief by the name of Brian Weaver, maybe the best car thief in the upper Midwest. We'd learn later the 'Vette was stolen, but he'd put it in the name of some bogus auto sales business in south Minneapolis. That's what Weaver did. He stole cars from everywhere, typically right off dealer lots, and put them all in different names.

But Weaver was also a dope dealer, and a big one. And a very good friend of Pat's. Pat, in fact, had hired Weaver's brother Mark to work in his shop. Strangely enough, I remembered the Weavers from junior high. They'd gone to my school. Brian was a year ahead of me and I remember him hanging around questionable characters even back then. Mark played hockey and he was good. Had he applied himself, which he didn't, he could have played for a Division I school. And he might have gone even further. Maybe he could have gone pro.

Brian Weaver, in our minds, was just one more piece of the puzzle pointing to Pat Matter. In fact, the same day Weaver showed up at Selin's in the red Corvette and black leather coat, Pat showed up, too. So did Mike Eason, Seydel, Billy the Kid, and an associate of Billy the Kid's named Bob Metz, a heavyset guy who I noticed Jim Skaja was referencing in his surveillance notes as "F.F." "Jim," I said, "Why F.F.?" Fat Fuck, Jim told me.

By December 2000, we'd been able to put a wiretap on Selin's phone. By the end of March, 2001, we had indictments on Fettig, Selin, Romig, and Rankin, all for conspiracy to distribute methamphetamine. Eventually, Fettig would be sent to the federal penitentiary. Billy "the Kid" Romig, too—sentenced to twenty-two years. Selin pleaded guilty. Rankin also went away.

Then in January of 2001, Brian Weaver got busted. We got a drug buyer of his to cooperate. Weaver was pulled over in a truck he was driving and taken away. In the passenger side of the truck was Pat Matter.

But through it all, we had nothing tangible on Pat. What we did have, however, was more circumstantial evidence that pointed to Pat. Seemingly every*thing* and every*body* pointed to Pat. He was surrounded by a cast of characters that were all thieves and drug dealers. But how to prove a connection? Up until then, nobody was talking. But I knew where the evidence was. It was in Pat's financial records—the records from Minneapolis Custom Cycle and the records from the Minnesota chapter of the Hells Angels. The key, to my mind, was to follow the money. From there, I was certain we could prove money laundering, covering up what was beginning to look like a significant drug operation. We needed to seize the records.

Fortunately, we got help from an IRS special agent, and not the one who said we wouldn't be able to take Pat down. But Jim Shoup was present the day I had declared "bullshit" to his fellow agent and Jim came to me one day. Jim was a tall, husky guy. Everybody called him Shoup Dog or Shoup Doggie Dog.

"You still want to take Matter down?" he asked.

"You bet your ass," I said.

"Well let's do it." From that point on, Jim and I began putting together an affidavit for a search warrant for Minneapolis Custom Cycle, Pat's house, and the Hells Angels clubhouse.

In January of 2001, Pat's crew chief and Hells Angels Sergeant at Arms, Richard Rohda, got busted for possession of a stolen pickup truck. This justified a search of his house, but I didn't want the Hells Angels knowing a search was taking place by direction of our task force. I figured Pat must have sensed by now that we were out there and we needed to keep as low-key as possible. I asked one of our general detectives if he would execute the search warrant so that none of our names would be on it. But I went along on the search. In Rohda's house I saw a lot of Hells Angels files and paperwork. The files weren't within the scope of the search warrant so we couldn't seize them, but I made a mental note of them. Jim Shoup and I added Rohda's house to the list of places we wanted a search warrant for.

When we finished the affidavit, it was sixty-six pages long—a veritable laundry list of reasons that we believed we had probable cause to search for and seize Pat's records. We detailed everything we had uncovered since I'd first been assigned to Rocky's Special Operations Division back in August of 1997. Jim took it to Judge J. Earl Cudd, who looked at it and said, "You know, Agent Shoup, if an affidavit for a search warrant is more than two or three pages long, that normally tells me you don't have probable cause." Cudd had a point. Typically, the longer an affidavit, the more of it is just filler, calculated to make it look good. It's like a high school essay test. The kid who doesn't know the answer to the question is the kid who writes twelve pages about it, just sort of hoping that quantity alone will somehow hoodwink the teacher. But Cudd read the affidavit and signed it anyway.

Funny thing. Later, Pat would appeal the warrant and the appeals court would agree with him. There was insufficient probable cause, they said. But the appeals court also let the seized evidence stand, based on the "good faith" exception. Jim and I had operated reasonably and had put together the affidavit under a good-faith belief that we were acting completely in accordance with the letter of the law.

At any rate, in April of 2001, we executed the searches. I decided to focus on the clubhouse. Billings had checked out the clubhouse the prior day, or so I overheard him say to Tom Rainville. "Used a ladder to get in." It probably should have seemed odd to me, him gaining access to the clubhouse when we were all set to execute a search warrant on it the very next day, but I didn't think too much about it at the time. I guess I figured he was just checking out our potential points of ingress. I also didn't think about the fact that his daily commute to work had him practically driving right by Pat's residence, as well as the clubhouse.

L-R: Tom Rainville, Me & Bob Bushman holding HA colors and jacket.

The next day we hit the clubhouse and confiscated boxes of files and records and notes. Boxes of stuff were seized at Pat's house, too, as well as at Richard Rohda's house, and Minneapolis Custom Cycle. We brought it all back to an office we'd set up just for the task force. Sixty-four boxes total. A supervisor with the Bureau of Criminal Apprehension turned to me at one point and said, "Isn't this a great case our guys in the BCA put together?"

"Excuse me?"

"The case our guys put together. Pretty cool, isn't it?"

"Um … this is a multi-agency case. I'm not sure where you've been, but there's been a lot of collaboration going on with a bunch of different people from a bunch of different places." I kept my voice even, but I was pissed. Pat's not off the mark with his thoughts about the right arm of law enforcement not knowing what the left is doing. Most of the time that can be explained by one word: ego. But in this case, we'd risen above that. Several agencies had come together and checked their egos and had worked in concert for a common cause. And we'd continue working that way, too. In time, we'd have the resources of the ATF working with us in the person of Special Agent Mike Litman, and the resources of the Minnesota State Patrol in the person of Sergeant Denny Roske, just to name a couple of the agencies and people that would ultimately be involved.

"Oh," said the BCA guy, slightly embarrassed. "Sure, sure. Of course."

But with the seizure of all the records, a lot of the work was just beginning. Jim Shoup's guys with the IRS, including Special Agent John "Prospect" Tschida, began their financial investigation. Me, I was more interested in gleaning intelligence about the inner workings of the Hells Angels. We'd taken a fax machine from the clubhouse and from the drum we were able to get about a year and a half's worth of faxes—everything from meeting minutes to club rules. We found a lot of files on the Outlaws, too. There was a folder on every Outlaw chapter in Wisconsin, Illinois, and Indiana. Each folder had detailed photographs of each chapter clubhouse and a full description of each member, complete with home addresses. These guys had done a lot of homework.

At one point during our investigation of all the records, the National Drug Intelligence Center came to help, bringing in sixteen intelligence analysts. Tom Rainville and I prepared everything for the analysts, briefing them on what we'd found. Then they sifted through it, cross-indexing everything to make it easier to search through the material. In the end, we had fifteen, six-inch, three-ring binders of stuff. The NDIC was ecstatic. It was the largest amount of information ever obtained on the Hells Angels. Tom and I were singled out by the

NDIC for our efforts.

With all the intel, we could confirm more names of people we were certain were involved in the distribution of drugs. And we began questioning everybody. With what we'd learned from the search, we could come at it from a position of strength. We already knew what the people we interviewed knew. And real quick, they knew that we knew. And they began to talk.

We brought the usual suspects back into the picture, too. "Dewey" Selin talked and told us that Pat bought dope from Brian Weaver. Selin also told us that he knew that Fettig was planning to roll over on Dewey as well as Billy the Kid Romig. Selin had gone to Pat about it. Pat apparently didn't have much sympathy for him, telling him that he was bringing too much heat around the Hells Angels and then stripping him and Romig of their prospect patches. We also got a statement from Michael Metsala, a Los Valientes member who dealt drugs with Selin and Romig and Fettig, and who got to know Pat pretty well. He told us he bought dope from Pat on at least one occasion and led us to believe he was Pat's personal Hells Angels prospect.

By then, federal prosecutor Jeff Paulsen was working with us. I'd known Jeff for years. Jeff had a phenomenal work ethic and was a bulldog like me. When he set his mind to something, he saw it through. And he'd set his mind to get Pat Matter. I invited him to sit in on our Tuesday morning roundtable discussions, meetings I'd insisted we hold to make sure everybody was on the same page with the investigation. We had a lot of information pointing to Pat, but we wanted something more. Something specifically drug related.

And then I remembered the two kilos of cocaine that was stolen out of Mark Armstrong's garage. Pat's two kilos. I mentioned it to Jeff in January of 2002. We could start interviewing everyone involved, I suggested. Somebody would roll over on Pat, I was certain.

"When did it happen?" asked Jeff.

"February of '97."

"That doesn't leave us much time." Jeff wasn't kidding. The incident was just a month short of being five years old—the statute of limitations. We went to work. We brought back in the guys responsible for the bike and cocaine thefts in the first place. We talked to Burronnie Brosh who confirmed everything he'd told us before about Pat and about his threats. In a photo lineup, Brosh picked out Pat, Rohda, and Armstrong. We brought Brosh's girlfriend in, too, who substantiated the story of Pat coming to her door looking for Brosh.

Of course we still had the testimony of Ronnie Rowles as well. As a matter of fact, I'd interviewed Ronnie about the Armstrong case again that previous August. He was reluctant. He knew by the line of questioning where I was heading. "You fuckers are trying to get me to testify against Pat Matter!" he yelled.

I calmed him down and said I just wanted more information about the stolen bikes. Soon, Ronnie was telling me about Brian Weaver. "The King of Vinning," he called him, alluding to Weaver's practice of switching out VIN (vehicle identification number) plates. Ronnie stole cars for Weaver for which Weaver paid him a grand apiece. "I used to make good money," Ronnie said, "but I started using more dope than I made." Then Ronnie said that Brian Weaver and Pat Matter were partners.

"What do you mean partners?" I asked.

"Dope and vehicles."

"Yeah? How so?"

"No way, man. I can't say anything more about Matter. If I testify against Pat Matter, I'm going to wind up in a pine box."

As for the third Armstrong thief, the mastermind—Tony Morales—we never could get anything out of him. Morales wasn't willing to say a word.

With time running out, we knew we had enough to make an arrest. Did we have enough to convict? Testimony from the class of people we were dealing with, especially people facing jail time themselves, doesn't exactly guarantee success. But we hoped that by the time of a trial, we could get something more on Pat. For now, we had to act. On January 23, literally days before the statute of limitations was set to expire, Jeff took our case to a grand jury and secured an indictment for conspiracy to distribute cocaine and possession with intent to distribute cocaine. It was as good a time as any to arrest Pat Matter.

CHAPTER 13
Busted

I knew Chris's guys were out there. I could sense it. By the time of my arrest, I knew I'd made too much noise about the Armstrong thefts. I'd talked to, and threatened, too many people.

But I wasn't worried about being implicated in what was going on at Dewey's. Chris had a whole lot of people in his sights: Dewey and Metsala and Rankin and Weaver and Billy "the Kid" Romig and all the rest. And it would be natural for the cops to think it was all tied together and all a part of the Hells Angels and therefore, that it all started with me as president. Not that I wasn't doing my share of drug distribution. It's just that my interest in Dewey Selin's shop was limited entirely to the use of his dyno machine for my bikes.

In fact, I didn't care for the heat Dewey was bringing with all the activity of his shop. Truth be told, I wasn't in favor of him or Romig becoming Hells Angels. I didn't think they were tough enough, not the right caliber. They were basically punks is what my gut was telling me and by then I'd become a pretty good judge of people. Jay Rankin and Rooster were the ones who wanted Dewey and Romig in the club, and, looking back, it's not hard to see why. Jay and Rooster had been dealing drugs with Dewey.

One night I was at my shop after a night of drinking. I was depressed. I'd gotten word that Tank had just died. After he'd quit the club, he'd gone to live in Vegas, closer to his mother. Apparently he'd been helping her with some gardening when he dropped dead of a sudden heart attack. Richard was at the shop that night and so were Dewey and Romig. Richard and I told them both we didn't want them in the club. I made the suggestion that it might be best for them to hand in their prospect patches. I was in no mood to fuck around that night. I made the suggestion rather … forcefully, let's say. They handed in their prospect patches. All told, they'd prospected for us less than a month.

So my major concern was not what was going on in Dewey's shop. And I wasn't too worried about guys like Mike Metsala, either—the Los Valiente member who claimed in his statement that he bought dope from me. Metsala was a goofy fuck and I didn't trust him. I called him Buzz Lightyear because of these bugged-out eyes he had. He was certainly no personal prospect of mine, as he'd led Chris and his guys to believe. I did do some business with him, but I probably shouldn't have. He kept trying to get closer to me and my operation. One night he came by my house with a trunk load of AR-15s, grenades, and night-vision goggles.

"Interested?" he said, opening the trunk and smiling. Yeah, that's all I needed. For all I knew, Buzz Lightyear was working with the cops.

"Listen, you dumb fuck," I said, "get this shit out of here. And if you have an accident anywhere within five miles of my house, I'm going to beat your brains out."

By then, I wasn't interested in anything that could bring more heat from the cops. James Brady's house had been raided back in '98 and they found those stolen bikes Chris mentioned but the bikes had nothing to do with me. But Brady was a Hells Angel and there was guilt by association. That's exactly why I'd made it clear to the club that there was to be no more bike stealing. I was pissed about the stolen bikes and pissed, too, that Brady had lost his patch. Some of the club members and I met with him at a park by the river, near the clubhouse. We asked him where his patch was and he just kind of walked away, effectively quitting the club. But, yes, I fined him fifteen hundred bucks for the lost patch. As Chris mentioned, I had to make a little bit of a statement with a baseball bat where Brady worked. Word made its way back to Brady and he called my shop and said I could meet him at ex-member Ralph Schluter's house. I drove there with a prospect and Brady had about seven or eight guys in the place. I walked right past them all and asked Brady for the money. Ralph stepped in and said nobody wanted any trouble and that he'd take care of it for Brady. Then he handed me the fifteen hundred and we left.

And so I'd been trying to keep things clean with the club activities. But in truth, my major worry was that one day it would be the Armstrong thefts back in '97 that would bite me in the ass. Someone could talk. Someone I'd threatened. Someone who would testify that two kilos of cocaine that became a part of the burglary that night happened to belong to me. Chris wasn't the only one aware of the statute of limitations. I'd been counting down myself.

By 1999, the stakes had gotten higher. A lot higher. I'd learned that Trish was pregnant. We'd had Cole living with us from my first marriage and Trish had become interested in us having a child of our own. I'd been busy with the club and the shop. The relationship had been suffering a little because of it. I wasn't sure having a baby was the best thing to do. But I changed my mind in September of that year when Trish delivered a beautiful baby boy. We named him Connor. In 2000, we all went to Sturgis in my motor home and had a great time. I had wanted to get the relationship back on track. With Connor in the picture, it was becoming more important for me every day.

Me, Connor and Trish at Sturgis 1999.

As the statute of limitations started running out, I found myself thinking about the people who really knew about my operation, the people I'd allowed to get close, guys like Mike Eason and Richard Rohda. Mike, as it happens, was an ex-cop. It had taken me a long time to come to trust him in the first place. Now I found my trust was starting to wane. Then in January of 2001, Richard got arrested for that stolen truck, even though I'd kept telling him to get a legal truck to drive. Facing a stolen vehicle charge would give him reason to talk. I knew that if someone like Richard or Mike talked, I'd be fucked.

Me on bike and Mike Eason standing at Sturgis 1999.

I wondered about Mark Weaver, too, who worked for me as a counter man and who would order parts and make deposits and take the bikes in for inspections and titles. Little by little, he learned way too much about my operation. But the thing is you can't operate in a vacuum. You can't do it all yourself. You have to surround yourself with competent people and at the end of the day, you just have to hope you can trust them.

Then there was Mark's brother Brian. I'd known Brian since '95, having met him through Richard. We'd become close friends. He wasn't a biker type. He was clean cut. And he was a hustler and really knew his business. In the drug trade, he dealt mostly in marijuana, something I didn't really handle. Marijuana is a bulky product and I found it easier to deal in meth. In the stolen vehicle trade, Brian was the best. He knew everybody, too, so of course he knew Morales and Brosh and Rowles. He'd actually worked with them. He was the one who put me onto them, at least Brosh and Rowles. And he knew firsthand how hard I went after them.

Yes, I was with him the day he got busted in January of 2001. It was the day after Richard was arrested. Brian was helping me retrieve a truck of mine. It was a couple days after I had returned from Las Vegas. Trish and I had just gotten married out there. We figured it was about time. By then, I knew there was never going to be anybody else in my life but Trish. Brian and his wife had come out, too. While in Vegas, I delivered a custom show bike to a customer, after having it shipped in a truck that an employee of mine had driven there. We all flew home after the wedding, and the employee drove the truck back. Somewhere close to home, spun out on meth I can only assume, my employee pulled the truck onto the shoulder of the highway and took off on foot. The highway patrol came across the truck, still running, and called the shop, talking to Mike Eason and telling him we needed to come get the truck before they had it towed. Brian happened to come by and he and Mike and another employee and I found the truck and I had the other employee drive it back to the shop.

Then Brian and Mike and I started heading back. As we exited the highway near the shop we saw undercover cops everywhere, some standing along the exit ramps, guns drawn. "Pull over now or we will shoot!" they yelled. We pulled over and got out of the truck and they put us face first on the pavement. They told Mike and me we could go, but they took Brian away. Somebody had rolled on him, identifying him as a supplier of marijuana.

Apparently the cops had been following Brian, but of course I was sure they were after me, too. It was obvious they thought the truck had been used to transport drugs because when I got back to the shop, it wasn't hard to tell it had been searched. For one thing, the headliner had been cut. Someone was rolling on me, I just knew it. Someone was a rat.

I called a lawyer for Brian—Mark Peterson—and Mark and I went down to the station. We saw Brian in the backseat of a squad car, getting ready to be led inside and booked. When he saw us, he ducked down in the seat like he didn't know us. I didn't have a good feeling. Was he cooperating, ready to throw me under the bus to save his own ass?

A few months went by. Then one day in April of 2001, a couple strange things happened. Brad Jacobsen, with his partner A.J., came by my gym with two grams of meth. I was about to make a sizeable purchase from them and the two grams were for me to test. On the way back to my shop, I noticed I was being tailed by the cops. They finally pulled me over close to the shop, looked inside the car through the windows, didn't see anything incriminating, and cited me for speeding. Coincidence? It hardly seemed like it to me.

When I got home that night, Trish told me someone had broken into the house. They'd used a ladder to gain access to my second-story deck and then cut the screen and came in, knocking over some potted plants in the process. A change jar had been knocked off our bedroom dresser. Chris said he overheard detective Tom Billings say he'd gained access to the clubhouse with a ladder. I would contend that Billings said "house" and Chris just assumed clubhouse. Billings broke into my home that day to have a look around. As Chris points out, my house was on his commute home. He stopped that day, took a ladder I had lying beneath the deck, and made himself a guest of my house.

It might surprise people to learn that cops don't always play by the rules. That's not the only example. Billings' buddy Tom Rainville was the cop who arrested Mark Armstrong. According to what Mark told me, Rainville took $25,000 in cash from him during the arrest for "evidence." There's no reason that Mark would have told me that if it hadn't been true. Nobody's seen that $25,000 since. And then there was the incident where Rainville had been caught in a park getting a blow job from a young man. We all heard about it in the club and nobody could believe the guy was able to keep his job.

At any rate, the morning after Billings broke in, somewhere around 5:00 a.m., on a Friday the 13th, there was a pounding on the door. It was the cops. I stumbled out of bed and looked out the window to see no fewer than ten police cars lined up in the driveway. Then the phone rang. I picked up. "Pat Matter?" the voice said. "We need you to open the front door. We have a warrant to search your home. We can knock the door down, but it would be easier all the way around if you just cooperated and opened the door." The voice belonged to Rainville.

"Yeah, yeah, sure," I said. "My wife's coming down as soon as we get some clothes on." Then I hung up the phone and yelled at Trish to stall them.

"How?" she asked as she started heading downstairs.

"I don't care—just do *not* open that door until I say it's okay." Then I scrambled for the two grams of meth and bolted for the bathroom, flushing the meth down the toilet. It was all I had in the house that I felt could incriminate me. "Okay," I yelled down. "You can let 'em in."

When she did, they came storming in, guns drawn, shouting for us to get our hands in the air. Connor came in, crying from all the noise and confusion. A female marshal searched Trish and then let her take care of Connor. Then they sat us down in the living room and began searching through everything.

They came across twenty-five grand that I always kept on hand. I called it bait money and I made sure it could be easily found. I always figured that if the cops ever searched the house, the money would at least make them feel like they got something for their efforts. Maybe it would be enough to satisfy them. What they didn't know was that I had over $60,000 more, hidden beneath a false bottom in the bedroom dresser. It was the money I was ready to use to make the meth buy from Brad Jacobsen. Twenty-five thousand dollars could be explained. Could just be cash from the shop. Sixty-thousand-plus was another story. The sheer amount was incriminating. Who, but a drug dealer, keeps that kind of money around the house?

The cops were there till 2:30 in the afternoon. They went through everything. I tried to cooperate but I couldn't resist fucking with them a little. At one point Connor toddled in with a toy one-thousand dollar bill. "Better give that to me, Connor, before the policemen try to take *all* of Daddy's money."

Eventually the cops left. And then they came right back in. John VanSlyke—Slick, Chris calls him—was yelling for everyone to check out the dresser in the bedroom. "It might have a false bottom!" I'd find out later that while my house was being searched, so was Richard Rohda's. And Richard had the exact same type of dresser with the exact same type of false bottom. His wife clued the cops in on it and they'd called VanSlyke. So the cops found—and took—the sixty thousand. When it was counted later, the total confiscated, including the twenty-five grand, was $88,300. At the time, I didn't know it was Rohda's wife that talked about the dresser. I thought it had to be Richard. And besides, Richard knew about the pending drug buy. He was one of the only people around me who knew. I started thinking Richard was talking.

Of course the shop was searched, too. Mike Eason let the cops right in. And for days afterwards, Mike seemed nervous around me. Maybe, I thought, it was Mike Eason who was talking. But I also knew there had been no smoking gun found in any of the places that had been searched, including the clubhouse which is where Chris had gone. They'd seized all my financial records, of course, but I figured a money laundering case would be tough to prove.

Still, what if someone talked? Richard was facing charges. So was Brian Weaver. And someone had to talk, because why did my house and business and the Hells Angels' clubhouse get searched in the first place? And who tipped the cops off so that they pulled me over that day after I'd left the gym with two grams of meth? And then there was the matter of the break-in, which only later I would come to conclude was Tom Billings. And I knew that not long before, Richard and Brian had taken their wives and gone off on vacation to Hawaii together.

Richard stopped by my house one day shortly after the raid. "Someone's a fucking rat," I said to him, "and all I can figure is that it's gotta be either you or Brian."

"It ain't me, Pat," he said, but he turned a little pale when he said it. But then days went by and then weeks and Richard and I went to races together and spent a lot of time in each other's company and things seemed okay. Finally I decided it couldn't be Richard. But I cut myself loose from Brian. And about that time, I let Mike Eason go, too. He knew way too much and I just had a bad feeling about him.

By then I'd been talking with Alan Caplan, a lawyer out of San Francisco who was kind of the unofficial attorney for the Hells Angels. Caplan was a character and a half. He'd lost his leg in a motorcycle accident back in the 1980s. In his prosthetic leg he'd carry dope. He had permission from the state of California to use marijuana for medical purposes, but he hid it in his leg anyway, just so he wouldn't get hassled. At any rate, in December, Caplan got a call from prosecutor Jeff Paulsen asking if I wanted to come in and proffer. Fuck no, I said. Hell, I hadn't even been charged with anything. But what did Paulsen know? What kind of case were the cops putting together? I was two months away from the statute of limitations running out on the Armstrong thefts. Was Rowles talking? Was Brosh? Morales? If one of those guys tied the coke to me and talked about the threats and extortion, I figured it would be my word against the word of known bike and car thieves. But if you coupled their potential testimony with the word of someone like Brian Weaver or Mike Eason—someone close to me who knew my history and operation—then you'd have something pretty damn serious.

I sweated it out until February 14, one day shy of the statute of limitations running out, all the time wondering if the cops were going to act. I had my answer that afternoon. Valentine's Day. The cops came into the shop with an arrest warrant. Richard was there. He let them in the back door.

CHAPTER 14
Starting to Roll

When we arrested Pat, I stationed myself on the perimeter, in a car across the street, ready just in case. But it was a low-key arrest and Pat was cooperative. A gentleman. I met him face to face the next day at the Anoka County Jail where I escorted him first to the DEA for processing, then to the U.S. Marshal's office, then to federal court where he appeared before a magistrate and was ultimately released on bond.

We had our arrest, but we still didn't have the case we wanted. We began working on a superseding indictment, something that would trump the original charges, something with more teeth, something that could put Pat away for a long time. That was the idea all along. And there aren't many prosecutors who proceed on that basis. Most would have just said, look, we don't have enough on the guy—forget about it. Not Jeff Paulsen. Jeff was the best, most aggressive prosecutor I'd ever worked with. He was committed and he knew that eventually we could gather enough shit on Pat to make something big stick. But that would mean getting the people who surrounded Pat to roll over on him. Who knew how long that would take? Jeff made no secret to Pat's defense attorney Alan Caplan of our goal of getting a superseding indictment. Why Caplan didn't push to invoke Pat's right to a speedy trial remains a complete mystery to me. The more time we had to get our ducks in a row, the better our chances for conviction. I wasn't very impressed with Hells Angels counselor Caplan.

Brian Weaver began cooperating in March, just a month after Pat's arrest. We sat down with him, Shoup and Paulsen and a couple of the other detectives and I, and we listened as he recounted his part in the Armstrong thefts, how he told Pat who the thieves were, how he was with him when he first went to Bug Brosh's house. Weaver had become good friends with Pat; he described their relationship as "extremely" close. They spent time together and Weaver witnessed and overheard a lot of stuff that was related to Pat's drug business. He sold marijuana to Pat, but mostly for Pat's personal use. Pat got his meth elsewhere. Weaver didn't know how much quantity Pat dealt in, but he knew it had to be a lot. Pat was never short on cash. Once on a trip to Vegas, Weaver saw Pat lose over fifty grand. Fueled by meth, he'd spent all night gambling.

In May, Weaver helped us out some more, setting up his marijuana source so that we could bust him as he delivered a load into Minnesota. That source, in turn, rolled over on *his* source in San Francisco. It all helped to establish Brian Weaver's credibility. We'd been investigating him heavily and after his arrest while in the truck with Pat back in January of 2001, we'd built up a case that would have put him away for a while. We were going after people who'd surrounded Weaver, people he did business with, people who knew his operation—both the drug dealing and the vehicle thefts. It didn't help his prospects that in January of 2002, he was arrested for witness tampering. He'd threatened one of the guys who was getting ready to roll on him. We happened to have had the guy wired at the time. Weaver, apparently, wasn't as careful as Pat Matter, who'd made Brosh strip naked in the men's room of the 22nd Avenue Station bar to make certain he was clean before delivering his threats. And so the King of Vinning was going down. Facing that kind of pressure, a guy might say anything. But with the drug sources he led us to, Weaver's cooperation was clearly credible. And what he knew about Pat was like gold to us.

Brian's brother Mark talked in April. Why? Because Brian rolled over on him. There's no honor among thieves and evidently that extends to thieves who happen to be brothers. Mark Weaver had become involved in Brian's business. Facing jail time himself, Mark told us all about his duties working for Pat Matter at Minneapolis Custom Cycle. Pat was not an easy man to work for. Demanding, Mark said. "Especially when he was juiced on meth. He'd have me doing twenty things at once. It was like I was working twenty-four hours a day, seven days a week. And I had no business training. I felt like I'd been thrown to the wolves." Mark went on to tell us how the money would come into the shop in cash, in large quantities. Pat would come and go from the shop with a purple Crown Royal bag, filled with what Mark knew had to be dope. Often Pat was accompanied by Mike Eason.

Pat didn't really try to hide what he was doing from Mark. "I guess it's pretty obvious what's going on," he chuckled at one point. Pat would send Mark to the bank to make deposits, always in increments of less than ten thousand dollars so as not to raise any red flags. Mark would have to prepare bogus receipts for the money. From the files we'd seized in the April 2001 search of M.C.C., we were able to show multiple entries from 1999 and 2000 for amounts around $9,000 and $9,500, with customer names attached that Mark confirmed were made up.

Mike Eason had problems of his own. Pat's service manager had been fleecing the Social Security Administration, collecting payments fraudulently. We brought in a Social Security investigator. Eason began to cooperate. He knew more about Pat's operation than even Mark Weaver knew. Eason told us Pat would receive ten or twelve pounds of methamphetamine a month, sometimes twice a month. It was Eason's job to sit on it for Pat, for which Pat would pay him five hundred dollars a pound. Eason would rent storage lockers for Pat to stash the meth. Eason gave us the names of Pat's suppliers, too, including Brad Jacobsen. And customers—names we knew, like Rohda and Rankin and Rooster. Rooster was one of the biggest—a "mainstay," Eason called him.

Eason told us that one time he helped Pat bury a million dollars in his backyard. The two of them counted out $850,000 in cash, then Pat counted a bunch more and when he reached a certain amount, he held up one finger. An even million. Then they stuffed the cash into PVC pipes and drilled holes under Pat's deck with an auger and buried the pipes. After we questioned Eason, Tom Rainville and I drove him around town where he pointed out the storage lockers he'd rented, along with the places, typically restaurants or hotels, where Pat would meet his suppliers and pick up the meth.

The people closest to Pat were starting to roll. And we kept interviewing. Hells Angel Jay Rankin and his wife Roxanne were both interviewed. Rankin was facing drug charges but had, in the meantime, been arrested on a rape charge. Rankin talked about Pat, but he and Roxanne had been buying cocaine through a guy named Steve Lyman. One time they wanted to order more drugs from Lyman but they couldn't reach him by phone, despite repeated attempts. Finally they went to his house where they discovered Lyman dead in his bed. Then they searched the apartment and found three kilos of cocaine and $100,000, both of which they took.

Pat's investigator-polygrapher, Darrell Shaw, was interviewed as well. At the U.S. attorney's office, Shaw wasn't entirely honest with the answers to the questions he was getting. Jim Shoup lost patience with Shaw and kept standing up and leaning in across the table towards him and Jeff Paulsen had to keep pulling Shoup back down in his seat.

We kept up our surveillance, too, continuing to monitor the movements of Pat and everyone around him, continuing to gather up evidence.

We put it all together and on September 18, 2002, Jeff Paulsen filed our superseding indictment: seventeen counts including distribution of cocaine, distribution of methamphetamine, money laundering, and engaging in a continuing criminal enterprise. The defendants named were Pat Matter, Mark Armstrong, and Mike Eason. The most significant charge was the continuing criminal enterprise charge. CCE, otherwise known as the Kingpin Statute, is a federal law specifically targeting large-scale drug traffickers. First-time conviction means a minimum twenty years. Maximum of life.

Soon after that, the negotiations with Pat began. In a word, he was fucked. He had little choice but to offer a plea and it became just a matter of what kind of deal could be made. Naturally, we wanted Pat to implicate others. His suppliers and anyone else involved in his organization. We tried to make that part of the deal. We wanted Pat's cooperation and let him know how big a favor he could do himself by talking. Pat would have none of it. He didn't even want to think about it. I can't say I was surprised. Sure, he was now a legitimate business-man of sorts, at least with M.C.C. He was a husband and a father, too. But he was also a one-percenter. And there was a code.

By then, Pat had a local attorney, Jim Ostgard, working alongside Caplan from San Francisco. Caplan wasn't licensed to practice law in Minnesota, so Pat needed someone local. Pat and Ostgard talked back and forth with Jeff Paulsen, trying to hammer out a deal. In January of 2003, Pat agreed to plead guilty to the distribution of methamphet-amine in exchange for a ten-year sentence. Jeff had one condition. "If we find out you've got a homicide in your past," he told Pat, "then all bets are off." It was a reasonable concern. Pat wore a Filthy Few patch, after all. Eventually, Mel Chancey, one of the Hell's Henchmen whom Pat had ordered to "take care of" some significant member of the Out-laws back in 1994 after Pat's truck had been blown up, rolled over and came clean about the shooting of regional Outlaw president Pete Rogers. Fortunately for Pat, of course, Rogers had survived.

Pat had a condition, too. If the judge went beyond the agreed-upon ten years to twelve years or above, he could rescind his guilty plea and allow the case to go to trial.

Jeff also demanded Pat pay a hefty fine—$500,000. Later he would tell me he basically pulled the number out of his ass. He really didn't know how much to ask for. We figured Pat had a lot of money squirreled away; there was Eason's story about the million in the back-yard, but Eason could have been exaggerating. Jeff figured half a mil-lion sounded reasonable. Caplan agreed to it right away and Jeff wondered if maybe we should have asked for more. In Jeff's office, Pat signed the deal. But when it came to the part about the money, he turned to us and said, "For this, you're going to have to wait for the ground to thaw."

Paulsen set a date of April 1st—April Fool's Day—for Pat to turn in the money. Pat, having dug up the $500,000 from his backyard, turned it in. The next day, Pat officially pleaded guilty in the court-room of district court judge James Michael Rosenbaum. Rosenbaum was an intimidating figure, a no-nonsense hard-ass who ran a tight courtroom. He was the judge who sentenced Billy the Kid Romig to twenty-two years. Plus another ten years supervised release.

Pat's $500,000 cash turned into the U.S. Marshall's.

In the hallway outside the courtroom I came up to Pat and shook his hand. It's my way. I like to keep things professional. Nailing Pat was my job; it wasn't personal. And I was starting to get to know Pat. I saw the human side. I saw how he and Trish interacted and I could sense the depth of their relationship. Surveilling him at bike shows, I saw how he interacted with his customers. He had a charismatic charm and it was no mystery to me as to why his shop was a success. Things are never as black and white as they seem. Pat was a criminal, but that didn't mean he wasn't worthy of at least a little respect.

We filed into the courtroom and Judge Rosenbaum entered. He saw Pat's plea condition—that he be able to rescind his guilty plea if Rosenbaum were to sentence him beyond twelve years—and rejected the plea entirely, explaining that if Pat was indeed guilty of a continuing criminal enterprise, he'd be likely to enhance Pat's sentence, possibly beyond thirty years, maybe life. "This court is prepared to try this case on Monday," he declared. I stood there with my mouth hanging open. A judge has a right to reject a plea deal, of course, but we'd worked hard to negotiate in good faith with Pat. A recess was taken and Pat's attorneys huddled with Paulsen and it was decided that Pat would drop his condition and maintain the guilty plea.

Back in the courtroom, Rosenbaum questioned Pat directly. He wanted information. "Where did you get the methamphetamine that you sold, Mr. Matter?"

"From a source outside of Minnesota," Pat replied.

"Does that source have a name?"

"Yes, your honor."

"And what's the name?"

Pat hesitated. "Your honor, I'm responsible for my own actions. I don't know how——."

"Your charge is a conspiracy, Mr. Matter. You can't be a conspirator by yourself. Did you manufacture the drug?"

"No, sir."

"Well then you got it from somebody else. This isn't a game of keep-away. This is called a plea. So why don't you tell me where you got your supply of drugs?"

"Texas and California," Pat finally said. It was all he would admit to. I could tell it pissed Rosenbaum off. He accepted the guilty plea and then set a date for sentencing. Pat was allowed out on bond in the meantime. But the ten-year deal was wiped out. And I could see from Pat's expression that he felt he'd been screwed and that we had betrayed him. As Rosenbaum left the courtroom, Pat turned and glared at Jeff and me. I felt like I was about an inch tall.

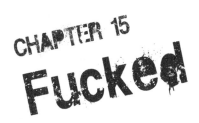

CHAPTER 15
Fucked

If Chris felt like he was an inch tall, he sure didn't show it. I won't pretend that I know what was in the man's heart that day, but his enthusiasm to put me away sure as hell seemed "personal" to me. Same with Paulsen. Especially Paulsen. Paulsen seemed to enjoy the whole process. Over time, I began to notice the fun he was having with the dates. My house, shop, and clubhouse were first raided on a Friday the 13th. I was arrested on Valentine's Day. The superseding indictment came down on the exact date of the twentieth anniversary of my joining the Hells Angels. I had to turn the money in on April Fool's Day. Funny guy, Paulsen.

Turning the money in was a story in itself. I brought the $500,000 in a duffel bag and they walked me over to the bank where it could be counted. To add insult to injury, the bank charged me for the counting. And then on the way out the door, a federal court clerk offered me a sucker. I guess that was me, all right. A sucker. Paulsen got a kick out of that, I'm sure.

As for Judge James Rosenbaum, it seemed clear to me that he was intent on making an example out of me. He was pissed when I wouldn't give him the names of my suppliers and he held it against me. And when he rejected the plea deal I'd made in good faith, I was fit to be tied. Making the deal for ten years hadn't been easy. I agonized over it. Trish and I talked at length about it. Rosenbaum was right when he said I was facing thirty years to life. If we took it to trial and I lost, I figured I'd probably never see her or Connor again. Trish's emotions ran the gamut. She was heartbroken that I was facing prison time, but she was equally infuriated at me for getting myself into that situation in the first place. She was stunned by the gravity of the situation. Then again, she knew my business even if she had chosen to pretend to herself that she didn't. My imminent incarceration was a cold slap of reality. It didn't help things when she discovered I had recently cheated on her. It was just one of those things that sort of came with the lifestyle. But I hated that I had hurt her, first with the cheating and now with the prison time. I loved her and Connor more than life itself. And I knew she loved me, even in spite of everything that had happened. Would she wait ten years? I had to believe she would. And so I made the deal.

When Rosenbaum rejected it that day and the court was recessed, I turned to Paulsen and said, "You fuckers sandbagged me. You knew all along that he'd reject the deal. Hell, you set it up that I'd get Rosenbaum in the first place!"

They'll disagree about that last part, but nobody can talk me out of believing it. Both Jim Ostgard and Alan Caplan told me as much after investigating the matter themselves. Judges are chosen at random off a spinning wheel. They do that to make sure that lawyers can't steer cases to certain judges who may be predisposed to rule in their favor. Interfering with the process is illegal. No less a body than the United States Supreme Court has said so. And yet it happens. Caplan told me about a Hells Angels case in Cleveland where a Justice Department strike force was accused of trying to circumvent the system, to steer one of Caplan's clients to a particular judge. In my case, there were a bunch of judges and I could have drawn any one of them, but somehow I ended up with the hanging judge—James Rosenbaum. There was nothing random about it. Paulsen steered me there.

I was screwed. I'd just lost half a million dollars as part of a deal that the government essentially welched on. I could have taken that money and left the country. I could have just let them have the $88,000 the cops confiscated during the search of my house and kept the rest and I could have been free. But I'd elected to stay and face the jail time we had agreed upon. Part of me wanted to just say, fuck it, let's take it to trial. I was seething during the recess and it took quite a while for

Caplan and Ostgard and Paulsen to calm me down. We walked out into the hallway and talked and after about a half hour, hearing thirty years to life echoing repeatedly in my head, I knew I had no choice but to drop my condition that I could rescind the plea, stick with pleading guilty, and take whatever Rosenbaum was going to dish out.

The thing is, back in March, I had called Caplan to see about my options. I wasn't willing to cooperate, but I'd been in Daytona Beach for bike week and, in particular, S&S Cycle's 45th anniversary. S&S had made me part of a tribute team. By then, I'd become good friends with George Smith from S&S and his son, company CEO Brett. I had a great deal of respect for both those guys and for their company. And they returned the respect. They appreciated the work I was putting out on my custom bikes and George himself had paid me a visit, asking me to be one of just five bike builders who he was going to have build nine custom bikes each—a total of forty-five custom bikes for the company's anniversary. It was also Harley-Davidson's 100th an-

One of the nine bikes I built for S&S for their 45th Anniversary.
One is currently in the museum at S&S.

niversary, so it was decided that the motors would be 145s, 100 for Harley, and 45 for S&S. The tribute bikes got a lot of publicity in Daytona during the anniversary. One of mine eventually made its way to the S&S museum where it sits today.

At any rate, Cole had come along with me to Daytona. He was seventeen at the time and at one point, he turned to me and said, "Dad, I don't want to lose you." And that's when I figured maybe I ought to explore my options. I couldn't help think about the people the prosecution had lined up to testify against me and I thought it was worth at least having Caplan contact Paulsen to make an inquiry. If I did cooperate, I knew I'd be kicked out of the Hells Angels. But I thought maybe there was a way I could do so while inflicting minimal damage. I'd called Caplan and Caplan called Paulsen. But Paulsen had turned him down. I'd put it together later that Paulsen was holding out, biding his time until I was really screwed. Paulsen knew exactly what he was doing.

Another option presented itself to me while in Florida. Cole and I went down to West Palm where I had a friend who was a SCUBA dive captain. Some of the S&S guys came along, including Charlie Hadayia, Jr., who had also become a good friend. Scott, my buddy in West Palm, took us out on a dive trip. In a moment when he and I were alone, he mentioned to me that if I wanted, he'd be willing to run me over to the Bahamas. "Just let me know when," Scott said.

I considered it. I knew I could grab a million bucks or so and head to the Bahamas where I could deposit the money into a bank account, an offshore account. Then I'd be able to transfer it to anywhere in the world I'd want to go. I could leave the States and be free. Truthfully, I'd thought about getting out of the country before. I'd considered Canada where I knew a lot of people. From Canada, who knows? But Trish had family and friends in Minneapolis. She wouldn't have left and even if she would have, I couldn't have asked her to live the rest of her life on the run. I could have left on my own, of course. But I wasn't willing to entertain the idea of living the rest of my life without Trish and Cole and Connor.

Jim Ostgard was able to push the would-be trial off and it bought me some time. Paulsen was in no hurry, of course. I imagined he felt that the longer I was out on bond and the more time I had to think about my upcoming sentence, the more likely I'd be to cooperate and implicate others. But for the time being I decided to dig in. I'd been willing to do ten years and now I figured I'd just have to be willing to do more. Caplan and Ostgard both assured me that if I stuck with the guilty plea, maybe the judge would tack on a couple more years at most. If I had to strap on twelve years, then that's what I would do.

In the meantime, I began to wonder about Alan Caplan. I was furious that he'd agreed to the $500,000 so quickly. He kept telling me that if I didn't pay what Paulsen asked, we wouldn't get the deal. But I had a hard time believing he couldn't negotiate the amount downwards. Caplan was costing me enough money with his fee. It started out at fifty grand. He kept assuring me we had a winnable case. And then as time went on, he kept asking for more here and more there. I had no choice but to trust him. He represented my way out. I paid what he wanted in cash and watched as he'd stuff the bills into that prosthetic leg of his. "We can beat this," he'd keep saying. By the time it was all over, I would end up paying Caplan $175,000. And for what? I could have pleaded guilty and been sentenced by a hanging judge all by myself, thank you very much.

The fact is Alan Caplan was, first and foremost, for Alan Caplan. He didn't care about me. He didn't really care about the Hells Angels. But he sure as hell cared about their business and he didn't want to lose it. The last I heard, he's still representing them. When I'd approached him back in March about talking to Paulsen, I could tell he didn't like the idea. But he knew after the plea deal was rejected that I'd be considering it again. And so a couple weeks after we'd been in Rosenbaum's courtroom, Caplan had me fly out to San Francisco to talk specifically about what I might say if I did cooperate.

On my first night there, we sat in a bar and we talked about the possibility of asking for another judge. But what would happen if we spun the wheel and it landed back on Rosenbaum? Then he'd really put me away, just for trying to avoid him. It was a conversation we'd had before with Jim Ostgard. Jim was dead set against the idea. He didn't want to make waves, knowing that since he was a local attorney, he'd no doubt be up in front of Rosenbaum again someday.

Then Caplan asked me what I'd reveal if I cooperated. "What would you give them?" he asked. I said I figured I'd talk about the drug dealing. Nothing more. After all, it's not like there were any club murders that I knew about. Still, I could tell Caplan wasn't happy about the possibilities.

"You know, Pat," he said, "the other idea is that you just take off. We'll take it to trial. See how it goes. But then, if things start looking bad, just split. Get your ducks all lined up. Get your money, get a driver. Leave during a recess in the proceedings. You'll probably get a forty-five minute to an hour head start. Get yourself down to Mexico. From there, you could take off for anywhere. Brazil, maybe." It wasn't that unrealistic. For not testifying against the club, they could set me up real nice in Brazil.

But of course I wasn't interested and it was becoming clearer to me how dead set Caplan was against my cooperating. I began to feel less and less comfortable around him. That night he told me yet another idea. He knew a local guy who could get me out of the country even before there could be a trial. He was a Hells Angel from Richmond, California, not far from San Francisco. Nickname of Bones. "Why don't we go talk to him, Pat?"

The next day we met Bones for lunch at a restaurant in Hayward. Bones was tall and thin. Well-groomed, well-spoken Italian guy. We made small talk over lunch and then, having coffee afterwards, he said, "Well, I guess we have some things to discuss."

"I'll let you guys talk," said Caplan, who was thinking of his legal career and didn't want to be any part of the conversation. "I'll be waiting in the car."

Bones turned to me. "So, you're wanting to get out of the country."

"I'm thinking about it." Of course I'd already turned down the idea in West Palm when a getaway to the Bahamas had been offered. I was only talking to Bones on account of Caplan.

Bones said he had a tuna boat. He and his crew could take me to

South America. "How much money would you be bringing with you?" he asked.

"Probably about a million."

I could sense Bones' wheels turning. Then I listened as he told me how he and his crew would get me on the boat and sail us to wherever I wanted to hide out. We'd go somewhere where there was no extradition treaty with the U.S. I got a bad feeling immediately. Bones would let me and my million dollars on the boat, all right. But I was pretty sure the boat would be the last place anybody would ever see me alive.

"Thanks," I said, "I'll think about it." Caplan took me back to the airport the next morning and I was never so glad to get on a plane.

Back home I started thinking about the potential trial, about who the prosecution would have as witnesses. I knew that Mike Eason was talking. I knew Brian Weaver was, too. I no longer trusted Richard Rohda, either. I couldn't prove it, but I just knew he had to be rolling. By then, I'd let him go from the shop. He'd been kicked out of the club, too. Rooster didn't care for Richard and when Richard brought an ex-member into the clubhouse one day, in direct violation of club rules, it was all the excuse Rooster needed to get Richard out of the club and I sure wasn't about to argue on Richard's behalf.

I figured Jay Rankin was talking, too. He'd also been bounced out of the club, for the rape accusation Chris mentioned. An accusation was all it was, though. There were never any charges made. Jay brought a girl back to the clubhouse one night and had sex with her. She left, and then came back of her own accord where Terry, another member, had sex with her, too. Then she wanted to go home but neither Jay nor Terry wanted to take her. I guess that kind of pissed her off. Finally a third member took her home and maybe she had a jealous boyfriend back there and felt like she had to make up a story or something. I don't know. All I know is that I was there the next day when a SWAT team blew through the front door of the clubhouse and came rushing in armed with AR-15s. They told us all to hit the floor and then they interviewed everybody separately about the alleged rape. But all the stories about the girl coincided. Not only that, we had footage from our security camera out front of the clubhouse door showing the girl voluntarily coming back in.

No arrests were made, but the whole thing was just bad business and I let Jay and Terry know about it. I didn't like even the suggestion of rape. Rape is the lowest. That these guys allowed a situation to happen where a rape allegation could even be made was just plain stupid. Then I flipped out when Terry said, "Well, fuck, Pat, look at what's going on with you. A rape accusation is nothing compared with your shit." I punched him pretty good. Then we all did and both he and Jay were tossed out of the club.

I imagine that didn't help my cause when Chris and his guys began to question Jay in regard to my case. I'd sold Jay meth. I'd slowed down, though. When the heat started coming down on me I told everyone in the club we needed to quit dealing drugs for a while. But truthfully, I don't know how much they were listening to me by then. Basically, they just changed their venue. Dewey's shop became the go-to place. And of course Jay was buying from Steve Lyman, too. I'd heard about Jay and his wife finding Lyman dead and taking off with the three kilos of cocaine and the hundred thousand dollars. I guess you could call Lyman Jay's silent partner. Anyway, Jay and Rooster and some of the other guys were going behind my back to get their drugs. Just because I was club president didn't mean I had control over these guys. As president, I was always honest with the members. I wanted a Hells Angels chapter that was open and democratic. But that honesty and openness wasn't always returned. Loyalty was breaking apart all around me.

As for Rooster, he pissed me off in another way, too. He told me he knew where Burronnie Brosh lived and worked and would take me to him. I'd threatened Brosh six years earlier, of course, after he'd helped steal my coke out of Mark Armstrong's garage. I figured he'd probably be a witness for Paulsen. He'd moved since then and Rooster knew where. He told me but it was just his way of trying to come across to the other members like some kind of tough guy. One night he took me to where Brosh worked in northeast Minneapolis. Tommy and Keith, two other club members, rode along. Rooster pointed to the building from the car. "There," he said. "Okay, I've done my part."

"Your part, Rooster?" I said. "What the fuck is that supposed to mean?" That's what it had come down to apparently for Rooster. Partial, half-assed involvement, unwilling to help me take care of business. I couldn't believe it. Tommy and Keith seemed surprised, too. Keith had only been in the club for a year, but he understood better than Rooster what it meant to be a Hells Angel. Keith had told me he'd handle Brian Weaver for me. "I'll knock on his door and when he answers I'll take care of him, Pat. Just say the word. And then I'll take you to Canada or wherever you want to go." Now that's loyalty.

"Thanks, Keith," I had told him. "I'll let you know." I had no idea what Keith had in mind by "take care of him." Maybe he just wanted to rough him up a little. But I didn't want to take a chance. Although I had built my whole reputation as a guy who wouldn't think twice about doing what he had to do, even if it meant killing someone, I wasn't ready to order the cold-blooded murder of anybody, even someone whom I was certain was going to testify against me. That wasn't me, even if others believed it was and I had let them believe it.

With Rooster, our relationship hadn't been the same since 1997. That was the year Rooster's wife Sherry filed for divorced. In the family court proceedings it came up that he had beaten her. He testified that he'd been out of town one time and when he returned he found that Sherry had been doing drugs, partying all night long. He saw drugs on the table and he snapped. That was his excuse to the court for the domestic assault.

I was there for the proceedings, mostly for moral support for Rooster. We were all seated around a conference table and Sherry was seated across from me. The revelation about the drug use just about made me fall out of my chair. A Hells Angel isn't supposed to testify in open court about anybody doing drugs. Rooster felt that since it was a civil case and not a criminal one, it didn't matter. But it did.

I wasn't the only one pissed off. Sherry didn't want the drug use coming out. And of course she knew I was Rooster's supplier. She looked across the table at me. "It's on," she said. "He brought it up. It's wide open now, Pat." Stupid move by Rooster. During a break I talked to Sherry in the lobby, told her I had no idea Rooster would bring up drugs. I started to worry that Sherry would talk to the cops. Later, I'd find my concerns were justified. Sherry had gone right to Roy Green, the cop who'd been harassing me at the time.

At the clubhouse a few nights after the Brosh thing, it all just sort of came to a head with Rooster and me. The dealing drugs behind my back, the unwillingness to help me, the '97 court incident with Sherry—it just built up and I let him have it. "Fuck you, Rooster," I said to him. "You've been riding my coattails and living off my reputation for years and you've never done a goddamned thing on your own in your whole fucking life!" We argued and I ended up taking my patch and slamming it down on the table and walking out the door. I was ready to quit the Hells Angels. Richie came out with my patch and talked to me as I was sitting on my bike, trying to calm me down. Rooster eventually came out, too. Finally I took my patch back.

I never did do anything with Brosh. Or Ronnie Rowles for that matter. I knew those guys would be testifying but I decided I wasn't going to worry about them. There wasn't a lot of credibility in those two and when it came right down to it, all they could really say was that I'd threatened them for stealing bikes. They could talk about the cocaine, but where was the proof it had even existed?

Eason and the Weaver brothers were another story. They knew a lot about me. Still, they were trying to save their own asses when they made their statements to Chris and his guys. And that meant some embellishing. Yeah, I might have done some meth that night in Vegas, for example, and I might have lost fifty grand, but Brian didn't mention that twenty thousand of it was house money I'd won on the slots. And maybe I could be a demanding boss, but Mark Weaver knew I was a fair one, too. And that Crown Royal bag? There was nothing in there but Crown Royal.

If we cross-examined those guys on the witness stand, I figured we could put dents in their stories. But what was working against me was the sheer number of witnesses. One or two guys with questionable credentials is one thing. A parade of witnesses who had come to know me well was something else. And the charge of running a continuing criminal enterprise was still on the table. To prove CCE, the prosecution would have to show, among other things, that I had supervised or worked "in concert" with at least five other people. Did they have their five? Mike Eason, Brian Weaver, Mark Weaver … who else? Richard Rohda? Someone else I hadn't even thought of? The possibility seemed pretty strong to me.

I was fucked and there was just no way around it. Trial would be suicide. I called Jim Ostgard. I wanted to explore the possibilities of cooperating again. I hadn't made up my mind to do so, but I wanted to test the waters. But Ostgard got nowhere with Paulsen. He even had a letter hand-delivered to him, outlining some potential items I might consider talking about. Apparently he'd talked to Caplan who'd suggested the items from our talk in San Francisco. In the letter, Ostgard reminded Paulsen of what the cost of my potential cooperation would really be for me: "There is no question in my mind that what Mr. Matter is willing to do will seriously put his life at risk," he wrote. But Paulsen was still playing hard to get. Still biding his time.

And so I waited for the next court date where I would re-enter

My motorcycle shop, Minneapolis Custom Cycle.

Completed motorcycles ready to be shipped.

my guilty plea and hope for the best from Judge James Rosenbaum. I tried to keep busy. The shop was still going strong and we even used the time to move the business into a larger building. The work kept my mind off things. I suppose there was a little denial going on; I even tried to tell myself that somehow Rosenbaum would change his mind and decide to accept the original ten-year deal. And even if the sentence was twelve years, I was sure I could get out sooner.

Finally the sentencing date was set: November 25. A few nights before the court date, we threw a big party at the Star Bar. It was my going-away party and Hells Angels from all around the country showed up. Part of the reason for the party was to help defray the cost of my legal fees. We sold t-shirts and raffled off jewelry and ended up with about $40,000. The next day I donated several thousand dollars to the Children's Hospital.

And the club, in a gesture of honor, painted a mural on the front wall of the clubhouse. It was a painting of me with Rooster and Sonny

Barger, taken from a photograph someone had snapped during the USA Run in Iowa back in 1995. Then El Forastero Fat Steve Larson came by my shop and gave me a big gold and diamond "1%" pendant. Must have cost at least three grand. "Our club wanted you to have this," he said. "We know you're going through some shit and we wanted to give this to you out of respect."

1995 USA Run, Okoboji, Iowa. L-R: Rooster, Sonny and Me.

On the morning of the 25th, Trish and I drove to court with Alan Caplan who had stayed at our house the night before. We stopped along the way and dropped Connor off at a friend's house. Connor was four and I knew he didn't understand what was happening. I hugged him as I left him with our friends and told him I loved him and hoped like hell he didn't notice my eyes watering up. "Be a good boy," I told him, "and I'll see you soon." But I knew Connor would most likely be a teenager before I'd see him outside the walls of a prison.

When we arrived at the courthouse we met up with Jim Ostgard and Caplan turned to me and said, "Now, Pat, we just want you to be prepared. Technically, Rosenbaum could give you as much as twenty-two years." *What?* Where the fuck did that come from? I couldn't recall either one of those guys mentioning that to me before. I glared at them both.

Inside the courtroom, Trish took a seat next to Cole. I noticed a lot of friends in the gallery. But I had asked the Hells Angels guys not to come by. I wanted them there; I needed their support. It went without saying how much I loved the club. But I knew the presence of the Hells Angels in the courtroom would have pissed Rosenbaum off.

Judge Rosenbaum came in and after some preliminaries, he began talking about "penalty enhancement for leadership role." This was bad and I knew it. It meant he could add years to the sentence because I was the leader of a criminal organization. But even Paulsen had to admit to Rosenbaum that my leadership wasn't anything the prosecution could prove. Sure, you could prove I dealt drugs, but nobody could prove I was the ringleader of a criminal organization. Paulsen didn't make his admission to the judge out of the goodness of his heart. Paulsen was concerned, and rightfully so, that a sentence handed down on questionable grounds could be appealed more easily. Rosenbaum didn't seem to care.

"I had the pleasure this morning," Rosenbaum said, "of reviewing Mr. Matter's website which might suggest he has an interest in a particular organization." The shop website was aimed at my customer base. We called ourselves the Bad Boys of Manufacturing and portrayed an outlaw image. My picture was posted with an "America's Most Wanted" caption. It was marketing. It was our brand. I had a sort of slogan that we printed everywhere: *Defying Rules and Tradition, I am the REAL DEAL. Pat Matter.* People loved it. We sold a ton of t-shirts just from the website alone.

Of course the whole thing rubbed Rosenbaum the wrong way.

He associated it directly with the club and in his mind, the Hells Angels was a criminal organization. I'd find out later he learned about the going-away party, too. He didn't care for that, either. I guess he thought it was a wise-ass thing to do, have a party on the eve of being sentenced to prison. And clearly he didn't let the donation to the Children's Hospital get in the way of his opinion of me.

"It is clear to this court," Rosenbaum continued, "that Mr. Matter instructed, he led, and he directed others in the distribution of drugs. He was the recipient of a portion of the profits of sales by other individuals, and there were at least five." And then he named the five: "Michael Eason, Mark Armstrong, Bradley Armstrong, Paul Seydel, and Richard Rohda. He was clearly an organizer and director of a drug dealing conspiracy."

Then he turned to me. "Sir, you have done a lot of very bad things. I am putting you in jail, the jail which you have earned. And though I feel bad for you, I feel worse for your family. But you know very well who imposed your sentence. It's based upon your acts and yours alone. The order of this court will be 210 months." And then Judge Rosenbaum stood and recessed the court.

I walked, shell-shocked, over to Trish who was crying and I hugged her and I hugged Cole and then they led me out of the courtroom while I did some quick math in my head. Two-hundred and ten months was seventeen and a half years. By the time I'd be released from prison, I'd be close to seventy years old.

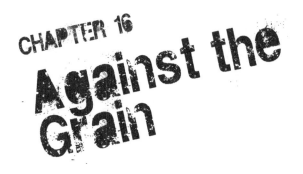

CHAPTER 16
Against the Grain

In the Anoka County Jail, I started thinking about the chain of events that had led to my sentence. There was plenty of time to think, after all. I remembered back to when Paulsen had called Caplan in December of 2001, asking if I wanted to come in and proffer. Fuck no, I had said. I was no rat. But maybe I could have given them something. Anything. I could have pled. I could have at least admitted to the two kilos of cocaine that they knew were mine from the Armstrong thefts and I probably would have gotten no more than five years.

Alan Caplan and Jim Ostgard came and talked to me. Both thought I had solid grounds for appeal because of Rosenbaum's enhancement for leadership role. No one had proven the Hells Angels was a criminal organization and as far as a leadership role, the Hells Angels was all Rosenbaum could tie me to. Caplan said he'd start writing up the appeal. But then he cautioned me: "Pat, solid grounds or not, less than five percent of criminal convictions in federal court are reversed on appeal." And then, turning to me before he left, obviously still more concerned about his larger duty to the club, he added, "You know, Pat, if you start thinking about cooperating again, you can't call me. I can't be your lawyer anymore."

Trish came to see me. She was devastated. And I wondered how I was going to live without her for the next seventeen and a half years. Would she be there at the end of the sentence? Deep down I believed that she would have stuck it out for the original ten years. She loved me, really loved me. But seventeen years was a lot to ask. I knew I'd never be able to blame her if she bailed. I'd survive her leaving, but I knew it would be heartbreaking. But that's the way it goes. When you love someone, you get hurt. That was one of the three truisms I had learned over the years. In my time, I had also learned that when you're real, everyone hates you for it. And when you trust, you get killed.

Trish told me that on the day of the sentencing, later in the afternoon, she'd gone to the shop. Rooster was there. He was taking motorcycle parts. Rooster told her the parts were his and that I had said he could take them. "Pat's only been gone a few hours!" she told him. I was infuriated. Just one more thing about Rooster that pissed me off.

Over the course of the next several weeks, my thoughts were all over the place. But being an old man before I'd see Trish or Connor on the outside again, if I ever saw them again at all, was the one thing that kept pushing itself into my mind. And while Thanksgiving came and went and then Christmas, I sat in my cell and thought about Brian Weaver and Mark Weaver and Mike Eason and God only knew who else—Richard Rohda, I was sure—who hadn't hesitated to turn on me. And I wondered why I was being such a hard ass about cooperating, what code it was that I was really clinging to, why it went so against the grain for me to think about ratting out people who probably wouldn't think twice about ratting me out. *No snitches in the club.* I loved the club. Did the club feel the same way about me? Rooster was in my shop before my body was even cold. Caplan? He was ready to send me off on a tuna boat and forget all about me.

In the end, it all came down to Trish and Connor. I hadn't been the best father in the world to my other kids. I had tried to keep in touch with Joe and Nikki and Chad from my marriage to Jackie as best I could. They'd all come up to spend a month with me every summer and I tried to call them every other week or so the rest of the year. I'd send Jackie money for clothes for the kids, too. But looking back, I knew I could have been more involved. Cole, of course, had spent time with Trish and me after Leslie had gone to prison. Even still, there were times in his life when I just hadn't been there. With Connor, I had the chance to be a good father, to be really involved in his life. But now I was facing the possibility of missing most of his childhood. With

Trish, I had found true love. Without Trish and Connor, I could have strapped thirty years to my back and carried it for the sake of the code. But there were other standards now. Other principles to live my life by. Fuck the code. Fuck the seventeen and a half years.

I couldn't call Caplan, he'd made that clear. But at the end of December of 2003, I called Jim Ostgard. "Jim," I said, "Let Paulsen know I'm willing to make a deal."

Sonny and Connor at my house. The choice to cooperate
didn't come easy. Sonny was a good friend.

CHAPTER 17
A Deal's A Deal

When Judge Rosenbaum rejected the plea deal we'd made with Pat, just about everyone on the prosecution side was beaming. Pat was the bad guy, after all, and hearing Rosenbaum take away Pat's ten years to make possible a much longer sentence made a bunch of guys who had worked on the case smile. And if Pat turned around and saw that, then I can imagine it must have seemed pretty personal to him. But I wasn't one of the guys beaming. We'd made a deal and I felt like shit that Rosenbaum had scuttled it.

Jeff Paulsen wasn't thrilled either. The judge hadn't promised a longer sentence; what he'd said was that he was ready to see the case go to trial. And with a trial, anything can happen. Juries are notoriously unpredictable. That's the reason you make a deal in the first place—to hedge your bets. And we were far from being ready for trial. Outside the courtroom, Pat and his attorneys walked down the hallway to talk to Jeff while I stood there and noticed Trish glaring at me with roughly the same expression that Pat had on his face. I wanted to crawl under a rock.

Between that day in April and the sentencing in November, we stayed busy. We had to be ready in case Pat changed his mind and decided to go to trial. We were still investigating and still working on witnesses, chief among them being Richard Rohda. Mike Eason was good, the Weavers were good. But Richard Rohda knew more about Pat's operation than anyone and he was also a Hells Angel, though we'd heard from an informant that he had been recently kicked out of the club.

We also had Sherry, Paul "Rooster" Seydel's wife. But she wasn't helping much. Yes, she was talking to Deputy Supposedly, Roy Green, but she wasn't saying much. He brought her in one time so that I could interview her. She showed up with her sister Diane who kept asking me questions about my personal life. "Are you single?" she said. "What do you do for fun?" I'd have been flattered if I had been stupid enough to think she wasn't trying to compromise me. Meanwhile, the real interviewing that day was being done by Sherry. All she wanted to do was question me about Seydel. "What's going to happen to Rooster?" she'd ask. "What do you have on him?" It was a waste of time.

There was, by then, no doubt in anyone's mind about the extent of Pat's drug distribution business. When he says he shut things down when the heat was on, he wasn't kidding. We could tell when those times came about. There would be pockets of time—six or nine months—where our undercover guys couldn't buy meth from anybody in the Twin Cities. Such was Pat Matter's stranglehold on the drug trade.

In February, Richard had been arrested again, this time for VIN switching and in May, just a month after Pat's plea deal had been rejected, he was sentenced to twenty-one months, the sentence to begin on June 30th. At three o'clock one morning in late May we received a 911 call from his residence. Richard, free on bond, had gotten into an argument with his wife. She was planning to sell the house and leave him as soon as his prison term started. In frustration and desperation, he pulled a gun and said he was going to kill himself. Then he walked into the laundry room where his wife heard a single gunshot. She dialed 911 but then hung up after Richard walked out of the laundry room unhurt. When two of our cops arrived, Richard was arrested for felon in possession of a firearm.

In jail the next morning, I went to talk to him. "Richard, Richard, Richard," I said. "What were you thinking?" Richard's world was falling apart. He was losing his wife, he'd been kicked out of the Hells Angels, he lost his job at Minneapolis Custom Cycle, and he was headed to federal prison. He began to sob. "Do you think maybe it's time to talk?" I said. He nodded.

We walked across the street to our investigative office and I interviewed him along with Bob Bushman and Detective Dave "Frenchy" Giguere. Richard told us a lot about Pat's drug dealing and a lot about the Hells Angels. Pat would get ten to twenty pounds of meth at a time. The guys in the club would buy what they wanted (Richard would typically take two pounds himself) either paying for it up front, or having Pat front them until they could turn around and sell what they took. Bushman asked Richard point blank if drug dealing was a big part of the Hells Angels business.

"Oh, yeah," Richard said. "But there's an unwritten rule that you can't go around with a drug dealer. It would make things bad for the club." It was more or less what I had come to believe about the Hells Angels. It wasn't a drug dealing organization per se, with the Hells Angels directing, as a club, the sale and distribution of large quantities of illegal drugs. But if you're a wannabe drug dealer, what better place to access like-minded people, every one of them, so far as I could tell, involved with buying and selling? And every one sworn to a code of silence.

We asked Richard about what Pat was thinking in terms of his pending sentencing. "He doesn't know exactly what he's going to do yet, if he's going to stay here or if he's going to leave," Richard said.

"Where would he go?" asked Bushman.

"He told me someplace where there ain't no extradition. And he has the money to do it."

"Where does he have the money?"

"Buried." Then Richard went on to tell us a story almost identical to Eason's story about helping Pat bury a large quantity of cash in his backyard.

I wondered about the risk of Pat taking off. I figured maybe he'd been considering that option. Bones, the Hells Angel with the tuna boat in San Francisco, was Alfred Abono, long-time club member and former president of the Richmond chapter. The guy was a large-scale marijuana dealer who once lived in a swanky house in Concord, California. I can't say, of course, but Pat was probably wise not to get on Abono's boat with a million dollars.

We started questioning Richard about getting kicked out of the club and he was clearly bitter about it. Bushman asked him if he'd be willing to testify against any of the members. Like, say, Pat. Or Rooster. Richard hemmed and hawed.

"Look," said Bushman, "the way I see it is that these guys have really done nothing for you. And you've been one of the more loyal members." Richard nodded thoughtfully. Then he said he'd testify for a grand jury but that he'd have to think about actually testifying in court against Pat Matter. But he agreed to set up a certain marijuana dealer for us. And he agreed to meet with us the next day at 9:00 a.m. Then he was released.

The next morning, 9:00 a.m. came and went. So did 10:00. So did 11:00. Dave Giguere and I drove to Richard's house. His car was in the driveway and I noticed his cell phone on the seat. We started banging on the door of the house but nobody answered. The whole scene just didn't seem right to me and I called the captain back at the station for permission to enter the premises. "Don't you dare break in," he said. I hung up and Dave and I looked at each other and decided we'd apologize to the captain later. We were going in.

Outside the garage, I noticed a well-used keypad for entrance. Richard was a grease monkey and it wasn't hard to see which keys had been hit and which hadn't. The problem was punching the dirty ones in the right order. Miraculously, the second combination I tried worked and the garage door went up. Dave and I entered the house and looked around the first floor, calling for Richard and getting no answer. Then we went upstairs where we saw him lying on a couch, unconscious, gurgling, vomit running down his shirt. I rubbed my knuckles along his sternum, a test for responsiveness, and got nothing. He'd stopped breathing. I cleared his airway and we called for an ambulance which arrived in minutes. Richard had overdosed on pills and beer and was barely alive.

Richard's suicide attempt landed him in the ICU for several days, but he recovered. I don't think he would have made it if we had arrived even one minute later. Following the hospital stay, he was treated for depression. At that point, he was so grateful we'd saved his life, he decided he'd work with us in any way he could. I felt bad for Richard. He'd been abandoned by his wife and by the Hells Angels, an organization he'd truly loved being a part of. In truth, we were the only friends he had left.

Now we had Mike Eason, Brian and Mark Weaver, Richard Rohda, and others. Pat was smart to stick with the guilty plea. Richard told us something else, too. Back in May, during his statement the day before his suicide attempt, we'd asked him about Pat's Filthy Few patch. Had Pat killed anyone? Paulsen, of course, had made a history clear of murder a condition of the ten-year plea deal. Richard had said he wasn't sure. But during an informal prep session at the U.S. Attorney's office a few months later, in August, we asked Richard again. "Yeah," Richard said, "in North Carolina. That's how he got his Filthy Few patch. Lightning Les was the only other guy who knew about it."

Had I been on my toes that day I would have remembered that Lightning Les had been killed way back in July of 1980, two years before Pat had even become patched as a Hells Angel. But when North Carolina was mentioned, we surmised Richard was referring to the incident at the Electric Keg in Charleston when Pat and Rooster got in the fight with the sailors.

In the statement Richard had given to us back in May, he had told us that he'd helped Pat dig up a gun one time that he'd kept hidden. The gun had a silencer. According to Richard, Pat said he'd used the gun years before. But of course all I could find with respect to the Electric Keg incident was the charge for assault. And by then, I'd figured out the truth about the Filthy Few patches anyway. I knew that the numbers didn't add up; too many people were wearing Filthy Few patches for the amount of killings. Richard himself had told us back in his May statement that in 1997, at the Sturgis Rally, Sonny Barger was handing the patches out like candy. He figured two hundred or so had been given out. Of course Pat had received his Filthy Few patch long before that. I had to consider the possibility that Pat had killed for the club, but I could find no evidence to back up Richard's claim. For me, it was a non-issue. Pat might have viewed it differently.

By then, we were going after Pat's suppliers. We knew about Brad

Jacobsen, of course, and also about Brad's partner A.J. Delbosque. Together, they were probably the biggest dope dealers in the state of Minnesota. Delbosque had recently died of a heart attack but Jacobsen had carried on. He was a high-roller, globetrotting to places like Amsterdam and Frankfurt and Switzerland. We knew that if Pat ever decided to cooperate, he'd be a key to taking Jacobsen down.

We wanted Paul "Rooster" Seydel, too. He was the last of the guys we'd been surveilling at Dewey Selin's shop who was still out and about. And we knew how close he'd been to Pat, though we didn't realize at the time that a rift had formed between the two. We executed a search warrant on Seydel's house and Shoup was questioning him at his kitchen table and I overheard Seydel talk about selling drugs and was surprised to hear him say, "But I'm not as big as Pat."

On November 25, I felt an inch tall all over again. Like Pat, I was expecting something around a twelve-year sentence. But Judge James Rosenbaum's very demeanor that day had me soon thinking it was going to be more and when he started talking about Pat's leadership role in the Hells Angels, I knew Pat was screwed. I watched Pat hug Trish and then watched as he was led away for seventeen and half years and once again I wanted to find a rock to crawl under.

A few weeks later, Pat called Ostgard, and on December 30, we sat down with Pat and Ostgard in Jeff Paulsen's office. It was Rainville, Shoup, Billings, and me. Jeff wasn't necessarily thrilled that everyone was there, but we all had our questions for Pat, too.

Pat began to talk. He seemed nervous and uncomfortable. I could tell it was exceedingly difficult for him to be cooperating with law enforcement. But he was honest, if not completely forthcoming. "I'll answer your questions," he said, "but I'm not going to volunteer anything unless it's specifically asked."

And so the questioning began. Pat confirmed names. He gave us his Texas and California sources, the ones he refused to name in front of Rosenbaum. But his main suppliers had indeed been Brad Jacobsen and A.J. Delbosque, also known as George and George. When they were in town with a supply of meth for Pat, they'd call his shop from a payphone. Typically, it was Jacobsen. "It's George," he'd say, and then they'd arrange a place to meet, usually at a hotel. Pat would be given a key to a car in the parking lot where he'd retrieve the meth from the trunk in a gym bag and then leave the key on the floorboard. The financial transaction would come later, separately. Drugs and money never changed hands at the same time.

Pat would take the meth and deliver it to club members: Rohda and Rankin and Seydel and others. But nothing much happened at the clubhouse. Members might have talked discreetly, but Pat feared the presence of bugging devices. "We'd talk in little huddles," he said, "outside in the back courtyard of the clubhouse or in more open areas—parks, and by the river." Pat sold to Mark and Brad Armstrong as well. And he admitted to laundering money through Minneapolis Custom Cycle.

A month later, we sat down with him again, this time at the Anoka County Jail, and took another statement. Pat was ready to testify in court.

With Pat, we finally had enough to nail Jacobsen and Seydel. In March of 2004, Pat testified in front of a grand jury. In August, he would testify against both Jacobsen and Seydel in federal court, the two being tried jointly. Jeff Paulsen didn't want to go to trial twice. He figured both could be found guilty in the same proceedings.

A week before the trial was to begin, I got a call from Jeff. "Chris, I need you to come to my office. As soon as possible." Jeff's office was across the street. I went right over. "Chris," he said, "I'm going to need you to second-chair the case for me." The second chair acts as a sort of second prosecutor; it's the top support position. The responsibility is huge. In a federal trial, it's almost always a federal agent. I knew IRS agent Jim Shoup had been slated for second chair.

"Me?" I said. "I mean, sure. But why? Where's Jim?"

"We got a little problem with Jim. He just came to see me. You know Brad Jacobsen's wife?"

I nodded.

"Well, Jim's been having an affair with her."

It was a stunning and unfortunate turn of events. Somewhere along the line, in the course of our investigation, Jim had come to know Donna, Jacobsen's wife, and the two began seeing each other. Jim was going through a bitter divorce at the time, with a custody dispute. He was lonely, depressed. Needless to say, Donna, wife of an accused drug dealer facing years in prison, had problems of her own. But of course the affair was wildly inappropriate. Not only would we lose Jim as second chair, we'd lose him as a witness. His credibility had been severely compromised; the defense would shred him upon cross-examination, throwing the affair in his face and making the jurors question anything he'd have to say.

I filled in for Shoup. In August of 2004, we went to trial in the federal courthouse in St. Paul. The media was all over it. "The Drug Dealer who Supplied the Hells Angels" was how Jacobsen was described in the headlines. With Seydel as a Hells Angels member being tried at the same time, and with Pat Matter as Hells Angels chapter president breaking the club code and testifying against both, the case drew national interest.

Well-represented in the courtroom was the national interest of the Hells Angels, too. Members from all around came to see the trial, in full colors. On the first day I was walking into the courtroom with Tom Billings. Tom was battling pancreatic cancer, a battle he would ultimately lose. Keith Hare from the Minnesota chapter called out to him. "Hey, Billings, I hear ya got cancer. Well, it couldn't happen to a nicer guy." I felt myself seething. That was personal and it was way over the line. I wanted to say something but I saw that Tom had managed a smile and had just kept walking. I bit my tongue and kept walking, too.

When Pat got up on the stand to testify, the Hells Angels in the gallery did what Hells Angels do to witnesses in court. They stared him down. Pat tried not to make eye contact, but I know he had to feel the glares. He'd been in prison for close to ten months by then and he looked pale. It probably made him appear more nervous than he was, but it sure as hell couldn't have been comfortable up there for him. But once he got going, he seemed fine. His words were clear and his testimony convincing.

Jacobsen's attorney was Earl Gray, a big-name defense attorney in St. Paul. He tried to discredit Pat by getting Pat to reveal his criminal past and to talk about all the money he'd made illegally. He showed the jury photographs of Pat's house and asked Pat how much he thought it was worth and how much the shop was worth. He asked Pat how much money he had put away. One by one he reiterated all the charges on Pat's original indictment and asked Pat if he was guilty on each of them. The strategy, of course, was to make Pat unsympathetic to the jury right from the start. From there, Gray attacked Pat's personal credibility. Pat held his own.

"All through your life, you've never told the truth to anybody, isn't that right, Mr. Matter?" Gray asked.

"I don't know who that's according to," Pat replied.

"Well, for instance, you got married two years ago, correct?"

"Yes, I did."

"Within two weeks you were out in Las Vegas with prostitutes, weren't you?"

"Prostitutes? No."

"Well, let's go on to your business. All through your life your business has been a lie, correct? From the get-go the money that you used for any of your businesses was either drug money or stolen parts money, correct? You haven't really earned any money, have you?"

"I don't know what you call earning."

"Earning money would be a legitimate job."

"Okay."

"And throughout your life, you've been involved in many assaults on people, is that right?"

"I've had some barroom brawls, yes."

"Barroom brawls with the Hells Angels. It's usually all you guys against one or two people, correct?"

"I don't know about that. Hells Angels pride themselves on one-on-one fighting."

Gray picked out some minor details about the arrest and about Pat's drug dealing and statements he'd made to the police and about dates and times, some of which Pat naturally had trouble remembering.

"Hard to remember all your lies, sir?" Gray accused. He was doing what defense attorneys do. But about the specifics of Pat's testimony against Jacobsen and Seydel, Gray didn't have anything he could attack. The testimony was true; all he could do was attempt to impugn Pat's character.

I testified, too. I wasn't exactly new to it. I'd testified in federal court a lot over the years. I liked it. I've often said that it's on the witness stand where a detective really learns his job. There's nothing quite like being grilled by a defense attorney over evidence to make you learn to be diligent and careful about how you handle an investigation. You need to cross all the "T"s and dot all the "I"s and being attacked on a witness stand in a federal court is a great way to confirm—or disconfirm—your methodologies. It's a hell of a classroom.

I knew Earl Gray from prior cases going back twenty years and he knew me. But that didn't stop him on cross-examination from purposely misstating my rank and mispronouncing my name.

"Now, Deputy Omt," he began.

"That's Detective," I corrected. "And it's Omodt. You know that, Earl."

Gray smiled and said, "Of course. Now, Detective Omt …." I let it slide. I knew he was trying to rattle me. But it would have taken a lot more than that.

With the Hells Angels present, tensions around the federal courthouse ran high. During a recess, a marshal walked by the seat where one of the Hells Angels had been sitting in the gallery—Richie from the Minnesota chapter. The marshal noticed a residue. A bomb-sniffing dog was brought in and when the dog alerted to the residue, the courthouse was immediately evacuated. Turned out that Richie had been on some kind of special diet. He'd been perspiring. And whatever it was that he was on began to sweat out of his pores, leaving the residue on the seat. We laughed about it later, but it was a pretty serious atmosphere around the federal building for the duration of the trial.

One night, on the way home from the courthouse, I happened to pass by the Hells Angels clubhouse. The mural that Pat mentioned—the one of him with Sonny Barger and Rooster—had been defaced. It was an inside job. The painting was intact but for one thing—a big, freshly painted black spot took the place of where Pat's face used to be.

In the end, the jury deadlocked. It was disappointing. We'd have to retry the case in front of a new jury. Seydel had had enough. He decided to plead rather than risk another jury. Jacobsen decided to stick it out and we began to try the case again in January of 2005. We still had Pat's testimony, but wished we had more. A smoking gun of some description. As the second trial got underway, I started thinking about the phone logs we had from Minneapolis Custom Cycle. And about Jacobsen's extensive traveling. We had his records: flight records, U.S. Customs records, hotel information, and rental car reservations. I put together a detailed spreadsheet. I considered the timing of the incoming calls to M.C.C. from "George." Detective Rainville and I reconciled them with Jacobsen's travel itinerary. It all lined up perfectly. Every single time "George" called Pat's shop, Brad Jacobsen was in town. Without exception. And at no time—without exception—did "George" ever call when Brad Jacobsen was out of town. We had him dead to rights.

During a recess, Paulsen took the spreadsheet to Gray. Gray huddled with Jacobsen. When the judge returned to the courtroom, Gray stood. "Your honor, we'd like to approach." Then he told the judge what we had hoped: "My client would like to change his plea, your honor." Brad Jacobsen was subsequently sentenced to fourteen years.

Now it was our turn to help Pat Matter. Back in front of Judge James Rosenbaum, Paulsen asked for a downward departure on behalf of Pat under Rule 35: a court may reduce a sentence if the defendant provides substantial assistance in investigating or prosecuting another person. Pat's sentence was reduced from seventeen and a half years to twelve years but I was still thinking about the original ten years that Rosenbaum had dismissed. The original deal we had made. Now that Pat had testified in open court, there had to be other cases where he could do the same.

About that time I got wind that the case for what became known as the River Run Riot was coming to trial in Las Vegas. In April of 2002, at the Laughlin River Run, an annual motorcycle rally in Laughlin, Nevada, a riot broke out between members of the Hells Angels and members of the Mongols motorcycle club. Dozens of members from both clubs fought it out in Harrah's casino. One Mongol was stabbed to death and two Hells Angels were shot to death. There were multiple injuries. The subsequent investigation led to forty-two Hells Angels indictments, including for murder, drug distribution, money laundering, pretty much anything. It was shaping up to be a real mega-trial and I wondered if maybe the prosecution could benefit by having an ex-Hells Angel president on hand to testify, to give some background and expertise on how one-percenter clubs operate. I had a contact in Nevada in the International Outlaw Motorcycle Gang Investigators Association and I called him up. "I've got somebody here, if you think the prosecution could use a witness who pretty much knows everything about the Hells Angels. A chapter president."

My contact said he'd make a couple inquiries. Within an hour two federal prosecutors from the case had called back. "Sure," they said. "We'll take him."

Pat agreed to go. In the end, his testimony in Nevada would help shave two more years off his sentence. It would come at a price. Again, he was breaking the code. Pat would ultimately have to go into witness protection. But his sentence would be reduced to ten years and that's all I'd really wanted. After all, a deal's a deal.

CHAPTER 18
WITSEC

Yeah, a deal's a deal, but it sure as hell took a lot for me to get that one. Three times prosecutor Jeff Paulsen promised ten years. The first two times the promise was broken, with Rosenbaum rejecting the initial plea agreement and, after I testified, Paulsen telling me the downward departure he would ask for would definitely result in the original ten years. It didn't. Rosenbaum came back with twelve and it was only because of my trip to Vegas to testify at the River Run Riot trial that I was able to get the ten. And even then it was only because I insisted on getting Paulsen's promise in writing. In fact, I had to insist on the downward departure in the first place. Paulsen dragged his feet. I imagine he and Chris and the rest wanted to stretch it out as far as possible, try to find somewhere else they could use me, get as much out of me as they could before giving me anything in return. I'd made the mistake all along of assuming the government would live up to its promises. Bad assumption.

Looking back, it seems pretty clear that Paulsen knew all along that Rosenbaum was going to reject the ten-year deal. Chris says the Filthy Few patch was a non-issue. I'm not so sure. Paulsen's a smart guy. I think he made sure Rosenbaum knew that I wore the patch and what the patch meant. Chris couldn't find any evidence that I'd ever killed anyone because I hadn't. Why did I have a Filthy Few patch? Because Rooster ordered us a couple. That was all it took. And then Richard said something to Chris about an incident involving Lightning Les which was pretty damn convenient since Lightning Les was dead and unavailable to confirm it. And when it counted, when he was under oath in front of the grand jury, Richard didn't say a thing about it.

But the fact that there was no evidence that I'd ever killed isn't what made its way to Judge Rosenbaum. When Rosenbaum rejected the deal, he was operating under the assumption that he was dealing with a murderer, an assumption Paulsen had no interest in dispelling. Paulsen knew I wasn't going to roll for ten years. He needed more. Rosenbaum gave it to him. That's the way these guys operate. It's underhanded and dishonest and they play around with years of your life but they rationalize it to themselves because in their minds the ends justify the means.

The day I sat down with Paulsen, Chris, Rainville, Shoup, and Billings was the worst day of my life. I didn't trust any of them and I was giving up so much of what I'd loved and believed in over the course of twenty-one years as a Hells Angels president. It was a sickening feeling. But I told the truth about everything they asked. I knew I had to; they knew it all anyway. They had statements from Eason and Rohda and the Weavers. All I did was add my confirmation.

In January of 2004, I was moved from the Anoka County Jail to Waseca Federal Prison, seventy-five miles outside of Minneapolis. In March, I was transported back to Anoka so that I could testify in front of the grand jury. It was no secret that I was in Anoka. The club was nervous, thinking that I was rolling. Richie came to visit. "Pat, man, what the fuck's going on? What are you doing back in Anoka?"

"I'll be pleading the Fifth," I told him. "It's okay." But I didn't plead the Fifth. And then in late August, I was returned to Anoka once again, to be closer to the federal courthouse for the trial of Jacobsen and Seydel.

During the trial, Hells Angels members sat in the very front row. Sure, I felt their glares. But what made me most uncomfortable went beyond the glares. Behind their eyes I could feel their sense of betrayal. I'd loved these guys. I'd have died for them. And I hated what I was doing. Absolutely hated it.

Tom Rainville came to see me during a recess while I was being held in the marshal's tank. "Now, Pat," he said, "you gotta say the right things up there. We're counting on your testimony, you know."

"I'm telling it the way it was, Tom. I'm telling it the way it happened." I didn't need the lecture from Rainville and it pissed me off. I wanted to say something about young men in parks, but I let it go. I got a similar talk from Jim Shoup before the trial had started. Gotta tell the truth, he said. And then I came to learn about his affair with Jacobsen's wife. Jim Shoup was giving me a lesson on integrity? I'd already made up my mind that Paulsen was less than honest when he steered me to Rosenbaum. Then of course there was Billings who had broken into my house. And there was Roy Green who'd been stalking me. And Andy Shoemaker and the cops who continued to harass me and the club, going so far as to concoct a fake rape story. Even my attorneys had told me that the guys after me were "the worst of the worst." And it was *my* honesty that somehow they were all concerned about?

It was the revelation of Shoup's affair that I believe cost the prosecution that first trial. And the taxpayers a ton of money. Paulsen brought it up during his opening argument, trying to get it out on the table before the defense could make a big deal out of it. But it didn't help. I think the jury's opinion was tainted from that point on.

After my testimony, Waseca didn't want me back. They couldn't guarantee my safety. Paulsen wanted to put me in witness protection, the Federal Witness Security Program: WITSEC. I didn't want to go. I was fine with Waseca. I knew I could take care of myself. But Paulsen signed me up and they brought out a polygraph examiner from Washington, D.C., the first step towards WITSEC. They want to know a guy isn't looking to get into WITSEC under false pretenses, maybe looking to identify someone else in the program. I refused the polygraph test, effectively turning WITSEC down. It pissed Paulsen off, but at that point I really didn't care much about prosecutor Jeff Paulsen.

I stayed for a time, then, in Anoka. People there knew I had talked. One time a young kid, maybe twenty-seven or twenty-eight, looking to make a name for himself, came up to me in the dayroom and said, "You know, when you get out of jail, we're going to come looking for you." I didn't know who he meant by "we" but he made a bunch of noise like he was some tough-ass. I said I didn't think so and punched him so hard I knocked him out. He flew backwards and his head hit some concrete steps and it scared the hell out of me. I thought maybe I'd really fucked him up. He turned out to be okay, but for hitting him, I had to spend two weeks in the hole, locked down for twenty-three hours a day.

It was Jim Ostgard who approached me about testifying in Vegas. He'd talked about it back when we were still thinking my testimony against Seydel and Jacobsen would get me a downward departure to ten years instead of twelve. Two more years off for my testimony in Vegas would have meant eight. But of course, that's not the way it worked out. I wouldn't be surprised if Rosenbaum had known all along about Laughlin, giving me the twelve years instead of ten as an incentive for me to testify in Vegas.

At the hearing where he reduced the sentence to twelve years, Rosenbaum listened as Ostgard detailed the risks I had run by cooperating. "His concerns have been of his family," Ostgard said. "There's always going to be someone out there looking to harm Pat, and that's something he would not have had to live with if he had decided not to cooperate."

Rosenbaum was mostly unmoved. "It's appropriate to recognize what you have done with your cooperation," he said to me, "but all the saints in heaven can't make your history disappear, and I'm not inclined to do so either. But I will reduce the term to 144 months."

I hadn't attended the Laughlin River Run in 2002. That was after the search of my places and my arrest, and I'd been trying to keep a low profile by then. But I knew something was cooking with the Mongols. Earlier, I'd been in Daytona Beach on business, receiving the Component Bike Builder of the Year Award from *Easyriders* magazine. Dave Nichols, the editor, said, "Pat, I'm going to make you a millionaire." The publicity helped. We picked up a couple dealers around that time, too, including Kim Suter of K.C. Creations in Kansas City and Eddie Trotta of Thunder Cycle Design in Ft. Lauderdale. Dave's prediction came true. And it was all legitimate business.

Anyway, in Daytona Beach for the award, I had run into another bike builder, Johnny, who owned L.A. Choppers in California. Johnny was a Mongol. "Pat," he said, "we need to cool things down with our clubs before some bad shit happens. The Laughlin Run is coming up." I took the message back with me, but nobody seemed interested in listening. Things got ugly in Laughlin.

My knowledge of the Hells Angels-Mongols feud, along with my knowledge of the inner workings of the Hells Angels, along with my knowledge of outlaw motorcycle clubs in general, all became pretty valuable for the prosecutors in Vegas. Chris had an ATF agent by the name of John Ciccone fly up to talk to me. In return for my testimony, he guaranteed we'd be able to clip those two additional years off my sentence and get us back down to the ten. "I wish I'd have known about you before," he said. "I'd have had you down to ten from the very start." Ciccone spoke directly and honestly. By then I wasn't much in the mood to trust anybody. But for some reason I trusted Ciccone. I agreed to testify.

"But you'll have to go into WITSEC," Ciccone said.

"Then I need an assurance that I'll be sent to Sandstone." Only a few prisons around the country are set up for witness protection. I knew Sandstone was one of them, and at roughly a hundred miles from Minneapolis, I knew it was the closest one to Trish that I could get. Ciccone said he would see to it and Paulsen said he'd go back to Rosenbaum. And that's when I got the deal in writing. But we'd still need Rosenbaum to sign off on it.

The trip to Vegas was a model of efficiency. I was whisked to the airport in a van that was escorted by another van and two chase cars, cutting through traffic at eighty to ninety miles per hour. The accompanying agents were all armed with fully automatic weapons. At the airport, I was led onto the plane—a regular commercial flight—with an agent's jacket draped over my cuffed hands, and then seated in the back. When we touched down in Vegas the plane stopped short of the gate and the passengers were all told to remain seated while they led me up the aisle and down a gangway onto the tarmac where another van and a couple more chase cars were waiting for me. I can only imagine what the other passengers thought.

On the way to the jail where I was to be housed, in Henderson, just outside of Las Vegas, a marshal told me to make sure I didn't tell anyone my name. "We can't have your identity getting out," he said. At the jail, he led me inside and sat me down at a desk in a room where a woman was to take my information. Then he walked out the door.

"Name?" the woman asked.

"I can't give that to you." She looked up from her paperwork and repeated the request.

"I can't give you my name," I said again. Then she punched a buzzer and within moments a half dozen cops burst through the door.

"Won't give me his name," she said.

"Got us a wise-ass?" one of the cops said. Then they all moved closer to me and I was certain I was about to get my ass kicked. Fortunately the marshal was right outside the door and when he saw the commotion he came into the room.

"It's all right," he said. "We're gonna give him a name." I guess at that point the cops all put two and two together and figured out I was a government witness. I didn't have any more problems in the Henderson jail.

For five days I testified in Vegas. Forty-two Hells Angels were on trial and they were trying them in four separate groups. But the judge limited me on what I could say. I could only tell about my own experiences. I wasn't allowed to testify to anything that could be extended to the club as a whole. "It's like the Catholic Church," the judge explained. "The experience of one bad priest shouldn't be used to impugn other priests." The analogy brought a snicker from the courtroom. I'm guessing it's not often the Hells Angels are compared to the Catholic Church.

Alan Caplan was one of the attorneys for the defense. Because he'd been my attorney, he wasn't allowed to question me. Nor could I testify about my experience with him or about the $175,000 I'd paid him. But that didn't stop him from telling all the other defense attorneys just what to ask me.

I wasn't even allowed to testify accurately about the rules of the club. One of the prosecutors asked me directly about what the rules said about who wasn't allowed in the Hells Angels. "You can say 'no blacks,'" the judge told me, "but you can't say 'no niggers.'"

Six Hells Angels ended up being convicted and I was surprised it was that many, based on how far the judge bent over in favor of the club. Of course that was all right by me. I didn't feel quite as uncomfortable testifying as I had during the Jacobsen-Seydel trial. Maybe I'd gotten more used to it. Then again, I didn't really have to testify against anyone in particular, either.

At one point I was asked how many of the defendants then in the courtroom I knew. I knew all of them, but only one of them very well. And so I thought it was true enough to answer "Just one." The glares from the club members in the gallery kind of softened after that. I'm not sure how much my testimony helped the prosecution. I began to think that maybe the club had reached the judge, that he'd been paid off. Either way, I had done what I had promised to do and from Vegas, it was off to Sandstone. I was now in the Federal Witness Security Program.

I was also a hundred miles and ten years away from Trish. By then, I had given her power of attorney. "If in ten years you're still here, you're still here," I had told her. "I understand either way." If she wanted to, she could take everything I owned: the shop, the house, the cash I'd managed to hold onto. But the way I felt, if she left me, she might as well take everything anyway. Everything? Fuck. She and Connor were everything.

CHAPTER 19
A New Start

Pat had another condition for testifying in Vegas besides being moved to Sandstone. It was that we keep in touch with Trish for him. Keep an eye on her; make sure she was getting along okay. He asked me specifically. Little by little, Pat had come to trust me. I was glad. I knew how he felt about Trish and Connor and I found myself moved by it. Family is important to me and I wanted to do what I could to help Pat keep his intact. Ten years is a long time. My experience had been that women never wait around that long. If a guy goes to prison, you can bet good money that by the time he gets out, his wife or girlfriend will be long gone.

I was surprised by how restricted Pat was by the judge in the Vegas trial. He could barely say anything. I wondered why a judge would limit the testimony of someone with so much in-depth knowledge of the inner workings of the Hells Angels. There are cops who are experts on the Hells Angels; I'm one of them. But there's no amount of expertise that can compare with a twenty-one-year stint as chapter president. Like Pat, I too wondered about the judge's relationship with the defendants and what might have gone down behind the scenes. It's all speculation, of course, but it was just bizarre to a lot of us that Pat's testimony was as hampered as it was.

As for the first Jacobsen-Seydel trial, I saw it pretty much the way Pat saw it. The prosecution could never really overcome the Shoup revelation. Maybe there was more to it, who could say? But the affair sure didn't help. I felt bad for Jim. I had a lot of respect for him as an investigator and, more importantly, we'd become close friends. On the other hand, a whole bunch of us had poured our blood and sweat into the investigation and it was unconscionable that he'd risked the whole thing by allowing himself to get involved with Jacobsen's wife. Going through a tough divorce wasn't an adequate excuse. We were lucky the jury deadlocked and didn't instead issue a verdict of not guilty.

Soon after the Shoup affair, my chief deputy called me into her office and told me we could never work with Shoup again. It was an order, and one that I'd have to exercise just a few years later. In 2007, I was sent to head up the Minnesota Financial Crimes Task Force. Jim got wind of it and called me, wanting to come aboard. I beat around the bush and eventually said I didn't think it would be a good idea. We hung up and shortly afterwards Jim's boss called me on Jim's behalf. "Jim really wants to be on the task force," she said. I came clean and said I liked Jim but I'd lost faith in him. I didn't feel I could trust him. Besides, I had an explicit directive that we couldn't work with him.

Five minutes later, Jim called again. I guess his boss had just told him what I'd said because he was furious. "What the fuck, Chris?!" I said I was sorry, but I was just being honest and as far as him joining the task force, there really wasn't anything I could do. Jim hasn't spoken cordially to me since. There was one particularly awkward moment when we ran into each other at a state conference. I was getting an award for an insurance fraud case I'd initiated on a former Hells Angel. The case had eventually been kicked up to the federal level where none other than Jim Shoup had worked on it. He was getting an award, too. For the very same case. Small world. Sometimes too small.

As for Pat, I continued to keep in touch with Trish, as he'd requested. I was one of the few people on his call list. Trish, of course, was another. WITSEC is pretty strict about calls from the inmates to the outside world. I heard from Pat about once a month at the beginning, less frequently as time went along. A lot of times we ended up communicating through Trish.

I'd seen Pat in Anoka before WITSEC and learned about the incident where he'd knocked a guy unconscious—the kid who said something about coming to look for him after they got out. One of the jailers there said the kid deserved it. "Pat's been a model prisoner," he told me. "If everybody here was like Pat, we'd never have a problem. We didn't want to put him in solitary, but the regulations say we had to. But between you and me, we were all happy he'd punched the kid out."

The next time I saw Pat was about a year after he'd gone into Sandstone. By then I'd accepted a promotion to lieutenant and had moved into Internal Affairs where I would spend about three years. Back in 2003, the IRS had seized the Minneapolis Hells Angels clubhouse on the grounds that it had been used as a place to deal drugs and therefore to further a criminal enterprise. We'd joked about turning the building into a Fraternal Order of Police post, just for the irony. The Hells Angels sued to get the clubhouse back and the case finally made its way to civil court.

Jeff Paulsen was involved and so was Jim Alexander, an attorney from the U.S. Attorney's office. I became involved, too, although most of my time was taken by my work with Internal Affairs. In preparation for the trial we again interviewed Richard Rohda. We had to interview Pat, as well, and that meant making a trip to Sandstone. I knew that's where he was, though I'd been sworn to secrecy about it. It was my first experience with a WITSEC unit. To go there, we had to get clearance through Washington D.C., and it took almost two weeks to process all the paperwork. When we arrived, we were thoroughly searched. Sandstone WITSEC was the most secure, most serious place I'd ever seen in all my years of law enforcement.

If the IRS had had their way, I wouldn't have been involved in the trial at all. Jim Shoup had apparently tried to cut me out. One week before the trial I was officially interviewed. In the course of the interview it became clear how much I really knew about the Hells Angels and about what went on at the clubhouse. Of course Jeff Paulsen understood my level of knowledge but it was Alexander who was in charge of the case and Alexander had been busy working arm in arm with the IRS. Tied up in Internal Affairs, I had kind of slipped through the cracks. And unfortunately, a lot of what I could offer during the official interview couldn't be used. The discovery process had already taken place. Alexander was pissed the IRS hadn't involved me earlier and he made me second chair, effectively cutting the IRS out of their own case. We ended up losing that civil trial, unable to overcome the IRS bungling. The clubhouse was returned to the Hells Angels where the Minnesota chapter uses it to this day.

At the trial, I saw a lot of the Hells Angels I had come to know over the years. They'd come to know me, too. During a break I went into the courthouse cafeteria and saw Southside Billy sitting at a table by himself and I grabbed a cup of coffee and sat down across from him. "Hey, Billy," I said. Billy's health had recently deteriorated and he had to make use of an electric scooter to get around. Strange sight, when you're used to thinking of these guys riding Harleys.

"Hey, Omodt," he said. "How ya doin'?" We made small talk and then finally Billy said, "You know, Omodt, I just want to apologize."

"For what, Billy?"

"For my life."

"What do you mean?"

"The whole Hells Angels thing. The drugs. The brawls. But you know, I had just come back from Vietnam and I didn't have a friend in the world. These guys looked out for me. It's the only brotherhood I'd ever known."

"You don't have to apologize to me, Billy. I get it."

"You're the only cop I ever met who does."

"Well, I guess it's never been personal for me. Just my job, you know?"

Billy got quiet and then said, "You're a nice guy, Omodt."

"Thanks, Billy. It's all I really know." It was a nice moment and I was glad to be able to underscore my feelings that investigating these guys was never anything personal. I respected them as people, notwithstanding their criminal behavior. I could separate the sins from the sinners, as they say. Not making it personal wasn't always a two-way street, as the comment from Keith Hare to Tom Billings at the Jacobsen-Seydel trial demonstrated.

Billings died from his cancer shortly after that trial. Towards the end he was under hospice care at his home with his wife. Once a week, I would get a bunch of the guys together and we'd go visit him. Jeff Paulsen would come along, too. Tom was one of the hardest-working cops I'd ever known. He could have retired years before, but he loved being a cop too much.

L-R: Jeff Paulsen, Tom Billings and me visiting Tom
shortly before he passed away.

About that time, I started thinking about my own retirement. I was closing in on my fifties. I remember, as a young cop, seeing guys working through their fifties and on into their sixties. Old-timers. For the most part, they all seemed ornery and miserable to me. Tom Billings was an exception, and so was Don Enger, my old mentor back in the Edina, P.D. They loved being cops. But that wasn't the case for most of the old guys and I had promised myself I'd be careful with my money and get out relatively young. Back in 1994, I'd gone back to school part time and had gotten a degree in business management, just to keep my options open. I figured a few more years of detective work and I'd be on my way out.

It was in 2007 that I was sent to the financial crimes task force. My job was to oversee the place. It needed it. What I found when I got there was a mess. The property room was a disaster. Evidence was routinely commingled. There were basically no policies or procedures in place and it took me about a year to straighten everything out. About six months later, I was promoted to captain and sent downtown to oversee the jail. I appreciated the promotion and was grateful for the bump in salary, but I can't say I cared much for the setting. There were over 350 employees and a prison population of well over 600 on any given day. I was happy when, six months later, I was asked to be commander of the Metro Gang Strike Force, a multiagency task force created to battle gang problems and drug-related crime.

But what I found there was worse than what I'd found at the financial crimes task force. Based on my experience there, I'd requested an audit of the Strike Force as a condition of taking the position, but due to a lot of foot-dragging, the audit didn't take place until after I came in. One day into it, the auditors ushered me into a conference room and closed the door and told me what they were finding. Evidence was commingled, case files were missing or nonexistent or completely devoid of content. The property room was a free-for-all. Yellow sticky notes were posted on seized property with the names of the cops who were claiming the property as their own whenever the cases would be finished up. When search warrants had been executed, seemingly anything of value had been seized. Some of the seized property couldn't even be accounted for.

I had my work cut out for me. Migraine headaches, a lifelong problem of mine, started coming regularly—two to four a week. But I never took time off, never let anyone know how miserable I was. The headaches were no doubt stress-induced. I started to hate the position. Straightening out the Strike Force wasn't police work. I thought back to when I had started as a cop. All I'd ever wanted was to be a detective. Now I found myself in charge of an agency that was an absolute mess, full of negligence, if not some degree of corruption. But I was determined to stick with it. If I'm given an assignment, I'm going to see it through. One thing I'm not is a quitter.

Part of the problem I discovered with multiagency task forces is that sometimes the people who get sent to them aren't the best cops. Agencies will sometimes send their worst guys just to get rid of them. They'll send good ones too, of course. Task forces are filled with decent cops. But if there's a bad apple in someone's department—a "problem child" as they're known, maybe a troublemaker or someone who's just incompetent—lots of times that guy will be packed off to a task force somewhere and someone else will have to be responsible for him. For the Gang Strike Force, that someone was now me. A couple years later I would be asked to teach at the Minnesota Chiefs of Police Executive Training Institute where I would lecture police chiefs from around the state on how to properly run a task force and how to properly select your personnel. Get the best guys, I'd tell them, not someone else's castoffs.

In the meantime, I had to face accusations that I'd misused Strike Force time and money. The Discovery Channel followed us around one time for a special they were doing on motorcycle gangs. It was during that 2009 USA Run in Minnesota. The accusations, made by a disgruntled IRS agent I had worked with previously on the financial crimes task force, were that filmed encounters with gang members had been staged using Strike Force resources and that I was acting out of personal gain. I'd been out of control, pulling over motorcycles left and right. In reality, I pulled over exactly one group of motorcycles the whole week. It was all bullshit and I was livid. The agent was threatening to go to a local TV station and in fact a reporter from the station came by asking questions. I told him the truth and said he could have access to whatever records he needed including my own personal tax returns. He went away but I insisted on an internal investigation to clear my name and I was subsequently exonerated fully.

The truth is that I was selected as special liaison between law enforcement and the Hells Angels for the USA Run based on my knowledge of one-percenters and my experience with the Hells Angels. I spoke to the state sheriffs as an expert and set up training for area cops on what they could expect, and how to appropriately interact with the club members during the Run. Maybe the accusations came out of envy that I had such a prominent role. In any event, what I was learning was that the higher up you go, the bigger a target you become.

Interestingly, during the run, a bike was confiscated on a DUI. I heard about it and requested permission to examine it. Bob Henderson and Steve Cook came along. We could tell right away it was a stolen bike. We knew what we were looking for. So here we were in 2009, and I was still finding evidence that the Hells Angels were stealing bikes.

Inspecting a stolen Harley in Carlton County at the USA Run, 2009.

Back at the Strike Force, it continued to be an uphill climb straightening everything out. And it was made worse when news leaked out about a conference in Hawaii that six of the guys on the

Force had managed to sign themselves up for. The bill came to $18,000 and they'd paid for it with seized money in direct violation of forfeiture laws. The press got wind of it and I started getting phone calls from reporters. The publicity was horrendous and my headaches weren't getting any better. I met with the commissioner of public safety to let him know what really needed to be done to clean up the Force. "Shut the doors for at least six weeks," I suggested. "Let me institute all new policies and procedures. Let's rebuild it from scratch."

But soon after, a couple agencies pulled their detectives out on account of the bad publicity and the commissioner decided that the best thing to do was to just shut the whole damn thing down permanently. Subsequently, with my assistance, the state and the FBI did an investigation. I showed the investigators around. At one point we opened a safe where we found three guns.

"Drop guns," the agent said. Drop guns: guns a cop might drop at a crime scene to conveniently "find" and connect with a suspect.

"How do you know?" I asked.

"Why else would they be in there?" It was a good point. I could never be certain that that was the purpose of the guns, but if it was, it was even more confirmation in my mind that the Force needed nothing less than a complete overhaul. Of course in the meantime it had been my name that had been dragged through the newspapers.

On top of all that, the St. Paul Police Federation filed suit against me. That made the papers, too. They claimed it was me who'd leaked to the press the names of the guys who went to Hawaii. I had done no such thing. Why would I have? The names had actually been released by mistake by the State and the State admitted doing so in a deposition. The suit was dropped immediately. But of course that part never got printed in the papers. What made the suit more sad than infuriating for me was the fondness I had always felt for the St. Paul P.D., going all the way back to my boyhood and my admiration for my grandfather who had proudly served as a St. Paul cop.

I was sent back to the sheriff's office, but by then I'd been made more than a little cynical. Up until I'd made lieutenant, I couldn't wait to get to work in the morning. But from that point on, my career as an investigator, the work I'd really loved, had effectively ended. I knew that cases like Pat's were in the past. And the new administration that had, back in 2007, come into power in the sheriff's office—the office my own father had built—seemed bent on destroying itself with incompetence and political opportunism. A once-proud agency of law enforcement became a quagmire of political favors and political vindictiveness. All around me I saw people wanting to get out. Good people. By the time I was sent back in 2009, I was one of them. I hung on three more years and in August, 2012, at the age of fifty-two, I retired. The instability of the department had become so bad that between 2007 and 2012, I had either been transferred or made to change offices a total of eight times. It got to the point where I didn't even bother to unpack my personal effects. My plaques didn't go up on my office walls and the family pictures didn't appear on my desk.

My daughter, Rachel, threw a retirement party for me and about a hundred and fifty people showed up. Bob Bushman was emcee and several people spoke, including Jeff Paulsen who made a speech about how much I'd done to investigate the Hells Angels. "Nobody knows more about them than Chris," he said. "He was the one guy I always felt I could count on." Don Enger spoke, too. He called me one of the best investigators he'd ever had the pleasure to be associated with. It felt good to be appreciated and I was touched. It helped with the bad taste I'd had in my mouth from my last year or so on the force.

It was strange to wake up on that first day of retirement. As much as I'd been ready to walk away, I had a fear of not being a cop. It's all I'd known since my internship in the Edina police department, which had seemed about a million years before. But by the third or fourth day, I began feeling as if the world had been lifted from my shoulders. The stress was gone. And there were a lot of things I had planned, including spending time with my family and coaching youth athletics, things I'd always made time for. But now I had a lot more time.

And I wanted to continue something else, too. For a few years, I'd been speaking in seminars and conferences around the country on how to investigate outlaw motorcycle gangs and the Hells Angels in particular. I spoke mostly to groups of biker investigators and undercover cops. Steve Cook, the Kansas City detective who had been such a great source of information back in 1997 when we had started investigating the Hells Angels, had by then become a good friend of mine. We had stayed in touch. Steve had started a law enforcement training company and had enlisted my help with the seminars. In 2002, we'd co-founded the Midwest Outlaw Motorcycle Gang Investigators Association. We got to thinking that our presentations could be made a lot more effective if we had an actual Hells Angels member in attendance, someone to talk about the club's activities, to provide some inside scoop, to answer questions. Someone like Pat Matter. Pat was getting out of prison and I knew he'd need something to do, a way to make a few bucks. And maybe a new start.

My dad, Don, my mom, Helen Ann and my children, Rachel, Matt and me
at my Lieutenant promotion ceremony 2004.

CHAPTER 20
Sandstone

Sandstone was one unique place. I liked Waseca a lot more. There was more to do and you were less confined and you got yourself on a routine and time seemed to pass faster. At Waseca I had a job working for the electrical shop. I had a five-man crew and our responsibility was the recreation building. But there was never much work required so we'd report there in the morning and walk the track or just hang out and then report back to the shop at 3:00 p.m. each day, finished with our responsibilities. We were back in our cells by 3:30, then 4:30 we ate and after 5:00 your time was your own to shoot pool, play ping pong or cards, or do whatever, until you had to be back in your unit at 8:30. There was a lot of space and a lot of activities. I'd been well-respected in Waseca, too. It was before I'd testified, of course, and everyone knew who I was, knew I was a Hells Angels president. They had read the local papers, the reports describing me as the Godfather of the Hells Angels.

Visitation was all day on Saturdays and Sundays and from 5:00 p.m. to 8:00 p.m. on Fridays and Mondays. Trish came every week without fail. She was my angel. Connor came, too. He was four and he couldn't understand why I couldn't go home with him and Mommy. He'd hang on to my pants leg and cry when it was time to escort the visitors out.

When Waseca wouldn't take me back after the Jacobsen-Seydel trial, I was stuck in Anoka. A county jail is a bit more austere than a federal prison. You're restricted to your pod. At Anoka there were six pods of about sixty guys each, mostly in two-man cells. There's not nearly as much to do, nor space to do it in. I went in at 180 pounds and soon ballooned up to 220. I started exercising as best I could in the limited environment. I'd walk from one end of the unit to the other, up the stairs and down the stairs. I started doing pushups and sit-ups all day. Eventually, I got myself down to a lean 162.

Anoka had a different kind of clientele than Waseca, too. The population was more transient. Prisoners were coming and going more frequently. But I made a few friends. There were others in there who had also cooperated and we had each other's back. I played a lot of spades to pass the time, and often against a couple of the deputies and a sergeant. I was well thought of by the jailers, mostly because I kept quiet and to myself. Unlike visitation in Waseca, visitation in Anoka was only one day a week for twenty minutes, and it was always behind glass.

Sandstone was more like Anoka with the relative lack of amenities and space. There was a small yard and small dayroom. The yard at Sandstone, where eighty WITSEC prisoners were housed, was smaller than my backyard. Seventeen times around was a mile. Where Waseca had probably twenty pool tables in the recreation hall, Sandstone had one in its dayroom, along with a couple card tables. There was a small cafeteria and a gym with a basketball hoop and some treadmills and a few weights. The cells were twelve feet by twelve feet with a toilet, bunk beds, and a couple small lockers. You started out doubling up with somebody else and eventually you worked your way up to one of the single cells.

But the population of Sandstone was less transient than Anoka. And much more dangerous. Some of the worst criminals in the country were there, guys who'd been convicted of four or five murders or more. There were tough black gangsters from Washington D.C. and top members of the Mexican Mafia. Everyone there had cooperated somewhere along the line; that's why they were there. So you weren't supposed to know anyone's name. And some of them, I didn't want to know.

But I knew Salvatore Gravano. "Sammy the Bull" of the Gambino crime family had worked with the FBI to bring down John Gotti and a bunch of other guys—thirty-six mobsters in total. Sammy was the highest ranking Mafioso ever to turn government witness. He admitted to the murders of nineteen people but because of his cooperation, he did less than five years. But when he was released in 1994, he couldn't stay out of trouble. He got back into drug trafficking and in 2002 was sentenced to twenty years, spending a few of them at Sandstone. He thought he'd gotten a raw deal with the twenty-year sentence. And I thought to myself, *raw deal?* You killed nineteen people. But I didn't talk to Sammy much; I didn't really have any interest in getting to know him. One time out in the yard, I was casually swatting some flies and one of the inmates said, "Pat, you're sure killing a bunch of them." Sammy was sitting out there and I said, "Yeah, nineteen, I think." Sammy said, "Nice number, Pat."

The Aryan Brotherhood was represented in Sandstone, too. Paul "Cornfed" Schneider was there. Schneider was a hit man for the white supremacist group. Theirs is a criminal gang organization that operates both inside and outside of the federal prison system. Some of their members make Sammy's guys look like Cub Scouts. Schneider was a giant of a man, ripped and tattooed and he made an intimidating presence. We all knew Schneider's story. He'd been doing life for murder when he was asked to testify on behalf of another Aryan Brotherhood member. During a break in the trial, he stabbed the defense attorney with a homemade knife. It was maybe an eighth-inch thick and six to eight inches in length and he'd hidden it by jamming it into his calf, right through the skin. The papers said he'd had it hidden in his rectum, but we knew the real story. Schneider was insane. The lawyer survived the stabbing ("I didn't like his smart-ass attitude," Schneider explained when asked about a motive), but Schneider almost lost his leg to the ensuing infection.

From Pelican Bay State Prison, Schneider ran a drug smuggling operation and managed to conspire to kill a sheriff's deputy, for which he was given a second life term. Pelican Bay is known for housing the worst of the worst, mostly in solitary confinement. Schneider wanted out and rolled on his fellow gang members and was sent to Sandstone. One time in Sandstone he'd threatened to kill another inmate and when word got to the jailers, they came in the middle of the night to move him to another unit—six big guys from the riot squad to accomplish the task of moving one prisoner.

David Headley was in WITSEC, too. Headley's name before he changed it was Daood Sayed Gilani. He was from Pakistan and he conspired in the plotting of the Mumbai terrorist attacks in India. One hundred and sixty-eight people were killed in those attacks. David and I played bocce ball together.

So these were the types of people I was now associating with. Sandstone seemed to just embody evil. There was a feel about it, an aura that hung heavily about the place. I looked around the yard one day and thought to myself, *Well, Pat, I guess you made the big time. You wanted to be a tough guy and here you are, living with some of the most notorious people on the planet.* People can think what they want about the Hells Angels. But outside of a sociopath or two like Thunder, we never had anybody approaching the class of what I found at Sandstone.

I tried as best I could not to associate with anyone. I didn't make a single friend, nor did I try to. My attitude put a lot of the inmates off. They were cutthroats and hustlers and if you didn't need anything from them, they didn't care much for you. They buddied up to the new guys coming in, doing their laundry or getting them food from the kitchen, but of course they wanted things in return. Money or sometimes sexual favors. The guys looking for sex we called the Rainbow Coalition. It's funny, but those guys didn't consider themselves gay. I guess they figured just because you wanted a blow job from another guy, that didn't make you a homosexual. Not if you were in prison and there weren't any other options. But it seemed pretty gay to me and I left them alone. Gay or not, those guys were far from sissies. There were some badass dudes in the Rainbow Coalition.

The thing is there were some guys who just didn't belong in Sandstone. There were a few who'd cooperated on cases that didn't seem nearly important enough to warrant witness protection and I often wondered if the people running the WITSEC program were just trying to keep Sandstone filled. There were dudes who were clearly trying to turn their lives around. And yet they'd been dumped in this place, with lowlifes and some the worst that humanity had to offer. Guys set to get out in a year or so, maybe convicted of minor drug distribution, were housed with criminals who were doing life for cold-blooded murders.

I asked Chris to keep in contact with Trish. Maybe I was beginning to trust him, but it was hard. It was hard for me to trust anybody. I felt Chris had ulterior motives for keeping in touch with me, one of them being their need for me to testify at the clubhouse trial. And frankly, I allowed Chris on my call list for my own reasons, besides checking on Trish. I needed to keep on him about the Rule 35 downward departure of my sentence. I had it in writing from Paulsen but even after all this time it still hadn't gone in front of Rosenbaum. After I testified at the clubhouse trial, it finally did.

They drove me back to St. Paul for the Rule 35 hearing. A couple of the attorneys from the Laughlin trial had sent letters to Rosenbaum on my behalf. "There were a lot of Hells Angels in attendance at the trial," one of them wrote. "Pat Matter put his life on the line." But the thing that swayed Rosenbaum the most was John Ciccone. John actually took the time to fly in from California for the hearing. He could have just sent a letter, but he came personally and spoke for close to half an hour about my testimony at the Laughlin trial and then said, "Your honor, I'll tell you what you should do—"

"Nobody tells me what I should do in my courtroom, Mr. Ciccone," Rosenbaum huffed.

"Well, I'm going to tell you anyway, your honor. This man deserves at *least* two years off his sentence. This is a high-ranking member of the Hells Angels. We don't get guys like this to cooperate every day as you might imagine. If you don't reward him for it, we may never get another. And besides that, it's just the right thing to do, your honor."

Finally, I got up to speak. I had a few words prepared but I didn't get too far before Rosenbaum cut me off. "I've heard enough, Mr. Matter. I'm giving you your request for downward departure."

"Thank you, Your Honor."

"Mr. Matter," he said, looking down at me from his bench. "I didn't hate you when I sentenced you originally. But nor do I love you now. But I'm allowing the two years off your sentence." Truthfully, I don't think he would have done so without John Ciccone. Rosenbaum was probably still under the impression I had worn a Filthy Few patch because I'd murdered someone. Nobody had bothered to tell him otherwise. John's presence made the difference. I don't know if John liked me or not, but he did everything he said he'd do and he sure had my respect.

Fortunately, John hadn't held it against me that I'd refused to testify for other Hells Angels cases. He had asked me to do so a couple times, once for a racketeering trial for Smiling Rick, a good friend of mine and president of the Washington state Hells Angels chapter. Paulsen had previously asked me to testify, too, in Chicago at the trial of Mel Chancey and David "Pulley" Ohlendorf. I could see where things were heading. "No way," I'd told them. "I'm not making a career out of being a federal informant."

I'd learn later that the prosecution team in Chicago would use my proffer in Minnesota to bluff the defense team into thinking I was coming to testify. But I had no intention of doing so. John was disappointed but he seemed to understand and respect my decision. Paulsen might have respected it, too. I think he and Chris were finally beginning to see that I was a man of my word. I'd been honest and straightforward in all my dealings with them. It was more than I felt I'd received in return.

Some of the prisoners at Sandstone were baffled that I didn't cooperate more. I guess they figured once you're in witness protection, what's the difference? But that's not how I felt about it. Rolling isn't anything I took lightly and guys who did pissed me off. Besides, I wasn't going to get any more time off my sentence by then. "But at least you get out of this place for a couple days to testify," one of the inmates said. "You get to take a trip."

I just shook my head. "Is that really where you're at?" I said.

In June of 2008, I got some bad news. My sister Lucille had died. I'd kept in touch with her, talking with her by phone on a weekly basis.

Her death came as a real blow. In January of 2009, I got some more bad news. My brother Rusty died. Rusty hadn't been well. He'd had a stroke. He couldn't talk. From time to time, I'd kept in touch with his wife, but we never really got along, she and I. She knew Trish had been visiting me and somehow she figured out where. She also happened to know Rooster, who'd been doing time in Duluth. She'd written him letters and apparently in one of them she mentioned me and Sandstone. Special Investigations, the security arm of the Bureau of Prisons, became concerned that my security had been blown.

Worse, the Hells Angels USA Run happened to be coming to Minnesota that year. It was deemed too dangerous for me to stay at Sandstone, for me and for the prison guards. It was an overreaction. The unit manager told me, "I'm not going to get killed for you, Matter." Everybody was blowing the supposed security breach way out of proportion. Nobody was going to get killed for anybody. Did they think the Hells Angels were going to storm the place? It was ridiculous and though I didn't care much for Sandstone, I had my reasons for wanting to stay. First and foremost was Trish, who'd continued to visit me every single week.

But there was another reason. Earlier in the year, I'd been diagnosed with prostate cancer. I'd had problems dating back to my time in Anoka. I'd been taking medication and getting my PSA checked every six months. In February they told me it was cancer. Stage three. I was all set for surgery and treatment in Minnesota, at the Mayo Clinic at Rochester. Now they were talking about moving me to Butner, North Carolina, to the Butner Federal Correctional Complex and running me through the prison healthcare system there. I resisted. I even called John Ciccone who made a call on my behalf. But WITSEC moved me anyway.

In Butner, they needed to keep me out of the general prison population so they put me in solitary. All told, I'd be down there for six months; in an isolated cell, locked up for twenty-three hours a day, with one hour for walking around a five-foot by twenty-foot caged area.

Besides the guards, the only other person I could talk to was the guy in the adjoining cell, also in solitary for his own protection. And it's no wonder. Anthony "Gaspipe" Casso was a former underboss of the Lucchese crime family. Casso was regarded as a homicidal maniac even by Mafia standards. He'd taken out some big names. One that got away was John Gotti, the same mobster Sammy the Bull had brought down. It's a small world sometimes in the federal prison system. Anyway, Casso was doing thirteen consecutive life sentences. We talked from time to time, mostly small talk. It gave me something to do, besides pushups, which I did religiously. I could talk by phone twice a week with Trish. We never missed a phone call. It's what kept me going.

At Butner, they treated my cancer. In Minnesota I'd been scheduled for *da Vinci* surgery, a minimally invasive procedure with robotic technology. That wasn't available at Butner. In Butner the surgery would be manual, open surgery. I asked the prison administrator about the surgeon. He hesitated and kind of frowned, then said, "I'm not sure I'd have the surgery if I were you. You might want to consider the radiation." They had laser radiation available to treat the cancer. Open surgery was risky. Urinary incontinence, impotence—all kinds of nasty side effects, and those were risks with a good surgeon. I didn't like the way the P.A. hesitated when I asked him about the local guy. I opted for the radiation. Forty-two treatments total, one a day, five days a week. The procedures left me with permanent scar tissue and a need to self-catheterize to this day. But I survived the cancer.

By then, I'd talked to Chris. I wanted out of Butner, out of solitary. I wanted back in Sandstone. Chris said he'd talk to Paulsen and get me back to Minnesota. Chris came through. I trusted him more now. I had to finish my treatments, but eventually I was sent back to Sandstone. It was September of 2009.

Solitary confinement for six months in Butner made Sandstone seem crowded. It was difficult having so many people around. It made me uncomfortable and anxious. In time I adjusted. From then, I just kept counting the days. I stayed to myself and avoided the drama and bullshit of the other inmates as best I could. I lifted weights and kept in shape. The weeks went by. Then the months. Finally the years. I got some time off for good behavior and in August of 2012, I was released.

It was the same month Chris retired. He'd asked me about talking at police training seminars. Wondered if I'd like to share my story. Why not, I figured. I sure as hell had a story to tell.

It was strange walking through the gate for the last time. I'd been out before, for things like medical trips and for the clubhouse trial and the Rule 35 hearing. But I'd been heavily escorted, sometimes with ankle chains. Now I was walking out a free man.

My prison counselor drove me home. Trish wasn't allowed to come to Sandstone to pick me up. It's against WITSEC procedures. The counselor was a good guy and we'd gotten along really well. When we pulled up to the house he shook my hand and wished me luck. "And if I ever run into you again," he said, "I'll shake your hand again." I said thanks and walked up the drive and stepped into the house. Trish was there. Connor was there.

Everything was there.

CHAPTER 21
One Hell of a Story

Two weeks after Pat was released from Sandstone, he accompanied me to Peoria to speak to the Midwest Outlaw Motorcycle Gang Investigators Association. It was a three-day conference and a half day was blocked out for us. Richard Rohda came along. By then, he'd been speaking at conferences with me. Richard continued to be appreciative of my saving his life on that day he attempted suicide. We keep in touch to this day.

L-R: Richard Rohda, Ed "Fingers" Jauch, Pat, Steve Cook and Me.

Richard was good, but Pat was the hit of the conference. I wasn't so sure at first. I could tell he was uncomfortable. I told him beforehand that I was going to make it easy for him. "I'll speak for a little while," I told him, "and then you can speak and don't worry about getting stuck. I'll be right up there with you and I've got a list of questions that I can ask you to keep the presentation moving along and on track. All you have to do is be honest." And then I thought of another concern Pat might have had. "And don't worry about anybody at the conference using anything you might say. They won't be able to use any information you impart as part of a search warrant affidavit or anything of the kind, if that's what you're thinking."

"You can't get me to testify again," he said tersely.

"Absolutely not, Pat. That's not what this is about at all. These conferences are for informational purposes. Nothing you say here can be used in any way as evidence." That seemed to satisfy him but it just confirmed my thoughts that in all my years of law enforcement, I'd never known anyone so hostile to the idea of testifying against others. And it made me realize just how strongly he must have felt about Trish and Connor, to have put them above the code he'd lived by his whole life.

At the conference, once he got going, Pat had the audience captivated by his stories. Law enforcement officials who'd seen it all were riveted by the accounts of his time in the Hells Angels. During a break, Pat was mobbed by guys with questions.

One of the guys Pat met at the conference was my good friend, Ed "Fingers" Jauch. Ed's a cop in Illinois who once infiltrated the Outlaws. He was well aware of who Pat Matter was. The two had a mutual respect for each other and shared some great stories.

On the plane ride back home Pat told me he was apprehensive about his future. "I'm really not sure what I'm going to do now," he confided.

"Pat," I said to him, "my advice, no matter what you do, is to surround yourself with good people. Do that and you'll be fine."

My eighty-four-year-old father picked us up at the airport. It was he and I and Pat and Richard. The former Hennepin County Sheriff, a former Hennepin County sheriff's captain, a former Hells Angels president, and a former Hells Angels sergeant at arms. Both Richard and Pat knew who Dad was and he enjoyed hearing their stories and we all had one hell of a fun conversation.

Pat took to heart my advice about surrounding himself with good people. Not long after that trip, he joined Trish's church. And I made it a point to keep in touch with him. At first it was to check up on him, make sure he wasn't sliding back to old ways and old friends. But after a while, I started keeping in touch with him just because I wanted to. Pat Matter became a good friend of mine. From time to time we even ride our motorcycles together. Sometimes he brings Connor along.

The thing about police work, at least for me, is that seeing people turn their lives around is a lot more satisfying than seeing them get tossed into prison. I don't pretend to have all the answers, but there's got to be a better way to rehabilitate people than our current penal system. Pat was strong. He came out of the system okay. But prison culture is poisonous. People frequently come out as better criminals or worse people or both. Once exposed to the prison system, it's a rare person who turns his life around. Nearly half find themselves incarcerated again within three years. That needs to be fixed.

Part of the problem is the mandatory federal sentencing for low-level drug possession. I'm no fan of drugs. I'm not convinced that legalizing marijuana, for instance, with the possible exception of medical marijuana, is an appropriate thing to do. States that are doing that, like Colorado, are still going to find they have an active black market on their hands. The dope that's more potent than the law allows will still be sold illegally, and I know from experience that the potent stuff is often the gateway for more dangerous narcotics.

On the other hand, why throw the little guy into the prison system where he doesn't stand a chance? Early in my time in narcotics I was working the bus depot, and I watched as a young guy with a gym bag got off a bus from Chicago and suspiciously skirted out a side door. I had a hunch. I followed and approached him and identified myself and asked if he might just have some drugs in the bag. He got nervous. He started sweating. "You do, don't you?" I said. He came clean and I found some crack cocaine in the bag, less than a pound that he was delivering for someone. But of course I had to arrest him. He was just a kid, really, and I knew he was only a cog in a much bigger wheel. Nothing more than a mule. But because of mandatory sentencing laws, that kid got tossed into federal prison for ten years. I felt sick about it.

I was glad to start working on bigger cases, like the Hells Angels case. It's the kingpins that have to be dealt with; the guys at the top of the big criminal enterprises. And make no mistake—the Hells Angels is one of the biggest. What started as a small gang of Harley-Davidson enthusiasts outside of San Bernardino just after World War II has evolved into an international crime syndicate. The man on the street—hell, most of the cops out there—doesn't realize the extent of the Hells Angels' activities. There are other one-percenter clubs, of course, but the Hells Angels stands alone atop them all. The Outlaws don't like to hear that, but it's true and I suspect they know it.

Meanwhile, the war continues. Pat's friend Bear, Roger Mariani, was killed in April of 2006, shot to death in a hail of gunfire on Interstate 95 in Connecticut. The case remains unsolved, but seized shortly afterwards was an SUV with an Outlaw jacket, a handgun, and a black notebook labeled A.H.A.M.D.—All Hells Angels Must Die. In August of that year, several Outlaws were gunned down by Hells Angels members in Sturgis. And since then, it's been shootings and stabbings and bar fights between the clubs on a pretty consistent basis.

It's funny how the one-percenters all get lumped together, though, in the minds of most people. Or how motorcycle club members in general get lumped together, for that matter. I'll have cops call me from time to time, trying to pick my brain about a certain Hells Angels member. "Do you know anything about so and so?" they'll ask.

"Never heard of him. What makes you think he's a Hells Angel?"

"Well, he's got a leather jacket and rides a Harley. He's a tough guy. Oh, and he's got a lot of tattoos." And then of course I have to educate them on just how difficult it is to become a Hells Angel. It takes a hell of a lot more than a leather jacket and a Harley.

What I learned is how insulated the club is. It's not easy to get at these guys. We were able to do so in Minnesota but it took years and a lot of tenacity. But I don't know a better way than how we did it. Every now and then a cop will go undercover and infiltrate a Hells Angels' chapter. As you can imagine, that's not an easy thing to do. Some cops like to think they're infiltrating, but what they're really doing is riding their Harleys and growing their beards and getting tattoos and hanging out at the bars where the Hells Angels hang out. They take a lot of covert photos and bring them back to their bosses and tell them how close they're getting. I call them photo cops. Their efforts are pretty much worthless.

From what I've seen, real infiltration isn't typically worth the cost. The cop puts himself at incredible risk and just about everyone I've seen who was able to do it successfully has had his personal life ruined in the process. It's a ballsy approach and those who have done it, those who have really infiltrated the Hells Angels, have my respect. But the results have been marginal. Better, in my mind, to use old-fashioned investigative work. Sure, it's not as glamorous and it's more paperwork and it's a lot of tedious surveillance and late hours poring over tax records and other documentation; but if you just take the time to follow the money trail, you'll crack the case. At worst, you'll get a guy to talk. And then another, and then another. Keep at it long enough and you'll get the kingpin. "No way you can take Matter down," I was told. Glad I didn't listen.

If it takes patience, it also takes a commitment from the higher-ups and some freedom for the detectives to proceed as they see fit. Rocky was the best boss I'd ever had in this respect. He allowed us a lot of latitude and even allowed me flexibility in my schedule on days when I had custody of my kids. I made it up to him by coming into the office two hours early on some mornings, or working late into the nights. I loved what I was doing so it was easy for me. But my experience is that guys like Rocky are few and far between and getting ever more scarce. After Rocky retired, my last days as a detective were full of micro-managing and close supervision. It was a major reason I took the promotion to lieutenant and left the detective work that I loved.

There was a lot of bureaucracy and a lot of politics involved, too. I happen to know that the pride of police workmanship I saw all around me in the glory days of the Special Operations Division is now missing.

So, too, are any investigative efforts into the Hells Angels; they are still in operation in the same clubhouse. But then again, I can't imagine that without Pat Matter, that particular chapter is anything more than just a shadow of its former self. Through the grapevine, I've heard that the chapter has had four or five presidents come and go since Pat left in 2003. And there are a lot of other bike clubs around now, too. Rumor has it that some of the Hells Angels have even had their patches taken, something that never happened while Pat was president. At a bike show not long ago with some Hells Angels in attendance, I overheard people talking. "If Pat Matter was still around, we sure as hell wouldn't have all these other clubs."

The Hells Angels still wield some influence in Minnesota, though. Not long ago, Pat and I made plans to have lunch with Donnie Smith, a good friend of ours and a world-renowned custom-bike builder north of Minneapolis. Pat calls him a hero and a lifetime friend. I have a ton of respect for him, too. Donnie holds an annual custom bike show that's the largest in the Midwest and he often sells to the Hells Angels. In fact, it was at Donnie's show that I heard the comment about the other clubs. Bob Kenney, the Harley-Davidson expert from the Connecticut State Police whom we'd flown out to help us inventory all the stolen bike parts back in 1998, always flies in for the show and so does Bob Feinen, formerly of Dairyland Insurance. Both have become good friends of mine over the years. Anyway, Donnie came to lunch with Pat and me, but he felt compelled to call the Hells Angels first. He wanted to get permission.

Still, it was Pat who was the proverbial straw that stirred the drink and I imagine a lot of the heart went out of the club when Pat left. Turns out the glory days of the SOD unit coincided with the glory days of the Minnesota chapter of the Hells Angels. Good times all around.

But better days are ahead for Pat. My sense about him when I first met him that day at the Anoka County Jail was right on the money. There was more to Pat than met the eye. Pat was always more than just a criminal, and it's gratifying to have seen him rise above all that. Of necessity, he made some compromises to his own sense of integrity that I know he feels he shouldn't have had to make. He'll always believe that questionable steps were taken, by Jeff Paulsen and others, to make sure that he'd be sentenced to a degree that would compel his testimony against others. Is he right about that? Not to my knowledge. Until Pat's case, my experience had been mostly limited to the state justice system. The federal system, with the spinning wheel by which judges are picked randomly? I didn't even know that's how it was done. Is it possible to steer a defendant? I suppose it is. Does it happen? Probably. Did it happen in Pat's case? I can't say one way or the other.

I'll say this, however: Jeff Paulsen was the best prosecutor I ever worked with, bar none. But I focused on my job and I let the others focus on theirs. It's possible that Jeff believed Pat killed. He wouldn't have acquired that belief from me, but with what we knew about the Hells Angels at the time, it would not have been completely unreasonable for someone to think that Pat may have had a murder in his past. We'd been trained to think that Filthy Few patches meant killing for the club and our training had also included the widespread belief that a .22 with a silencer—the exact kind of gun Richard Rohda told us that Pat used—was the gun of choice for the Hells Angels. It was poor training and I'd like to humbly submit that I've helped improve upon what law enforcement knows today about how the Hells Angels operate.

Richard Rohda turned out to be a questionable witness with a penchant for exaggeration. And he passed along a lot of hearsay, too. But at the time that he was kicked out of the club, he was Hells Angels Sergeant at Arms and the first Hells Angel we could get to talk. It was reasonable to believe that his statements about the club were credible. But the bottom line is that I didn't believe Pat killed and I don't think, absent any real evidence, that Jeff Paulsen would have led Judge Rosenbaum to believe it, either. But there were other cops involved, of course. It's not out of the realm of possibility that someone might have talked to Rosenbaum and colored his vision of Pat.

As for the "worst of the worst" that Pat's talked about—Shoup, Billings, Rainville, etc.—I'll just say I'm proud of the work we all did. Look, it should come as no surprise that cops are human beings and not immune from making mistakes or questionable judgments. I'd like to think every man and woman in law enforcement represents a model of excellence, but I know that sometimes people fall short. I'm not naive. I saw it in my time with the Metro Gang Strike Force. People bend rules.

I got a small but interesting reminder of this not long ago. I had lunch with Bob Kenney who was in town for an International Outlaw Motorcycle Gang Investigators Association conference. Over lunch, he showed me a picture he'd taken at the conference of a black denim vest that they had on exhibit. It had Hells Angels colors and a Filthy Few patch. Later I described it to Pat. It was his. Someone had swiped it during the search of his house in 2001. It had never even been entered into evidence. Now it was hanging on display like a trophy.

But for every cop who bends a rule, there's a bunch more that are out there doing things the right way. It really is a thin blue line, as they say, that holds society together, and being a cop isn't easy. On balance, I'd say the law enforcement work that's being carried out every day across the United States is something to admire.

And as for the case of the twenty-one year president of the Minnesota chapter of the Hells Angels, everything came out all right in the end, if you ask me. We all got what we needed. We busted a Hells Angels kingpin and the Hells Angels kingpin got the opportunity to put a life of crime behind him. And in addition to all that, we got one hell of a story.

CHAPTER 22
Choices

I understand that cops are human beings. I understand that people make mistakes. But I don't understand how cops get away with breaking rules they're sworn to uphold. If you break the Hells Angels code you get bounced out of the club. And if you, as a member of the Hells Angels, break the law, you get punished more severely than your average citizen, often with gang enhancement. If you're a cop, the same laws don't always seem to apply. Shoup has an affair and creates a mistrial and his "punishment" is a year off work *with* pay. Rainville is charged with indecent exposure and pleads it down to disorderly conduct and gets to keep his job, eventually retiring to sunny Arizona. Mark Armstrong never reported the $25,000 that Rainville stole. But if he had, who in law enforcement would have taken his word over Rainville's? Crooks get punished for bad behavior. Cops get rewarded for bad behavior.

I broke the code and cooperated because the deal I'd made with Jeff Paulsen had been broken. Richard Rohda said I wore a Filthy Few patch because I'd murdered someone in North Carolina. Paulsen must have known that Richard was prone to exaggeration but the story made its way to Judge James Rosenbaum. However it got there, nobody bothered to correct Rosenbaum's perception. Richard was a tool for those guys.

As for Paulsen, the last I heard, he'd been reassigned from prosecuting high-profile cases at the U.S. Attorney's Office. For what reasons, I don't know. But it was reported in the *Star Tribune* and Jim Ostgard told me over lunch not long ago that it had to do with not properly following procedures. That would not surprise me. I'm sure Chris would tell you it was probably just all politics.

I'm not saying everybody involved in law enforcement is bad. I met some really good guys at the conference Chris took me to. Still, I was surprised at the behavior of some of them. The night before, a lot of the attendees had gone out to a Hooters and I watched while dozens of cops got drunk and loud and obnoxious. Anybody walking in would have been hard-pressed to tell they were officers of the law. Some were undercover guys with long hair and beards. Put denim jackets on everyone and it would have looked like an outlaw motorcycle club party. I was just two weeks out of the confinement of Sandstone and the whole sight made me uncomfortable. Chris had one of his migraines and I could tell he didn't want to be there, either.

And then of course I found myself considering the guys who'd investigated and prosecuted me, and the means they'd used, and I wondered who was really worse, the Hells Angels or those investigators. I don't think I'm alone in my ideas about how these people operate. I think of the civil trial over the clubhouse. The prosecution had me, a former Hells Angels president, on the stand testifying that drugs had been sold in that clubhouse and they still lost the case. The jury saw right through it, saw right through the police harassment and the dirty tricks. Maybe the IRS bungled the case as Chris says, but I heard that they polled the jury afterwards and the general consensus was that the jurors did come to believe that drugs were sold at the clubhouse. But they didn't care; they felt it was still unfair to seize the clubhouse.

But I didn't write this book for the purpose of bashing law enforcement. Nor did I write it to offend the Hells Angels. The Hells Angels is the most elite motorcycle club on the planet and I was proud to be a part of it. Prouder still to be a chapter president for twenty-one years. I wrote the book because I just wanted to tell my story. I sold drugs and I dealt in stolen motorcycle parts and I'm not going to make any excuses. I know how destructive methamphetamine can be. I made a lot of money, but I know I hurt a lot of people along the way. As Judge Rosenbaum told me, it took a lot of dark for me to see the light. But there's only one ultimate judge out there and that's who I have to answer to now. Nobody else. The pastor at my church, Pastor Steven Briel, a great man and a true friend, reminds me of this.

Suffice it to say, I don't miss any of my old lifestyle. I lived it well, but it was exhausting. I lasted more than twenty years slinging illegal drugs with a neon sign on my back. That sign was my Hells Angels patch. Catch me if you can. It was an open challenge and it meant I spent a lot of time looking over my shoulder and distrusting people. At times over the course of my career, I found myself fighting a war on three different fronts—against the cops, against the Outlaws, and against the Hells Angels.

Of course law enforcement threw themselves into the challenge full bore, but it still took them years. Ultimately, they had so much money and so many man-hours into me, they had to nail me. And they'd do whatever it took, even if meant cutting some corners. My attorneys kept telling me how much of a trophy I was to these guys. I guess it shouldn't have surprised me when Chris told me about my denim vest hanging up on display. I always suspected it had been swiped during the search. Now it's being used as an exhibit, with patches and logos on it that are all trademarked, by the way.

Outside of the drug distribution, there's not much about the club activities themselves that I regret, though I wonder sometimes if I should have been so insistent on pushing the Hells Angels into Chicago, into Outlaws territory. It helped reignite the war. I might have done things a little differently there, knowing how volatile the situation became.

But I loved being a Hells Angel. The good times I had would take another book. But that was a time in my life that's in the past. A different time. And I was a different man. In a sense, I feel as though I've grown beyond those days. Now, there are other things in life I appreciate.

I don't keep in touch with any Hells Angels now, of course. I cooperated. The Hells Angels won't talk to me and I don't imagine

One of the good times in the Hells Angels with Willie Nelson and with Willie's bodyguard, San Jose Hells Angel Larry "LG" Gorman on Willie's tour bus.

My wife and Willie Nelson. Trish was pregnant with Connor at the time.

that will ever change. As for testifying, I'd have willingly done ten years and kept silent. Had it not been for Trish and Connor, I'd have done thirty. It took Rosenbaum's seventeen and a half to get me to roll. I had a choice to make and I made it. We all make choices. We all live our lives the best we know how and we do what we have to do. That's just the way life works and I'm not going to apologize for it. I'm not in this world to live up to anyone else's expectations.

I have kept in touch with Richard Rohda. He's admitted to me that he was the one who told the cops I'd killed someone. "I know that, Richard," I said to him. I'd never wanted to throw it in his face, but I appreciated the confession. Brian Weaver came to my house one day soon after I'd been released and told me in tears why he felt he had to cooperate, facing the amount of prison time he was facing. "It's okay, Brian," I said. What else could I say?

And of course I keep in touch with Chris. It might seem an unlikely friendship, but Chris always handled himself around me with professionalism. But it took me a long time to learn to trust him. I was certain he must have been privy to the idea of steering me to Rosenbaum. But for the record, I came to believe he just didn't know how the system for picking federal judges worked. And over time, through everything we went through, we ended up respecting each other and forming a friendship that I value. We talk by phone almost every day. He still picks my brain for information on the Hells Angels. I guess he can't stop being a detective and sometimes I have to ask him jokingly if I'm still under investigation. Looking towards the future, I'm sure we'll be making ourselves available for more seminars, for law enforcement agencies or for anybody else who wants to learn more of the truth about the world of outlaw motorcycle clubs.

I still ride a Harley every now and again. Sometimes with Chris. Sometimes Connor and I will go out for a ride. He enjoys the Harley, likes the feel of it and the power and the freedom of being out on the open road. He's fourteen now, with his whole life ahead of him. The other day he told me what he'd like to do when he grows up. He wants to be an anesthesiologist. I told him that sounded just fine to me.

The End

breakingthecodebook.net

twitter.com/therealdealllc

facebook.com/BreakingTheCodeBook

Afterword

By **Pastor Steven C. Briel**, St. John's Lutheran Church, Corcoran, MN

Martin Luther once commented that God works behind many "masks" to do His work today. This book is an amazing story of God working behind the 'mask' of a good cop to pursue one of His fallen but baptized sons to bring him out of darkness back into the marvelous light of His forgiving grace and love. "There's only one ultimate judge out there," Pat comments briefly in his book, "and that's who I have to answer to now." He attends Church regularly now where he hears the judge of heaven and earth pronouncing him forgiven for Jesus' sake and where he receives the body and blood of Jesus in the Lord's Supper to confirm God's pardon and forgiveness. If God can forgive and restore a man such as the one whose shocking but true story is told in this book, then God can have mercy on anyone! As the great Apostle St. Paul himself once wrote, "Christ Jesus came into the world to save sinners, of whom I am the foremost" (*1 Timothy 1:15*). Isn't this true of us all?

Index

Photographs are indicated with ***bold italic*** page numbers

Harry (Cleveland Hells Angel), 26
Harvey (Bridgeport Hells Angel), 46–47
Haymaker, Mark, 119, 132
Headley, David, 215
Hells Angels
  Arizona, 136
  Charlotte, 22, 24–25, 37, 39, 41–42, 44, 50, 60–62, 69
  Cleveland, 41, 44
  Durham, 45, 60, 62
  Minnesota, 2, 21–24, 30–31, 33–34, 47, *47, 191*
  New York, 41, 75
  Omaha, 35–37, *38,* 42, 58–59
  Richmond, CA, 183
  Rochester, 95–96
  Sacramento, 126
  Washington, 217
Hells Angels South Run, 45
Hell's Angels-Three Can Keep a Secret if Two are Dead (Lavigne), 65
Hells Angels USA Run, 39, 45, 51, 54, 57, 175, *208,* 218
Hells Angels World Run, 51
Hell's Henchmen, 70, 76, 83–84, 86, 92–93, 96, 98, 160
Hells Outcasts, 36
Henderson, Bob, 208
Herald, Bob, 96
Hexeberg, Jan, 140
Hiney, Dean (Hells Angel), *138*
Hog. *See* Swanson, Denny "Hog"
Honda 450, 31
Hoover, J. Edgar, 29
Hot Bike (magazine), 70
Humboldt, IA, 69, *102*

I

Internal Revenue Service (IRS), 90, 121, 136, 139, 141, 144, 187, 203–204, 207, 230
International Outlaw Motorcycle Gang Investigators Association, 228
Invader Motorcycle Club, 42, 60

Iowa Boys' Reformatory, 6
Irish (Oakland Hells Angel), 52–53
IRS. *See* Internal Revenue Service (IRS)

J

Jacobsen, Brad, 48, 59, 152–153, 185–190, 192, 195, 197, 202
Jahnke, Jim, 128–129
James-Younger Gang, 23
Jauch, Ed "Fingers," *221,* 222
Jazz (Son of Silence), 128
Jesse James Days, 23, 34
John-John (New York Hells Angel), 46
Johnny (Mongol), 198
Johns, Leonard, 7
Johnson, Jim "Big John," 57
July 4th Massacre, 25, 42, 60, 62

K

K.C. Creations, 197
Kelly, Howard, 70
Kelly's Westport Inn, 106
Kenney, Bob, 117, 226, 228
Kerr Lake, 39, 41–42
Klinger, Johnny, 6
Klobuchar, Amy, 126, *127*
Kress, Lamont, *38*
Kristiana, Norway, 27

L

LaBerge, Butch, 81
L.A. Choppers, 198
Lancaster, NY, 95
Lancaster National Speedway, 83
Larson, "Fat" Steve, 175
Last Chapter, 17–19, 24
Las Vegas, NV, 48, 124, 147, 151, 157, 172, 192–193, 197–199
Laughlin River Run, 192–193, 197
Lavigne, Yves, 65
Lewis, Tommy, 69, 133
LG. *See* Gorman, Larry "LG"
Lightning Les. *See* Fitzgerald, Leslie "Lightning Les"

Tiny (Sioux City El Forastero), 46
Tommy. *See* Stroud, Samuel
   "Tommy"
Tramp, 11–12, 16, 18, 48
Trotta, Eddie, 197
Trust Me Racing, 135
Tschida, John "Prospect," 144

U
Ulicki, Mike, 6
USA Run, 39, 45, 51, 54, 57, 175,
   208, 218

V
VanSlyke, John "Slick," 105, 110,
   118–119, 154
Voss, Barry, 77–78, 123

W
Weaver, Brian, 131, 140–141, 145–
   147, 150–152, 155–156, 169, 171–
   173, 179, 185, 233
Weaver, Mark, 140, 150, 158, 172–
   173, 179, 185
Websie (St. Louis El Forastero), 26,
   116
Wellstone, Paul, 34
Wendover, UT, 99
West, Billy, 37, 48, 58–59, 122–123,
   123, 123–124, 204
Wildey, Dallas, 20, 37
William (Durham Hells Angel), 45
Wilson's Tavern, 17–18
Wingerson, Rick, 7, 9, 11–12, ***13,*** 13–
   14
Winston-Salem, NC, 43
Wolf, David, 95
Woodburn, OR, 95
World Run, 51
Wylde, Jack, 17

Y
Yamaha 175, 31
Yamaha CT3 Enduro, 31
Yank. *See* Frndyk, Taylor "Yank"

CPSIA information can be obtained at www.ICGtesting.com
Printed in the USA
LVOW01s0946090814

398085LV00018B/225/P